W9-CKL-935

# THEORY CONSTRUCTION IN MARKETING

## IN MARKETING

### SOME THOUGHTS ON THINKING

# THEORIES IN MARKETING SERIES
## GERALD ZALTMAN, EDITOR

# THEORY CONSTRUCTION IN MARKETING

## SOME THOUGHTS ON THINKING

### GERALD ZALTMAN

*University of Pittsburgh*

### KAREN LEMASTERS

*University of Arizona*

### MICHAEL HEFFRING

*University of Calgary*

1807 1982

**JOHN WILEY & SONS**

*New York • Chichester • Brisbane • Toronto • Singapore*

*HF*
*5415*
*.Z264*

*658.8001*
*Z1A*

Copyright © 1982 by John Wiley & Sons, Inc.

All rights reserved. Published simultaneously in Canada.

Reproduction or translation of any part of
this work beyond that permitted by Sections
107 and 108 of the 1976 United States Copyright
Act without the permission of the copyright
owner is unlawful. Requests for permission
or further information should be addressed to
the Permissions Department, John Wiley & Sons.

**Library of Congress Cataloging in Publication Data**

Zaltman, Gerald.
  Theory construction in marketing.

  (Theories in marketing series, ISSN 0273-2955)
  Includes index.
  1. Marketing.  I. LeMasters, Karen.  II. Heffring,
Michael.  III. Title.
HF5415.Z264       658.8'001       82-7002
ISBN 0-471-98127-3                AACR2

Printed in the United States of America

10 9 8 7 6 5 4 3 2 1

*55990 Buord 10\1\18v*

*. . . Science is* primarily *an activity of extending perception into new contexts and into new forms, and only secondarily a means of obtaining what may be called reliable knowledge.*

**David Bohm, noted Physicist–Philosopher***

*"Science as Perception-Communication," in F. Suppe (Ed.) *The Structure of Scientific Theories* (Urbana: The University of Illinois Press, 1977), p. 374. See also David Bohm, *The Special Theory of Relativity* (New York: Benjamin Press, 1965), Appendix.

This book is dedicated to

Simon and Charlotte Zaltman (G.Z.)

Raymond M. Hass (K.L.)

Steuart Henderson Britt (M.H.)

# ABOUT THE AUTHORS

Gerald Zaltman is the Albert Wesley Frey Professor of Marketing at the University of Pittsburgh where he is also Co-Director of The University Program for the Study of Knowledge Use. He holds a Ph.D. in Sociology from The Johns Hopkins University and an MBA degree from the University of Chicago. His active research interests include the adoption and diffusion of new goods and services, the development and application of market intelligence, and the philosophy of the social sciences. Gerald Zaltman works actively with private and public sector agencies throughout the United States and abroad on marketing related problems. He has received numerous awards for his research contributions in marketing and the allied social sciences.

Karen LeMasters is an Assistant Professor of Marketing at the University of Arizona. She holds a Ph.D. in Marketing from the University of Pittsburgh. Her major research interests include sociological approaches to consumer behavior, the marketing of health care services, and public policy issues relevant to the elderly.

Michael Heffring is an Associate Professor at the University of Calgary. He holds masters degrees in business and sociology from Northwestern University and a Ph.D. degree in Marketing from the University of Pittsburgh. His active research interests are in the areas of lifestyle research and marketing planning in the public and private sectors.

# PREFACE

This book is about building theories in marketing. It covers the outcroppings of what are involved in this fascinating process. We think, however, that these outcroppings or iceberg tips will be provocative, helpful, discomforting, and maybe even fun to think about. We do not attempt to review in any systematic or comprehensive way contemporary issues and thinking in the philosophy of science even though we address many of these matters.

It is our hope that, after reading this book, students will have some additional thinking tools to add to those they already use in developing their ideas. If this occurs, the intent of this book will have been achieved. If the student is challenged to pursue the topics further, we will be especially pleased.

But who is supposed to receive these benefits? Here we must confess to a small dilemma that has persisted throughout this undertaking. It is best expressed in the form of two scenarios. One is made prominent from comments by various readers, those close to this project, and our own past experience. This scenario envisions the book being used almost exclusively by aspiring and present academic researchers. It reflects the idea that interest in theory building is largely limited to academics. In fact, we believe that this book will be of substantial value in doctoral seminars and as a reference book for academicians.

The second scenario is made prominent by the increasingly accepted idea that marketing practitioners are the primary innovators in identifying and addressing marketing problems. At a minimum this suggests that a substantial chunk of creative thinking in marketing originates within an important subset of practicing marketing managers. If this is the case then an important audience would be aspiring and present marketing managers. Thus this book would be helpful to, say, MBA students in advanced marketing management, marketing research, and marketing policy courses as well as to practitioners.

The dilemma posed by these two scenarios stems from the advice we received that we couldn't appeal to both audiences at once. Presumably this reflects something about:

- Our writing style.
- The reading competencies of nonacademics.
- The intellectual appetites of nonacademics.
- The proclivity of some instructors to assign the equivalent of strained foods as reading material to students.
- All of the above.

The two scenarios reflect a two-communities theory long prominent in the history of ideas. This theory expresses the notion that the community of scholars and the community of practitioners are very different cultural groups. What is appropriate for one culture isn't always appropriate for the other. There is substantial validity to various ideas in the two-communities theory with respect to the marketing profession. However, the theory may wrongly cause us to act as if constructive thinking were very disproportionately lodged in one or the other community. We are rejecting this position and the idea that we should choose between the communities as traditionally defined. We prefer to define the intended audience in a somewhat different way.

The development and use of interrelated ideas (concepts, hypotheses) for explaining, predicting, and controlling events is an inherent human trait. Children do it. Adults do it. Both academics and practitioners in marketing make a living by doing it. Of course variation exists among people in how well it is done, the way in which it is done, and the degree of their interest in and understanding of how it is done. But done it is. We do not accept conventional assumptions we hear expressed so often to the effect that "Managers want solutions not theory" or "Theory is best left to academics." Such assumptions and the attitudes they produce are inconsistent with the working of the human mind and the creation of innovations in marketing thought. The request by managers to "be relevant" is often misinterpreted to mean "be atheoretical." Being relevant means providing more useful explanations, predictions, and controls. These are precisely the functions of theory. In a field like marketing the development of theory cannot really be separated from practice. Although this book isn't for everybody we feel that it is the degree of concern with thinking and learning processes rather than job categories that should distinguish readers from nonreaders.

Who then is this book intended for? It is intended for people who feel they are doing important things in marketing and who are open to improving their activities by examining how they think about these activities. This segment clearly encompasses people in both the academic and practitioner communities. It is not intended for persons who are not open to challenges to their way of thinking or who are not willing to expend the kind of effort required when reading about such challenges. This, too, clearly encompasses people in both the academic and practitioner communities.

In conclusion we offer two caveats to the reader. Some reviewers found the manuscript written in a "deceptively simple and easy" way, which might wrongly suggest that the issues we raise are less complex or even less important than they actually are. Some reviewers indicated that a second reading was required in order to perceive fully the complexity and novelty of the issues considered. If we have succeeded in writing a readable manuscript we do hope that the subtleties and complexities of the issues, especially as they are developed in the literatures we draw upon, are not underestimated by the reader. Other reviewers, equally knowledgeable in the philosophy of science, felt the manuscript might be written in too "demanding" a way for some readers. It is our hope that those who share this response will not dismiss the theory building enterprise as too complex to contend with.

Reviewers also fell into two distinct camps concerning the organization of material. One group felt the present sequencing of chapters to be "quite logical." The other group couldn't "see sufficient unfolding" from one chapter to the next. Although we believe we have a meaningful sequencing of topics, we do caution the reader against expecting the kind of orderly, cumulative progression that may often be found in textbooks on statistics or historical chronologies. As we have come to understand theory construction it is not a linear process. It is especially not an orderly process. At least it is not linear and orderly in the same way for different people or for the same person with respect to different problems.

**Gerald Zaltman**
**Karen LeMasters**
**Michael Heffring**

# ACKNOWLEDGMENTS

An undertaking of this kind is especially subjective and interpretive compared, say, with the presentation of statistical methods, product management concepts, or a description of consumer behavior. It is therefore particularly important to have one's own thinking critically reviewed by people representing a wide variety of perspectives. Moreover, these people should be willing to explain why they agree or disagree with a particular position. We have been singularly fortunate to have found many people who were willing to do this. The following people, in alphabetical order, provided this kind of extensive critique: Richard P. Bagozzi (Massachusetts Institute of Technology), Terry Chambers (Virginia Polytechnic and State University), Alex De Noble (Virginia Polytechnic and State University), Kjell Grønhaug (The Norwegian School of Economics), Theodore Levitt (Harvard University), Kent Monroe (Virginia Polytechnic and State University), Michael Morris (Virginia Polytechnic and State University), Donald Rahtz (Virginia Polytechnic and State University), Karl-Erik Wärneryd (The Stockholm School of Economics), and Arch Woodside (The University of South Carolina). Additionally, several individuals provided substantial critiques of selected parts of the manuscript. They are: Helen Anderson (The Stockholm School of Economics), Scott Armstrong (The University of Pennsylvania), Rohit Deshpande (The University of Texas), Elizabeth Hirschman (New York University), Alf Lindqvist (The Stockholm School of Economics), Lars-Gunnar Mattsson (The Stockholm School of Economics), Nancy Nighswonger (The University of Pittsburgh), J. Paul Peter (The University of Wisconsin), Seth Reichlin (The University of Pittsburgh), Mary Jane Saxton (The University of Pittsburgh), Kenth Skogsvik (The Stockholm School of Economics), Devanathan Sudharshan (The University of Illinois), Melanie Wallendorf (The University of Arizona), Solveig Wikstrom (The University of Lund), and David T. Wilson (The Pennsylvania State University).

It would have been nice to have the first draft we presented to these reviewers elicit the general response: "This is a nice finished product!" This was not the case. We were sent back to the drawing boards several times but learned a great deal in the process. We thank the people above for their persistence in drawing our attention to certain matters as well as for their substantial insights. The manuscript is immeasurably better because of them. Of course, we too were persistent in some matters and we know that everyone mentioned above will see evidence of this (they will probably use the term stubborn rather than persistent) should they try to assess whether we followed all their advice. Thus other readers of this book should not attribute any difficulties they perceive to any of the reviewers. That would be nice but certainly wrong.

While the task we and the reviewers undertook was as much fun as it was demanding, there are some key persons from whom we made considerable demands that could not have been much fun. However, we can only guess at this because they displayed great friendliness and supportiveness. For this reason we are especially indebted to the following persons who helped prepare the several drafts of the manuscript: Vanja Ekberg (The Stockholm School of Economics), Conrada Fabrizio and Kathleen Muldoon (The University of Pittsburgh), Kerstin Kristensson, Ingrid Rosenvinge, Stina Svard, and Gertrud Wollin (The Stockholm School of Economics). Our schools and colleagues at the University of Pittsburgh, the University of Arizona, and the University of Calgary have been very supportive and facilitative. In particular, the Graduate School of Business at the University of Pittsburgh provided the senior author with sabbatical leave to work on this project. Special thanks are also due to the Institute of International Business and its director, Professor Gunnar Hedlund, at the Stockholm School of Economics for substantial assistance to the senior author during the final revision of the manuscript. One small indication of the value of his stay at the Stockholm School of Economics is evident in the institutional affiliation of several of those whose help is acknowledged here.

G. Z.
K. L.
M. H.

# EDITOR'S PREFACE

Historically, marketing's intellectual concerns have focused predominantly on applied issues. Rather recently in the development of marketing, there has been greater understanding that applied or practice related issues are intertwined with theory: as one improves so does the other. Still, the amount of attention given to theory in marketing is relatively small, especially when compared to other disciplines. In fact, a common practice in marketing is to use theories developed in other disciplines. This practice has benefited marketing practitioners considerably and has advanced the discipline intellectually more quickly than the alternative route of independently discovering the presence of these theories in marketing phenomena. However, there are clear costs to heavy reliance on this approach. For example, insights unique to knowledgeable marketers may fail to be developed into theories. Additionally, phenomena unique to marketing may also fail to be developed into theories.

One way of avoiding these costs is to be more venturesome with regard to theory building. This, in turn, requires certain tools in developing and refining theory. The first book in this series, Richard P. Bagozzi's *Causal Models in Marketing*, provided a general model for the construction and testing of theory. In this second volume, *Theory Construction in Marketing*, we address a number of critical issues related to the thinking processes that produce theories. An understanding of these issues is essential for practitioners and scholars who are concerned with developing better systems for marketing phenomena.

Other volumes will explore other issues and present other perspectives relating to thinking and action in marketing. It is hoped that collectively the different volumes will stimulate more creative and exciting thinking and practice in marketing which, after all, is what good theory is about.

**Gerald Zaltman**
**Pittsburgh, PA**

# CONTENTS

## CHAPTER THREE   CAUSALITY                                45

## CHAPTER FOUR   THINKER TOYS: CONCEPTS, PROPOSITIONS, AND THEORIES   71

# ONE

## POINTS OF VIEW

*This chapter introduces the reader to a discrepancy between traditional views of science, which are especially common in marketing, and contemporary views of science. The use of both points of view is encouraged. The importance of overcoming perceptual and intellectual blocks to creating so-called "generative" theories, which challenge existing thinking, is also considered. Finally, the chapter concludes with a discussion about the practical importance of having theory-building skills.*

The old physics assumes that there is an external world which exists apart from us. It further assumes that we can observe, measure, and speculate about the external world without changing it. . . . The concept of scientific objectivity rests upon the assumption of an external world which is "out there" as opposed to an "I" which is "in here". . . . The problem that went unnoticed for three centuries is that a person who carries such an attitude certainly is prejudiced. . . . The point of view that we can be without a point of view is a point of view. . . . The new physics, quantum mechanics, tells us clearly that it is not possible to observe reality without changing it.

Gary Zukav[1]

Virtually all of the positivistic treatment of science has come under sustained attack since the 1950's. . . . Gradually the cumulative effect of these challenges has been that . . . positivistic analyses are, or are coming to be, widely viewed as inadequate. Thus the last vestiges of positivistic philosophy of science are disappearing from the philosophical landscape.

Frederick Suppe[2]

## Augmenting Traditional Science

There exists a highly fascinating, and very dense, thicket of issues loosely clustered under the umbrella term "philosophy of science." These issues concern the very nature of human inquiry. Because we vary greatly in our thinking processes, the types of intellectual skills we possess, and the aspects of our world that intrigue us, we also vary greatly in our preferred modes of inquiry. This variation is a source of richness in the scientific intellectual endowment. Variety is the spice of intellectual life, too. However, above all else, scientists and managers are human. We tend to identify with certain ways of doing things; indeed, we build careers and develop deeply held self-images based on these different ways of doing things. When we encounter an approach that we perceive to be very different from what we are accustomed to, we often respond in the fashion customary for most people presented with any innovation: we reject it or at best keep it at arm's length for a good long while. Rudolf Carnap, a physicist and major figure in the philosophy of science, has observed: "I have found that most scientists and philosophers are willing to discuss a new assertion, if it is formulated in the customary conceptual framework; but it seems very difficult to most of them even to consider and discuss new concepts."[3]

---

[1]Gary Zukav, *The Dancing Wu Li Masters: An Overview of the New Physics* (New York: Morrow, Boston Books Edition, 1979), pp. 29–30.
[2]Frederick Suppe, "Swan Song for Positivism," in F. Suppe (Ed.), *The Structure of Scientific Theories*, 2nd ed. (Urbana: University of Illinois Press, 1977), p. 619.
[3]Rudolf Carnap, "Intellectual Autobiography," in P. A. Schilpp (Ed.), *The Philosophy of Rudolf Carnap* (LaSalle, IL: Lippincott, 1963), p. 77.

This reaction is not necessarily unhealthy. Every innovation of whatever sort is not appropriate for everyone, nor are all innovations necessarily good for anyone. Partly for this reason controversies are often engendered when different modes of inquiry are brought into contact with one another. Attack and defense and sometimes further enlightenment can ensue from controversy.

This very human response to differences in modes of inquiry underscores the fact that scientific methods used by researchers and managers are social products. They are the products of people who are influenced by many things: who they apprenticed with as students and as on-the-job trainees, their times and cultural heritage, their birth order in the nuclear family, social nurturance received while going through puberty, the schools they attended, and similar factors. That the procedures of science that are created by people become deified and placed on a plane above human frailty simply makes them comparable to other major social products of civilization.

Contemporary marketing thought presently champions or deifies one particular scientific method: traditional science. (There is no one type of traditional science but rather multiple variations of it.) This is also referred to as "positivist belief" and "storybook science" by contemporary thinkers in the psychology and sociology of science and in the history and philosophy of science. The methods of *traditional science* are characterized in principle by *the dispassionate, unbiased formulation and testing (disproving) of hypotheses in ways that may be easily replicated, such testing procedures and outcomes being communally available.*

Traditional science has been criticized not as being incorrect but simply as being very incomplete. It ignores the human or social dimension of knowing.[4] It expresses what many social scientists think physical scientists do. In practice, science is neither dispassionate, unbiased, value-free, nor always open.[5] Nor can it be so to the degree suggested by traditional thinking. For example, a sample survey of publications in *Management Science* covering the period 1955 to 1976 found that nearly two thirds of the papers pursued a strategy of advocacy in which a single dominant hypothesis (nearly always supported) is compared to a simple null hypothesis. The author demonstrates that this is the least objective of all the approaches used in the sample of articles.[6] In what has become a widely cited research effort Michael Mahoney provided one set of journal referees with a paper containing results in agreement with the dominant hypothesis among their

[4] Wolfgang Stegmuller, *The Structure and Dynamics of Theories* (New York: Springer-Verlag, 1976); Walter A. Weisskopf, "The Method Is the Ideology: From a Newtonian to a Heisenbergian Paradigm in Economics," *Journal of Economic Issues*, vol. 13, no. 4, 1979; Daniel R. Fusfeld, "The Conceptual Framework of Modern Economics," *Journal of Economic Issues*, vol. 14, no. 1, 1980.

[5] L. Vaughn Blankenship, "The Social Context of Science," in F. Nicosia and Y. Wind, *Behavioral Models for Market Analysis: Foundations for Marketing Action* (Hinsdale, IL: Dryden, 1977), pp. 2–24; C. West Churchman, *The Design of Inquiring Systems* (New York: Basic Books, 1971); Ian Mitroff, *The Subjective Side of Science: An Inquiry Into the Psychology of the Apollo Moon Scientists* (Amsterdam, The Netherlands: Elsevier), 1974.

[6] J. Scott Armstrong, "Advocacy and Objectivity in Science," *Management Science*, 25, no. 5 (May 1979), 423–478.

group.[7] An equivalent sample of journal referees were given the identical paper but with the empirical results reversed and thus disconfirming the dominant hypothesis. The first set of referees accepted the paper, giving it a high rating on relevance and methodology. The set of referees who were confronted with disconfirming evidence rejected the paper, giving it a low rating on relevance and methodology. It may also be questionable as to whether our perception of a truly unbiased scientist, isolated in a laboratory, is a useful one even if it could be accurate. Particularly in the social sciences, such lack of emotion may not be desirable. Consider the following statement by Churchman and Ackoff:

> Pragmatism does not advocate the scientist who removes all his emotions, sympathies, and the like from his experimental process. This is like asking the scientist to give up being the whole man while he experiments. Perhaps a man's emotion will be the most powerful instrument he has at his disposal in reaching a conclusion. The main task, however, is to enlarge the scope of the scientific model so that we can begin to understand the role of the other types of experience in reaching decisions and can see how they also can be checked and controlled. The moral, according to the pragmatist, should not be to exclude feeling from scientific method, but to include it in the sense of understanding it better.[8]

In fact, Blankenship argues that a view of scientific inquiry that ignores the impact on the research process of the personality, experiences, and values of researchers, managers (clients), and subjects (especially as all three parties may interact with one another) may yield invalid and unobjective market research.[9]

An inference that might be drawn from Churchman and Ackoff's notion is that inquiry is not a matter of "science" only or "art" only. Perhaps art and science are not two distinct values, but a blend, each enhanced by the other. In an essay on realism in marketing models, Churchman suggests that a good marketing model is one that is meaningful to both scientist and manager (artisan).[10] It must be the product of an intellectual perspective that combines a scientist's way of thinking about things with a manager's way.

Although we shall have much more to say on this topic later, perhaps enough comment has been provided at this point to permit an explicit statement of the contemporary view of science. *The contemporary view holds that scientists and their methods are very often not unbiased and value-free; that a posture of objectivity is not always a desirable way of discovering knowledge even if it were possible; that traditional notions of disproving or falsifying hypotheses are of limited*

---

[7] Michael J. Mahoney, "Publication Prejudices: An Experimental Study of Confirmatory Bias in the Peer Review System," *Cognitive Therapy and Research*, I (1977), 161–175.

[8] C. West Churchman and Russel A. Ackoff, *Methods of Inquiry* (St. Louis: Educational Publishers, 1950), p. 224.

[9] Blankenship, *op. cit.*, pp. 22–24. Various views on this position and other ideas in this chapter may be found in *Proceedings from the Workship on the Epistomology of Management Research* (Stockholm: *The Economic Research Institute at the Stockholm School of Economics*, 1980).

[10] Churchman, *op. cit.* See also Jerome R. Ravetz, *Scientific Knowledge and Its Social Problems* (London: Oxford, 1971), esp. Chapter 3, "Science as Craftsman's Work," pp. 75–108.

*value; and that "reality" may be structured in different yet equally valid ways.* This view, of course, contrasts sharply with the traditional view of science described a few paragraphs earlier. What is most important for readers to keep in mind as they read this book is that the contemporary view differs from the traditional view primarily in its *assumptions about how scientists go about doing their work.* Both views stress the importance of rigorous methodology and holders of each view employ the same array of research techniques. The contemporary view simply says that there are substantial deviations from traditional science assumptions, that these deviations need to be understood in order to better evaluate knowledge, and that many of these deviations might be capitalized upon in ways that can improve the process creating valid knowledge. No one view is inherently better than another. Each view has its special benefits and limitations. This book suggests that two views are better than one.

## Generative Theory

Substantial assistance is available within the marketing literature to assist the field in understanding the composition or structure of theories[11] and the testing of hypotheses and theories.[12] However, creating theory is not the same as understanding, modeling, and testing theory. Little guidance is available to the marketing student about creating theories. The need for creating more theories and better theories in the field is great. "An examination of the marketing literature of the last decade suggests a predominance of empirical studies with small samples and limited generalizability, a considerable number of method-ological papers, and very few conceptual papers proposing new concepts or theories."[13] Even if we employ theories developed in nonmarketing contexts, the unique attributes of marketing contexts may require a process of adaptation which is itself a theory development or creation activity. We uncover a new insight which results in a somewhat different theory. However, the borrowing of theories has not always proved fruitful, especially when adaptation is not attempted. Efforts at applying personality theory to consumer behavior is perhaps the best-known illustration of this point.[14] In many instances, it may be

---

[11] Cf. G. Zaltman, C. Pinson, and R. Anglemar, *Metatheory in Consumer Research* (New York: Holt, Rinehart Winston, 1973); Shelby D. Hunt, *Marketing Theory: Conceptual Foundations of Research in Marketing* (Columbus, OH: Grid, 1976).

[12] Cf. Richard P. Bagozzi, *Causal Models in Marketing* (New York: Wiley, 1980); G. H. Churchill, Jr., *Marketing Research: Methodological Foundations* (Hinsdale, IL: Dryden, 1976); Paul E. Green and Donald S. Tull, *Research for Marketing Decisions* 4th ed., (Englewood Cliffs, NJ: Prentice-Hall, 1978).

[13] J. Wind, "On the Status of Marketing Theory," *Journal of Marketing*, Fall 1979, p. 6.

[14] H. H. Kassarjian, "Personality and Consumer Behavior: A Review," *Journal of Marketing Research*, 5 (1968), 155–164.

more efficient—and in any event more fun—to play the role of an architect developing a blueprint rather than a carpenter primarily following someone else's blueprint.

What we are urging is a point of view that we hope augments traditional science by helping the reader to develop what Kenneth Gergen describes as a "generative capacity" in one's thinking. The theory builder is the creater, the generator of thoughts, ideas, and evidence about phenomena that are not yet entirely understood. The generative capacity of a theory is its ability to challenge the commonly accepted assumptions of society and to suggest alternative ways of looking at phenomena. More formally, it is "the capacity to challenge the guiding assumption of the culture, to raise fundamental questions regarding contemporary social life, to foster reconsideration of that which is 'taken for granted,' and thereby to furnish new alternatives for social action."[15]

The vast majority of theories lack this capacity, a deficit which has been attributed to the heavy emphasis placed upon the positivist-empiricist orientation. This orientation is characterized by a set of assumptions, one of which is reliance upon "objective" facts, and by the use of traditional logic, involving the accumulation of great quantities of data and extensive training in methodology but not typically in theory building. The problem with this approach lies in the formulation of research questions: "Neither the facts nor the logic can furnish the questions to be asked of the data or metaphor for conceptual organization."[16]

Through the use of generative theory and creative imagery, the scientist can alter his or her mode of conceptualization from that which is commonly accepted so as to effect social change. In other words, by creating theory we can also create new social forms and world views. This does not mean that theories that primarily describe events or activities are not useful. Such theories are especially valuable for communicating accumulated knowledge about, say, management decision making to persons who are inexperienced in the area of practice covered by the theory.

A special characteristic of the traditional approach has been the requirement for verification of theory by data. Although much empirical research has been produced in marketing, few authors have stressed the generalizations that can be made about the phenomena studied. This condition has led to the conclusion by some observers that we appear to have very little real knowledge of marketing.[17]

Also, the meaning of concepts within a social context varies according to the degree of consensual validity attached to them, dictated in part by the norms and values dominant at the time. Although hypothesis testing has a central role in scientific inquiry, use of it for verification of a theory that already makes sense

[15] Kenneth J. Gergen, "Toward Generative Theory," *Journal of Personality and Social Psychology*, 36, no. 11 (1978), 1344–1360.

[16] *Ibid.*, p. 1347.

[17] Robert P. Leone and Randall L. Schultz, "A Study of Marketing Generalizations," *Journal of Marketing*, 44 (Winter 1980), 10–18.

intuitively has often come at the expense of substantive and imaginative theory creation.

The traditional positivist view also assumes a kind of temporal irrelevance, independent of contemporary life patterns. The generative theorist, on the other hand, recognizes that observed behavioral patterns are limited historically and can thus be changed. As marketing managers and government policy makers facilitate change in behavioral patterns among consumers, they are also creating the need to alter preexisting explanations or theories of behavior to correspond to the newer patterns of behavior. Thus the notion of generative theory makes special sense for marketers and government policy makers.

## Breaking Down the Barriers

The question now comes: how do you generate or discover theories? The focus of this book is to help develop strategies to generate and refine theories. To do so requires that current ways of thinking be examined and new ways of thinking explored. One way of approaching this is to isolate the blocks that hinder us from generating or rediscovering a theory or a new idea in the first place. These can include both perceptual and intellectual blocks.[18]

## Perceptual Blocks

Perceptual blocks are "obstacles which prevent a problem solver from clearly perceiving either the problem itself or the information that is necessary to solve the problem."[19] In terms of generating theory, these are obstacles that prevent the development or discovery of a theory or new idea to help solve a problem.

### Tendencies to Limit Problem Area Too Closely

Limiting the problem area arises out of prematurely narrowing the focus of a problem or by not realizing its multidimensionality. This block frequently occurs because we view a problem from only one *point of view*. For example, take the situation of a MacDougall's food outlet manager who is trying to increase sales. If he were generating a theory on how sales increases come about, he might base it on only his point of view. This might be represented as in Figure 1.1a.

He sees himself and the customer as the only participants. Further, he takes the rather utilitarian view that what is being exchanged is money for hamburgers.[20] It

---

[18] James L. Adams, *Conceptual Blockbusting* (San Francisco: Freeman, 1974).

[19] *Ibid.*, p. 13.

[20] The different types of exchanges mentioned come from Richard P. Bagozzi, "Marketing as Exchange," *Journal of Marketing*, 39 (October 1975), 32–39.

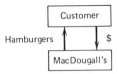

**Figure 1.1a**

becomes evident, however, that the problem can be changed if he takes a broader point of view, realizing that both his actions and the consumers' are being influenced by other factors (ads from competing food outlets, agencies putting out a "good" ad, quality of media programs, and others). This broader viewpoint might be represented by Figure 1.1b.

Thus, the two parties are linked both directly and indirectly. Explaining potential increases in sales could take into account not only customer–store relations but also customer–media, media–ad agency, and ad agency–store relations. Problems could arise at any or all of these points. Further, Figure 1.1b shows that you can limit yourself by considering only one type of motive for purchases—for example, utilitarian ($ — hamburger). If the *symbolic* nature of purchases is ignored, the importance of developing a strong outlet image would be missed.

It is the failure to recognize these indirect links as well as both the utilitarian and symbolic nature of purchases that results in a kind of "theoretical myopia." Thus, the hamburger outlet manager may locate the problem too narrowly and, in fact, develop theories and solutions to the wrong problem! De Bono develops a metaphor that illuminates this situation.[21]

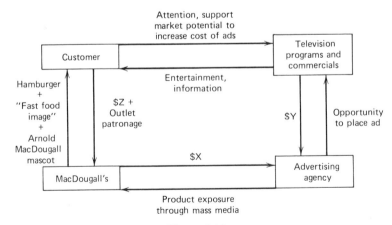

**Figure 1.1b**

[21] E. DeBono, *New Think* (New York: Aldine, 1969).

Logic is the tool that is used to dig holes deeper and bigger, to make them altogether better holes. But if the hole is in the wrong place, then no amount of improvement is going to put it in the right place. No matter how obvious this may seem to the digger, it is still easier to go on digging in the same place than to start over in a new place. Vertical thinking is digging the same hole deeper; lateral thinking is trying again elsewhere.

## Stereotypes

A stereotype denotes beliefs about classes of individuals or objects which are preconceived; that is, they result not from fresh appraisals of each observation but from routinized habits or judgment and expectation.[22]

*Market segmentation*, a concept that has provided stereotypes of consumers, has proven useful in predicting market potential and developing a unique marketing mix for various segments. As mentioned earlier, a generative theory recognizes that as people change, so must the range of situations in which a theory is tested. A large advertiser developed eight segments representing the market for certain beauty products. By tracing these segments over time the agency found some segments merged, others disappeared, and still others grew in size. If they had not made fresh appraisals, their stereotypes would have become outdated. These appraisals also resulted in new conceptualizations of segmentation.

The concept of *product life cycle* (PLC) has been adopted by many marketers and has been a useful stereotype of market behavior over time. It alerted marketers to relatively stable patterns that summarized the nature of exchange relationships for a product over time. The development of this concept illustrates two important points not observed in the segmentation example. First, the fact that patterns of market behavior (stereotypes) are predictable does *not* mean they are deterministic. Levitt brings this out clearly by pointing out that if you identify what point in the life cycle your market has reached, then you can extend it; instead of abandoning a product or market, use your creativity to extend the life cycle.[23] Second, it's important to criticize the concept (stereotype) itself. The PLC concept became so popular that it was integrated into standard operating procedures of many firms. Its use had become automatic. In many ways it became a self-defeating prediction.[24]

[22] J. Gould and W. Kolb (Eds.), *A Dictionary of the Social Sciences* (New York: The Press Press, 1969), p. 694.

[23] T. Levitt, "Exploit the Product Life Cycle," *Harvard Business Review*, 45 (November–December 1965), 81–94.

[24] N. K. Dhalla and S. Yuspeh, "Forget the Product Life Cycle Concept," *Harvard Business Review*, January–February 1976, pp. 102–112.

### Fixation

Fixation refers to an obsessive or unhealthy preoccupation or attachment to particular objects, ideas, theories, or people. Two examples will be given to show how fixation on one particular theory or problem can result in undesirable consequences. Using his many years in business as a background, Ford concludes that most companies can be distinguished as either problem oriented (PO) or objective oriented (OO).[25] PO's see objectives/goals in terms of the problems involved in getting to these objectives and their consequences; OO's interpret problems as merely challenges that have to be recognized and overcome. PO's are more likely to miss opportunities and lag behind industry in growth and potential. Ford typifies the problems of PO's as timidity, conservatism, having long time lags between setting objectives and target completion dates, improper delegation, and lack of problem-solving skills. Thus, fixation on one particular problem or theory leaves less time and inclination to pursue alternative theories and problems.

Hanan related the problems of fixation in an exchange setting.[26] A company had a PR program that had its sales force billed as "Problem Solvers," The result was that the sales force received thousands of problems from potential customers—most of which they couldn't solve. Of those they could solve, a vast majority of them weren't *profitable* to solve. His analysis suggests that people can become fixated with solving problems *because* they are problems rather than because the solutions are profitable.

### Saturation

Related to the problem of fixation is that of saturation. Fixation carried to its ultimate end would result in a mass of deductions from a theory that has been tested and retested (e.g., the eighty-fifth study of the price–quality relationship). With all this information there is a good chance we will have a case of information overload. Take the case of a company that has devised a marketing research system for collecting and disseminating information on its current markets. It finds that although it has distributed lots of "good" information, there seem to be actual declines in performance. People were spending more time trying to read and understand information and had less time *actually* to use it to pursue opportunities. Also some people skimmed it and partially understood it, then proceeded confidently onward, secure that they had learned a new idea. proceeded confidently onward, secure that they had learned a new idea. However, this particular reaction represents an intriguing aspect of saturation. Adams states "that one thinks he has the data, even though he is unable to

---

[25]C. H. Ford, "If You're Problem Oriented, You're in Trouble," *Business Management*, 35 (February 1969), 24–28.

[26]M. Hanan, "You Don't Know What Problems Are Until You Become a Problem Solver," *Sales Management*, 113 (July 1974), 32–38.

produce it when needed."[27] Thus, there is a high probability it will not be used or, if used, misapplied.

## Intellectual Blocks

At this point, it will be useful to discuss why a theory developer might think that a marketing phenomenon should be viewed a certain way. Doing so pinpoints intellectual blocks. These are blocks that "result in an inefficient choice of mental tactics or a shortage of intellectual ammunition . . . inadequate or inflexible use of strategies; or a lack of, or incorrect information."[28]

In generating a theory, a theory developer is basically constructing how he or she thinks the marketing exchange system works. But how often do we really examine *how* we generate our view of this exchange system? How often do we challenge our taken-for-granted assumptions concerning this view? Sometimes we question why we behave the way we do, but mostly we just behave. The successful researcher or practitioner often sees no reason to question his or her behavior. In fact, as Bowman suggests, most of us "plod along with pre-behavioral assumptions . . . and plod along quite profitably."[29] Yet the dynamics of the exchange system usually lead to other problems. Sanderson notes one of the paradoxes of success: ". . . such is the strength of past successful behavior in the direction of future activities that a particular mode of behavior will be extended to inappropriate areas without any qualms."[30] The same is true of theory development.

If success isn't a problem, then failure to generate more than one theory can be. This represents a type of intellectual block—the inability to develop alternative explanations of behavior. Recognition of this inability is particularly important if the representation of human behavior as being dynamic is adhered to. As time passes, as people change, explanations of behavior are also subject to change. A generative theory recognizes this. A great deal of this inability to develop alternative explanations might be derived from early courses in math and other problem-oriented disciplines. Children are socialized in a $2 + 2 = 4$ paradigm. They are rewarded (by grades, peer approval, status, parental admiration) for finding the right answer. In a great many ways this mode of inquiry is transferred directly into studies of marketing problems and theory development.

There emerges a new problem: one-solution mode of thinking. Since the

[27] Adams, *op. cit.*, p. 26.

[28] Adams, *op. cit.*, p. 63.

[29] J. S. Bowman, "The Behavioral Sciences: Fact or Fantasy," *Organizational Personnel Journal*, August 1976, pp. 395–397.

[30] M. Sanderson, "Successful Problem Finding," *Journal of Systems Management*, 25 (October 1974), 16–21.

premise of this book is that theories are representations of situations and that exchange involves different goals and different points of view, then it becomes important to develop alternative explanations and formulations.

In developing different approaches and formalizing ideas, we must be careful, however. As Toulmin notes, ". . . too often [this has] introduced us to particular conceptions and models, while failing to do what is essential, namely explaining in detail the function of these models, conceptions and the rest. The whole reason for formulating a problem using theory or conceptions is that it helps us to explain things we could not explain before."[31] This confusion many times arises because we don't explicitly recognize the fact that we are formalizing our observations. There is no recognition of the *language shift* that occurs in formalizing. This shift can involve using new words (ideas) in looking at old phenomena, as well as using old words in a new way. Confusion arises because we use new words to say the old phenomenon *is* something (sales growth of a product *is* a product life cycle), instead of using the new words to represent the old phenomenon *as* something (product life cycle is only *one* representation— other representations could have been made!).

Confusion also arises because we don't recognize the difference in meaning when using old words in a new context, that is, if we "borrow" the concept of entropy from physics, does it have the same *meaning* in the marketing context? Since many people get an initial theory by borrowing from another discipline, it is important to recognize that the terms that are used may not have the same meaning in the marketing area. Are the phenomena they refer to the same?

In summary, intellectual blocks prevent the development of different structural relationships between the concepts that are part of the theory. Furthermore, they prevent recognition that the theory is but one of many that could have been developed to address the problem at hand. Avoiding these problems requires not only flexibility in thinking strategies, but sensitivity to the different meanings that concepts might have in different settings.

## Viewpoints

We have indicated that traditional science has been criticized as being incomplete because it ignores the social dimensions of knowing. It thus tends to produce an inaccurate view of the world—whether it is the world of microbiology or new product testing —and of the way in which knowledge of the world is acquired. In the field of management science the stress on traditional science has tended to produce viewpoints or models that are unnecessarily discrepant with the real world.[32] William Souder, an industrial engineer, has described this discrepancy very well with regard to models used to evaluate research and development projects. His description is contained in Table 1.1.

[31] S. Toulmin, *The Philosophy of Science* (New York: Harper Torch Books, 1966), p. 12.
[32] Churchman, *op. cit.*

*Table 1.1*
**The Real World Environment Versus The Management Science View**

| The Viewpoint that Management Science Models Seem to Take | The Real World Environment |
|---|---|
| 1. A single decision maker, in a well-behaved environment. | 1. Many decision makers and many decision influencers, in a dynamic organizational environment. |
| 2. Perfect information about candidate projects and their characteristics: outputs, values and risks of candidates known and quantifiable. | 2. Imperfect information about candidate projects and their characteristics; outputs and values of projects are difficult to specify; uncertainty accompanies all estimates. |
| 3. Well-known, invariant goals. | 3. Ever-changing, fuzzy goals. |
| 4. Decision making information is concentrated in the hands of the decision maker, so that he has all the information he needs to make a decision. | 4. Decision making information is highly splintered and scattered piecemeal throughout the organization, with no one part of the organization having all the information needed for decision making. |
| 5. The decision maker is able to articulate all consequences. | 5. The decision maker is often unable or unwilling to state outcomes and consequences. |
| 6. Candidate projects are viewed as independent entities, to be individually evaluated on their own merits. | 6. Candidate projects are often technically and economically interdependent. |
| 7. A single objective, usually expected value maximization or profit maximization, is assumed and the constraints are primarily budgetary in nature. | 7. There are sometimes conflicting multiple objectives and multiple constraints, and these are often non-economic in nature. |
| 8. The best portfolio of projects is determined on economic grounds. | 8. Satisfactory portfolios may possess many non-economic characteristics. |
| 9. The budget is "optimized" in a single decision. | 9. An iterative, re-cycling budget determination process is used. |
| 10. One single, economically "best," overall decision is sought. | 10. What seems to be the "best" decision for the total organization may not be seen as best by each department or party, so that many conflicts may arise. |

*Source.* Souder, William, "A System for Using R & D Project Evaluation Methods," *Research Management*, September 1978, p. 33.

The stress on traditional science has also tended to produce an image or viewpoint of research methods that is unrealistic. Shulamit Reinharz provides a comparison of what mainstream sociological research claims to be and what it should acknowledge it really is. Her comparison is provided in Table 1.2 because it is appropriate to research methods in marketing as well as other social sciences.

The ideas in Table 1.1 and especially Table 1.2 are also consistent with recent important ideas in psychology concerning information processing and knowing. Substantial evidence is emerging and in some cases reemerging which suggest that affective judgments—feelings and intuitive responses—are relatively independent of and may often precede and subsequently influence cognitive processes.[33] The role of feelings in such processes as research and theory building would seem to be very central as well as overlooked. Table 1.3 presents a comparison of

**Table 1.2**
**Espoused Versus Actual Sociological Research Models**

| Mainstream Sociological Research Claims to Be: | An Alternative Method Would Acknowledge That It Is: |
|---|---|
| 1. Exclusively rational in the conduct of research and the analysis of data. | 1. A mix of rational, serendipitous and intuitive phenomena in research and analysis. |
| 2. Scientific. | 2. Accurate but artistic. |
| 3. Oriented to carefully defined structures. | 3. Oriented to processes. |
| 4. Completely impersonal. | 4. Personal. |
| 5. Oriented to the prediction and control of events and things. | 5. Oriented to understanding phenomena. |
| 6. Interested in the validity of research findings for scholars. | 6. Interested in the meaningfulness of research findings to the scholarly and user communities. |
| 7. Objective. | 7. A mix of objective and subjective orientation. |
| 8. Capable of producing generalized principles. | 8. Capable of producing specific explanations. |
| 9. Interested in replicable events and procedures. | 9. Interested in unique although frequently occurring phenomena. |
| 10. Capable of producing completed analysis of a research problem. | 10. Limited to producing partial discoveries of ongoing events. |
| 11. Interested in addressing problems with predefined concepts. | 11. Interested in generating concepts *in vivo*, in the field itself. |

Source. Reinharz, Shulamit, *On Becoming a Social Scientist*, San Francisco CA: Jossey-Bass, 1979, 11–12.

[33] Highly recommended reading on this point is, R. B. Zajonc, "Feeling and Thinking: Preferences Need No Inferences," *American Psychologist*, Vol. 35, No. 2 (1980), pp. 151–175.

*Table 1.3*
**Comparison of Newtonian Physics and Quantum Mechanics**

| *Newtonian Physics* | *Quantum Mechanics* |
| --- | --- |
| 1. Can picture it. | 1. Cannot picture it. |
| 2. Based on ordinary sense perception. | 2. Based on behavior of subatomic particles and systems not directly observable. |
| 3. Describes *things*; individual objects in space and their changes in time. | 3. Describes statistical behavior of systems. |
| 4. Predicts events. | 4. Predicts probabilities. |
| 5. Assumes an objective reality "out there." | 5. Does not assume an objective reality apart from our experience. |
| 6. We can observe something without changing it. | 6. We cannot observe something without changing it. |
| 7. Claims to be based on "absolute truth," the way that nature is behind the scenes. | 7. Claims only to correlate experience correctly. |

*Source.* Adapted from G. Zukav, *The Dancing Wu Li Masters; An Overview of the New Physics* (New York: Morrow, 1979), p. 41.

thinking processes associated with Newtonian physics and quantum mechanics. The most accomplished physicists are those who are able to blend both ways of perceiving subject matter. However, it would appear that issues in marketing are more akin to issues in quantum mechanics than they are to Newtonian physics. Hence it is especially important to acquire as well the kind of perspectives represented by physicists working in quantum mechanics.[34]

In both Table 1.1 and Table 1.2 a traditional viewpoint, which corresponds closely to traditional science, is contrasted with what is claimed to be a more realistic viewpoint. If the more realistic viewpoints are in fact more accurate with respect to the way decisions are actually made and how research is actually conducted, it is because they acknowledge more explicitly that decision makers and researchers are people working on problems that are often caused by people and in any event being solved by people and whose solutions are applied to people. If decision making and research in marketing are challenging and fun, it is largely because of this "peopleness." Thus our methods for exploring marketing should reflect the fact that market researchers and decision makers are people addressing people-related issues. Such a reflection greatly adds to traditional science. It produces more veridical insight, which is what good science is all about.

[34] We urge the reader to read Gary Zukav, *The Dancing Wu Li Masters: An Overview of the New Physics*.

## Being Multilingual in Discovery
## and Justification

A distinction is sometimes made between *discovery*, which is the process of uncovering ideas, and *justification*, which is the process of accepting or rejecting knowledge.[35] However, processes that are conceptually distinguishable can also co-mingle. For example, love, hate, and sex should not be confused with one another but it is the distinct contribution of psychotherapy that all three phenomena may co-exist in reference to the same person and affect each other in an ongoing relationship. So, too, does discovery occur during the process of justification and justification occur during the process of discovery. The intellectual distinction between discovery and justification is a useful and even necessary one, but we should not confuse their separation for intellectual convenience with the way they really co-exist in the everyday life of a scientist. The processes of discovery and justification are characterized in fact by multiple types of rules and procedures, and the basis for this diversity exists in the social and psychological foundation of scientific endeavors. Thus, while we are primarily concerned with discovery, we cannot avoid touching upon issues relating to justification. And in both cases multiple methods or procedures exist.

Perhaps the notion of language provides an appropriate metaphor at this point. We all know English is not the same as Spanish and neither of these languages is like Japanese. Each language has significant subtleties not shared by the others. Some thoughts expressed in one language can be translated into another language only at great cost in understanding. Some thoughts cannot be translated at all. Yet each language manages to solve a wide range of complex problems it shares in common with other languages and to do so in ways that are consistent with the very different social and psychological realities of people living in, say, Stoneham, Massachusetts, of Limón, Costa Rica, or Sendai, Japan. We cannot say that one language is inherently best for all people. Similarly, no one method of discovery and justification—"method" being the language of science—is best for all scientists. Particle physicists, archeologists, psychotherapists, endocrinologists, rural sociologists, and urban policy analysts live in worlds as different from one another as Stoneham, Limon, and Sendai. Accordingly, their methodologies may differ despite many common concerns or problems related to discovery and justification in explanation, prediction, and control. A subsidiary theme of this book is to urge an openness to different methodologies, to be a bit more multilingual with respect to our processes of inquiry.

In the chapters to follow we present a number of ideas that you may want to use to broaden your understanding of discovery and improve your own processes of discovery. There should also occur spill-over effects with regard to the testing

[35] Hunt, *op. cit.*

or justification of your discoveries. Most of what we present is highly consistent with contemporary analyses of the scientific enterprise. In this sense, there is not a great deal that is novel. However, if your exposure to the philosophy of science is along so-called traditional or positivist lines or if your exposure has been primarily through the marketing literature, many of these ideas may be perceived as new. They go beyond the storybook or fairy-tale version of scientific inquiry. In time the ideas in contemporary philosophy, history, and sociology of science, which are reflected in this book, may be viewed as being as removed from reality as storybook science presently is viewed. Thus, we encourage trial and even adoption of these ideas but with a low level of loyalty to them. The reader is urged to play with them and shape them into forms that are stimulating and relevant to his or her world view.

Thus far we have assumed an existing interest in theory construction among readers. No arguments have been advanced as to why the reader should have an interest in theory construction. For the more research- and teaching-oriented readers the presentation of such arguments may not be necessary. However, some readers may not be engaged in or contemplating a research- or teaching-oriented career. Readers pursuing a management career are often insufficiently exposed to reasons why they also should be formally concerned with improving their theory construction skills. Accordingly, the next section focuses on some of the reasons why practicing managers should be attentive to theory-building strategies. Chapter 6 will develop further the idea that many good managers are effective partly because they are also good theorists.

## The Practical Importance of Theory Building

The main purpose of this section is to provide a few reasons why practitioners should be concerned with theory-building skills.[36] We shall start, however, with a few brief comments about the interests of academics in this task.

There are several reasons why theory construction is important to the academic researcher. One reason relates to the socialization process. The socialization process in many academic settings contributes to a self-identity which finds the generalizing of knowledge rewarding. Theory building is an important part of this process. The reasons why such a socialization process emerges so strongly in academic settings need not be addressed here. Although generalizable knowledge may often be of value to nonacademics, its development tends to be confined to the academic community including the so-called "think tank" research community.

---

[36] This section is adapted from Gerald Zaltman and Karl-Erik Wärneryd, "Learning About Building Theory—Why Bother?" Working Paper, The Stockholm School of Economics, 1981.

As part of the socialization process, various norms reinforce the inclination for academic researchers to do research that (1) might be generalizable to multiple settings, or (2) aids the process of making other existing research relevant to multiple settings. Doing very applied highly context-specific research without regard to a possible broader relevance of that research is often (traditionally) not considered "nice" for an academic. It is like peeling bananas and wasting the fruit or, worse, peeling the banana and not bothering even to look at the fruit.

In the remainder of this section we shall discuss three reasons why practitioners should be concerned with building theory. The reasons selected here are very practical, job-related reasons. They have nothing to do with the ability to find an academic position if things go bad at work or the intrinsic gratification of being creative or of sounding impressive in the midst of banana peel research.

### Metalanguage

Language (in all its many forms) serves to convey meaning from one person to another. A related purpose of language is to provide a mechanism for individuals to interpret the meaning of events. By having labeled categories of thought, such as words, we can more readily think about as well as communicate about events related to those categories. The term "market segmentation" provides an example. Market segmentation is an instance of metalanguage categorizing a set of questions or activities. Having the general concept and term "market segmentation" makes it easier to discuss and implement marketing strategy. The concept also encourages managers to think more strategically about consumers: What is unique about different clusters of consumers? Can existing clusters be segmented further? Can certain clusters be grouped together? What is the optimal level of product and promotional differentiation given key market segments? These are questions some managers have always asked in one way or another. Most important, however, when the concept of market segmentation was crystalized or developed more formally and given a label which found common usage, the kinds of questions just listed began getting asked more explicitly and by more managers. Thus the language of marketing practice was improved upon by provision of a metalanguage ("market segmentation") which consists of a formally stated concept and commonly used term.

Metalanguage creates a clarifying effect. It pulls together and highlights what is already known or already being done on a more trial-and-error and perhaps less fully aware basis. The concepts of social marketing and marketing by nonprofit agencies are also metalanguage concepts. The terms did not create those activities: they merely stated more formally what some agencies were already doing with varying success. However, once the metaconcepts appeared, they did greatly enhance the quality of marketing thought in a larger number of nonprofit agencies. The development of these concepts made it easier for practitioners to understand and improve their behavior.

Being familiar with the concepts, processes, and terminology involved in theory building provides the practicing manager with a metalanguage. This metalanguage serves a similar clarifying effect with regard to a manager's own set of ideas, assumptions, and rules of thumb. It enables managers to think more easily and more creatively about their own thinking and the thinking of others. Metalanguage about theory construction represents a set of tools. These tools facilitate the diagnosis of marketing problems and the development and evaluation of their solutions much as X-ray and hematologic technology assist similar diagnostic and curative functions in medicine.

## Learning in New Situations

Let's start with the case of a brand manager who is responsible for a single product. He or she is concerned with knowing as much as possible about various contingencies affecting that product. These contingencies may range from fluctuations in the price of product components or ingredients, to changes in competitor behavior, to changes in consumer preferences. There may be a great many such contingencies. Moreover, a change in one area may require changes in several other areas. A successful brand manager will have an understanding of what the key factors are and how they are related for the specific product for which he or she has responsibility. This manager will be able to make certain predictions on the basis of this understanding. Depending on the predictions made, the manager may decide to alter one or more elements of the marketing mix over which he or she has control. The better the manager understands the intricacies of the various contingencies that must be dealt with, the more effective he or she will be in planning and implementing control activities.

Substantial success as a brand manager may result in a promotion to a product group or product line management position. The number of contexts the manager in our example is concerned with now grows from only one to several. However, there is another more significant change. Previously, say as manager of a specific food product, it was necessary to monitor the cost of milk, raisins, chocolate, various kinds of packaging materials, the reactions of distributors and consumers to changes in package size, color, and texture, the effects of cents-off coupons offered by competition and one's own firm, shifts in sales relating to new product offerings by competitors, unusually prolonged seasonal weather conditions, and so forth. How useful is this kind of information in the newer position? How comparable are the kinds of understandings, predictions, and interventions obtained when one is managing a single product to those required when one is managing a group of products each having its own manager? The answer to both questions is, "Not a whole lot." The product line manager is now more concerned with (1) managing people, that is, brand managers, and (2) evaluating and integrating or coordinating actions being proposed by various brand managers for their particular products. The product line manager is not worried so much about the necessity of increasing the promotion of brand A to offset inroads made by a competitor's new offering. The manager will be more concerned now with the impact of such an action on the available promotional budget for other products or brands in his or her group.

Thus there are different questions to be answered and different systems of explanation to be developed as one moves from one type of marketing function or position to another. The level of abstraction may change as well. In this case we mean that the scope of events becomes broader and the view of those events different. The manager of an entire product line must think more about factors affecting the entire line of products and less about factors unique to just a small subset. At a minimum it is the costs of component parts generally that is of concern rather than the cost of a major ingredient of just one product. The product line manager must now assess the impact of a potential new product on the entire line as opposed to its unique impact on brand A or on brand B. The unit of analysis is more often a set of products rather than the individual items within that set (see Figure 1.2). The brand managers of those individual items will, of course, keep those as their primary unit of analysis.

The person who understands and employs the metalanguage of theory construction will develop valuable understandings more quickly, make better predictions, and exercise more effective control as he or she encounters new responsibilities in higher level positions. Frequently, the higher the level of responsibility—for example, vice-president for marketing operations versus product line manager versus brand manager—the more general the level of explanations or understandings developed and the wider the array of different events or activities those explanations try to encompass. Often, too, theories found at higher levels of management may be more streamlined even though they are inclusive of a broader array of events. Thus, senior management is more prone to develop theories of action that are generalizable to many areas of the firm and yet are parsimonious. These two criteria are important to academic researchers as well.

The manager who is lacking skills in the metalanguage of theory construction will find it difficult to adjust to different tasks, especially those associated with higher levels of responsibility. The metalanguage of theory construction is common to all contexts since it is a way of thinking about thinking.

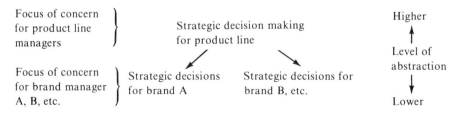

**Figure 1.2.** Different levels of concern and levels of abstraction.

### Frames of Reference

A frame of reference is the set of ideas and outlooks we generally use in viewing things. It is our set of unspoken assumptions, expectations, and decision rules. We often invoke different frames of reference for viewing the same event, depending on a variety of factors. When evaluating consumer response to a new product after its first six months on the market, we might focus especially on the ability of the product to enhance sales of other related products offered by the company as well as the absolute sales of the new product. In other circumstances the absolute level of sales may be relatively more important in our frame of reference. The frame of reference used to evaluate a particular product may vary from consumer to consumer. It may also vary for the same consumer over time depending upon past experience, severity of the need for the product, whether it is used privately or publicly, and so forth.

Thus frames of reference serve as a lens or filter and evaluating device between events and our interpretation of those events. This is illustrated in Figure 1.3. The reader may be familiar with the story of two shoe salesmen who were dispatched to assess opportunities in an underdeveloped country. One salesman returned to report that opportunities were very poor: "Only half of the people wear shoes." The other salesman returned to report that opportunities were very great: "Half the people don't have shoes yet." Clearly very different frames of reference were leading to very different interpretations of the same event.

There is general agreement among persons who study information use that information is more likely to affect our frame of reference than our actions in any direct sense. That is, if information has a direct effect on us, it is more often through its effect on our frames of reference than it is on our specific actions. Our actions may be affected, of course, but this effect is likely to be via our frames of reference. Information may change our frame of reference. The resulting change in frame of reference may alter an action because it alters the way we perceive events. For example, one study of the use of market research by managers found that formal market research studies influenced managers' ways of thinking about problems more than it influenced directly any specific

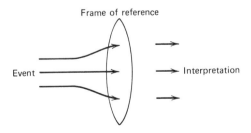

**Figure 1.3.**  Frame of reference as a lens between event and interpretation.

action on the problems the research addressed.[37] Many other empirical studies have found the same tendency.

Now, what has all this to do with the practical value of theory-building skills for managers? If our frames of reference are so critical to our interpretation of events and if the information we process generally influences decisions through its impact on our frames of reference, it becomes essential that we be able to evaluate and alter our frames of reference or ways of thinking about thinking. Skills in evaluating and building theory will enable managers to understand their frames of reference and improve them. The manager with an improved frame of reference is also an improved manager.

Management scientists devote substantial energy developing frames of reference to be used by practitioners. These frames of reference are called *models* or, frequently, *decision-making models*. There are models for product portfolio selection, models for selecting and introducing new products, models for allocating promotional resources, models for selecting retail locations, and so on. These models are often quite good, that is, they do well what they are intended to do. They are also little used by practicing managers. Managers still prefer to use frames of reference that they develop. There are many reasons for this, which cannot be treated here. There are, however, two important observations about this state of affairs which are relevant here. The first is that practicing managers are unlikely to change their posture toward the use of formal management science models. This makes it all the more important that they acquire the metalanguage of theory building and apply it to their own frames of reference. As this metalanguage is acquired and used, the reader will also find formal management science models more interesting and useful. This is especially helpful when entering a new position of responsibility. Reviewing existing management science models pertinent to the new position will enable managers to develop effective models or frames of reference of their own for that task much more quickly.

Frames of reference change with changing areas and levels of responsibility. Table 1.4 illustrates differences between corporate-level planning (top-down) and planning of managers who operate at a more specific business level (bottom-up) within the corporation. The same issue (or "event") is looked at rather differently. Each perspective or frame of reference has its advantages and disadvantages. The manager or planner who has the capacity to analyze (seek out and understand) frames of reference used in planning will develop more effective plans. With reference to Table 1.4, George Day suggests the same point: "Finally, the planning process itself should have the capacity to seek out, understand, and exploit the differences in market definition between top-down and bottom-up approaches. The pay-off will be clearer strategic thinking and faster response to

[37]Gerald Zaltman and Rohit Deshpande, *The Use of Market Research: An Explanatory Study of Manager and Researcher Perspectives* (Cambridge, MA: The Marketing Science Institute, 1981).

*Table 1.4*
*The View from the Top-Down Versus the Bottom-Up*

| Issue | Top-Down View | Bottom-Up View |
|---|---|---|
| 1. Definition of market. | Markets are arenas of competition where corporate resources can be profitably employed. | Markets are shifting patterns of customer requirements and needs which can be served in many ways. |
| 2. Orientation to market environment. | Strengths and weaknesses relative to competition<br>• cost position<br>• ability to transfer experience<br>• market coverage. | Customer perceptions of competitive alternatives<br>• match of product features and customer needs<br>• positioning. |
| 3. Identification of market segments. | Look for cost discontinuities. | Emphasize similarity of buyer responses to market efforts. |
| 4. Identification of market niches to serve. | Exploit new technologies, cost advantages, and competitors' weaknesses. | Find unsatisfied needs, unresolved problems, or changes in customer requirements and capabilities. |
| 5. Time frame. | 2 to 5 years | 1 to 3 years |

*Source.* Day, G., *"Strategic Market Analysis: Top-Down and Bottom-Up Approaches."* Report 80-105, Marketing Science Institute, August 1980. Used by permission.

emerging threats and opportunities."[38] This kind of payoff is a pretty good reason for a manager to be concerned with theory building.

## Summary

This chapter has discussed two views about the conduct of science. One view has been referred to as the traditional view of science. The second has been referred to as the contemporary view of science. In actuality there are many variations within each view. Moreover, these variations are sometimes substantial even

[38]George S. Day, *Strategic Market Analysis: Top-Down and Bottom-Up Approaches* (Cambridge, MA: The Marketing Science Institute, Report No. 80–105, August 1980), p. 23.

though they could not be treated here. If the so-called contemporary view receives greater stress in this chapter (and possibly others), it is because it is not very conspicuous in the field of marketing. Many readers may not yet have had significant exposure to current ideas in the sociology, psychology, and philosophy of science. Inquiry into and the practice of marketing should improve if both views are equally understood and appreciated by researchers, managers, and teachers. This chapter also identified a number of barriers which often block exposure to different viewpoints and limit our ability to develop a special kind of theory called *generative theory*. The concluding section of this chapter addressed the practical relevance of learning about theory. A basic idea in that section is simply that learning about theory will help a manager think about his or her frame of reference for handling responsibilities. This knowledge, in turn, should improve the exercise of those responsibilities.

# TWO
# BEING INTERESTING

*In this chapter we introduce the special idea of being "interesting" and offer some guidance for those readers who dare to be noticeably different. Being interesting and different is essential although not sufficient for constructing good theories. Readers may also use the conditions for being interesting as criteria for assessing the interestingness (or dullness) of the marketing literature they have encountered. For example, how much of what you have read in the last year has been interesting according to these criteria? Do you think there is an upper limit to the number or proportion of interesting ideas a field can accommodate within a specified period of time?*

Research usually is not searching for a new idea but trying to beat the dust out of an old rug.

Anonymous[1]

We are continually confronted with the perversity of friends and colleagues who, despite our best efforts to enlighten them, persist in misguided political, social, and even scientific beliefs; just as they find us, no doubt, intractable and obstinate in our preconceptions.

Lee Ross and Mark R. Lepper[2]

The human understanding when it has once adopted an opinion draws all things else to support and agree with it. And though there be a greater number and weight of instances to be found on the other side, yet these it either neglects and despises, or else by some distinction sets aside and rejects, in order that by this great and pernicious predetermination the authority of its former conclusion may remain inviolate.

Francis Bacon[3]

Being "interesting" is one of the necessary ingredients for the healthy development of conceptual and theoretical thought in marketing. This ingredient—which will be defined shortly—is not particularly prominent in contemporary marketing thought, although it is perhaps the one ingredient that best distinguishes impactful from unimpactful thinking. For example, Murray S. Davis suggests that the great theorists are not considered great because of the truth of their theories, but because their theories are interesting.[4] The truth of a theory may have only incidental relevance to its impact. If, indeed, being "interesting" is very important and yet is also insufficiently displayed, then perhaps the body of marketing thought might benefit substantially by a greater infusion of this ingredient. This infusion will not happen merely by calling for it. The relative absence of this ingredient may result partially from the lack of a well-diffused technology for being interesting. This section presents some possible components of such a technology. The thinking methodology for being interesting that is presented here is not a substitute for creativity, intelligence, or extended

---

[1] An anonymous senior creative director at Young and Rubicam. Quoted by Joseph T. Plummer in "The Ratio of Basic vs Applied Research: What Is the Optimum Balance?" American Marketing Association Conference on Research, New Orleans, September 8, 1980.

[2] Lee Ross and Mark R. Lepper, "The Perseverance of Beliefs: Empirical and Normative Conclusions," *New Directions for Methodology of Social and Behavioral Sciences*, no. 4 (1980), p. 17.

[3] Francis Bacon, *The New Organon and Related Writings* (New York: Liberal Arts Press, 1960; originally published, 1620).

[4] Murray S. Davis, "That's Interesting! Towards a Phenomenology of Sociology and a Sociology of Phenomenology," *Philosophy of the Social Sciences*, 4 (1971), 309.

and careful thought. However, it does offer ways of gaining new perspectives, and it is through new perspectives that scientific disciplines advance most.[5] This chapter concludes with several important caveats concerning the notion of being interesting as it is developed here.

## Definition of the Interesting

### Transcending the Taken-for-Granted World

The first requirement of an interesting theory is that it capture attention by appealing to a consciousness beyond the state in which most persons operate on a daily basis, a state in which knowledge is routinely taken for granted. For the marketing academic, this taken-for-granted world includes a body of literature containing the current "state of the art." In addition, for all persons shared experiences lead to what is termed "common sense." The value of using common sense as a basis for action is enculturated in life and has widespread social acceptance. Common sense defines a particular portion of the world to which our intellect is adapted. However, common sense can operate at a disadvantage, as it may obscure opportunities not apparent at the time.[6] A fundamental difference between the theorist who is great versus one who is mediocre is the ability and courage to challenge established patterns of thought. A mind that is flexible and open is continually assimilating new knowledge and forming broad conceptualizations that expand creative and perceptual powers. The work of Einstein illustrates how the creative mind can produce ideas that germinate and illuminate thinking for decades to come.

An interesting theory, then, is one that both challenges existing assumptions and that, if it were true, would cause many people to change much of their thinking or behavior. A clue to just how interesting a theory or idea may be lies in the answer to the following question: *How much current thinking will have to be altered by how many people if the theory were true?* If the answer to both aspects of this question is, "Lots!" then the theory should be a very interesting one indeed.

### Practical Applicability

A second requirement of an interesting theory is that it be of practical import. It should be perceived as useful or appropriate to the needs of the intended audience. "If (the) practical consequence of a theory is not immediately apparent

---

[5] Ian I. Mitroff and Ralph H. Kilmann, *Methodological Approaches to Social Science: Integrating Divergent Concepts and Theories* (San Francisco: Jossey-Bass, 1978), Chapter 1.

[6] We shall return briefly to the concept of common sense in Chapter 6.

to its audience, they will respond to it by rejecting its value until someone can concretely demonstrate its utility: 'So what?' 'Who cares?' 'Why bother?' 'What good is it?.'"[7] Creative thinking involves not only the ability to bring forth new ideas, but also the ability to help solve everyday problems. Creative thinking is not only thinking at a higher level of consciousness, freed from trivialities, but also the translation of these thoughts into positive action. For example, the sun as a source of light and life has been an object of worship since ancient times. To present a discourse extolling the symbolic virtues of the sun would be an esoteric exercise likely to be appreciated by only a few. However, to conceive of solar energy as one solution to the world's growing resource shortage and to present a blueprint or, better yet, slides of an actual office complex designed and functioning with reliance on the sun's rays would surely raise the interest quotient for the audience. The latter involves action. Habitual ways of thinking are broken through such an action. As Bergson notes:[8]

It is of the essence of reasoning to shut us up in the circle of the given. But the action breaks the circle. If we had never seen a man swim, we might say that swimming is an impossible thing, inasmuch as, to learn to swim, we must begin by holding ourselves up in the water and, consequently, already know how to swim. Reasoning, in fact, always nails us down to the solid ground. But if, quite simply, I throw myself into the water without fear, I may keep myself up well enough at first by merely struggling, and gradually adapt myself to the new environment: I shall thus have learnt to swim. So, in theory, there is a kind of absurdity in trying to know otherwise than by intelligence; but if the risk be frankly accepted, action will perhaps cut the knot that reasoning has tied and will not unloose.

## Firmly Held Assumptions

The theory builder should first be familiar with the assumption ground of the audience (the taken-for-granted world) and then successfully challenge part of this ground. Merely confirming what persons already know, for example, in a replication study involving a population with similar characteristics to the sample used in the original study, may add to scientific knowledge, but it does not qualify as "interesting." This suggests a third requirement of an interesting theory: that it challenge *firmly held* assumptions rather than either *weakly held* (at one end of a continuum) or highly central and even *fanatically held* (at the other end of a continuum) assumptions. As Davis notes, "There is a fine definite line between asserting the surprising and asserting the shocking, between the interesting and the absurd."[9] The interesting theorist must therefore not only be aware of the assumption base of the audience, but also be sensitive to which

[7] Davis, *op. cit.*
[8] Henri Bergson, *Creative Evolution* (New York: Modern Library, 1944), p. 211.
[9] Davis, *op. cit.*, p. 343.

assumptions can safely be challenged and which ones are best left alone because a challenge would prove too threatening, at least in the short run. Many theories labeled as "absurd" die instant deaths or go into comas lasting for years. History is richly imbued with examples of people who eventually achieve fame but only at immense personal cost. The mathematician Copernicus was one such person. His heliocentric theory in which the sun, rather than the earth, formed the center of the universe challenged the thinking of the Roman Church. Because Copernicus realized that his theory would be regarded as heretical, he published it late in his life. The twentieth-century scientist Einstein, with his curved-space theory, challenged the assumptions of Copernicus and won a place among interesting theorists. However, the scientific community is often slow to accept *radically* different ideas.

Managers in both private and public sector organizations are similarly reluctant to have their assumptions challenged. For example, a study of the use of market research in major product line decisions indicates that the more "surprising" the research findings, the less likely the research is to be used.[10] Surprising research results were those that were unanticipated and counter-intuitive and that contradicted firmly held assumptions. Such results, even if of a positive nature, tended to increase uncertainty, whereas the purpose of conducting research was primarily to reduce uncertainty. Managers tended to have comfort zones within which information should fall if it is to be accepted readily. If information challenged assumptions, it tended to fall outside the comfort zone and was likely to be rejected. In this respect managers and academic scholars are very much alike. The reader might refer back to the first section in Chapter 1 for the discussion of the Mahoney experiment. The reader familiar with both communities might wrestle with the question, "Who has the wider comfort zone, the practicing manager or academic scholar?" In this question a wide comfort zone implies a greater ability to accept challenging information.

The tendency to cling to existing beliefs, especially when they are challenged, has been the subject of considerable research in social psychology. Some of this research and its possible implications for the manager–researcher will be discussed below. An important theme present in this research is that biases in judgment are common[11] and since we are in the position of having to judge our judgment, we are probably in substantial error in our beliefs about our ability to make judgments.[12] A marketing manager or researcher may read a research report, make a judgment about the implications of that report, apply the

[10] Gerald Zaltman and Rohit Deshpande, *The Use of Market Research: An Exploratory Study of Manager and Research Perspectives* (Cambridge, MA: The Marketing Science Institute, 1981).

[11] P. Slovic, B. Fischhoff, and S. Lichtenstein, "Behavioral Decision Theory," *Annual Review of Psychology*, 28 (1977), 1–39.

[12] Hillel J. Einhorn, "Overconfidence in Judgment," *New Directions for Methodology of Social and Behavioral Science*, no. 4 (1980), pp. 1–16.

judgment in the form of a market decision, and then evaluate (judge) the quality of that decision. According to extant research, even undesirable consequences are likely to be interpreted as being supportive of poor original judgment about the research's implication.[13] Thus basically negative feedback is sometimes interpreted favorably, so prior assumptions cannot be challenged.[14] Moreover, poor judgments may be associated with very good outcomes because of factors unrelated to the judgment and beyond the control of the manager or researcher. Thus possibly wrong assumptions underlying judgments are reinforced. Conversely, a judgment might in some way be the best possible one but be associated with an unfavorable outcome, again for unrelated or uncontrollable reasons. In this case if we question and discard our initial assumptions, we would also be making an error. Table 2.1 is overly simplified but is presented to make a special point. We might expect that a large set of decisions made on a random basis might be equally distributed across the four cells. For example, a pigeon or a child in a kindergarten class or a coin might be employed to make judgments as to whether or not to introduce a new product or to increase promotional budgets or to hold or cancel a national meeting of sales personnel. Of course, pigeons, children, and coins "don't know any better" in this situation so we employ at much greater expense a very bright manager or management team to make such decisions.[15] Certainly they "know better." However, because they know better it is quite possible that fewer than one fourth of their decisions will fall into Cell 1. In fact, in many cases in Cell 1, the correct decision may have contributed very

*Table 2.1*

| Judgment | Outcomes | |
| | Favorable | Unfavorable |
|---|---|---|
| Correct | Cell 1 | Cell 2 |
| Incorrect | Cell 3 | Cell 4 |

[13] Charles G. Lord, Lee Ross, and Mark R. Lepper, "Biased Assimilation and Attribute Polarization: The Effects of Prior Theories on Subsequently Considered Evidence," *Journal of Personality and Social Psychology*, 37, no. 11 (1979), 2098–2109.

[14] See especially C. D. Batson, "Rational Processing or Rationalization? The Effect of Disconfirming Information on a Stated Religious Belief," *Journal of Personality and Social Psychology*, 62 (1975), 176–184.

[15] The reader may find interesting a study in which eight teams totaling 228 MBA students had their performance in a marketing simulation game compared to experimentally managed teams using either arbitrary rules such as "Never order market research" applied consistently or arbitrary rules applied randomly in making decisions. "The experimentally managed teams operated at approximately the same level as half the human teams. The surprising fact is that they did not perform significantly worse than their (human) counterparts." See Robin M. Hogarth and Spyros Makridakas, "The Value of Decision Making in a Complex Environment: An Experimental Approach," *Management Science*, 27, no. 1 (January 1981), 93–107, esp. p. 102.

little to the actual favorable outcome. (However, this would be no less true for pigeons, children, and coins.)

We are not advocating making decisions at random. We do know, however, that even with substantial data from various types of feasibility studies to guide decisions, new products often fail in national introduction or in major test markets.[16] These rates may be as high as 60 percent or more.[17] The basic difficulty is that we are prone to accept at face value evidence confirming our prior inclinations while critically evaluating disconfirming evidence. A survey of managers' responses to research studies relating to a major product decision found a strong tendency for managers to critically examine the research methodology only when they didn't like the results.[18]

Interestingly, managers in this study indicated that when unhappy with the results, they examined the methodology to find out what was wrong with it rather than whether it was valid or sound. Extrapolating from this study and that by Lord, Ross, and Lepper cited above, we can say that managers involved in new product decisions may identify with a favorable decision to launch the new product and on a less than conscious basis interpret mixed or negative evidence in such a manner as to support a decision to launch the product. With some good fortune the result might fall in Cell 3 of Table 2.1. Nielsen and other data sources suggest Cell 4 as being more likely.

## Conceptualization of the Interesting Theory

As depicted in Figure 2.1, the creator of interesting theories breaks out of the circle of thinking that constitutes the routine world. While most persons assume the boundaries of the given to be fixed, those who construct truly interesting theories challenge these boundaries. By perceiving that all boundaries are permeable, the theorist has taken a first major step toward the creation of an interesting theory. Otherwise, the circle will not be broken.

Analysts of social change processes, notably Boulding,[19] have drawn distinctions among dialectical/nondialectical and evolutionary/revolutionary processes which are germane to our conceptualization. Holistically, the three concentric circles within the assumption ground can be viewed as follows:

(A) Earth, composed of fanatically held or ideological assumptions. From this vantage point, a particular world view is projected in association with a

[16] Alvin J. Silk and Glenn L. Urban, "Pre-Test Market Evaluation of New Packaged Goods: A Model and Measurement Methodology," *Journal of Marketing Research*, May 1978, pp. 171–191.

[17] Nielsen Marketing Service, "New Product Success Ratios," *The Nielsen Researcher*, 1979, pp. 2–9.

[18] G. Zaltman and R. Deshpande, *op. cit.*, 1981.

[19] Kenneth E. Boulding, *A Primer on Social Dynamics* (New York: Free Press, 1979).

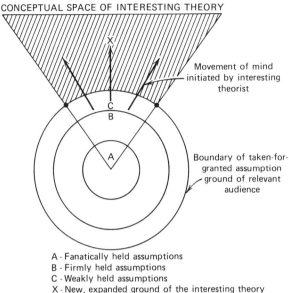

Figure 2.1. Escaping the world of routine thought.

power base. A direct challenge to (A) sets into motion a threat system and results in a dialectically revolutionary situation.

(B) Vast Expanse of the Universe, made of generative assumptions which are firmly held. Webster's dictionary provides a working definition of *generative*: "Having the power or function of generating, propagating, originating, producing, or reproducing." Herein lies the positive, energizing force of a set of assumptions serving as a generator of new ideas. The process of challenging these assumptions may be viewed as "nondialectically revolutionary" representing a "discontinuity in the total evolutionary process because of some mutation which has a profound, long-term effect on the whole system"[20] Area (B) is composed of firmly held assumptions.

(C) Cloud Cover, formed by peripheral assumptions. To the uninitiated, this layer may appear to be rigid, but the "interesting theorist" knows that the force generated by (B) will quickly penetrate and extend this area. A challenge to (C) alone is evolutionary, or a gradual change. The assumptions in (C) are weakly held.

How, then, is the theorist to challenge this mixture of assumptions and achieve a high interest quotient? Here we diverge from Davis and assert that the use of the dialectical approach could be misleading, as illustrated in Boulding's thesis: "The growth of knowledge is not advanced by the dialectical process at all; it is hindered by it . . . for when questions are posed in dialectical terms, that is, in

[20]*Ibid.*, p. 58.

terms of the conflict between two cultures or two power centers, each center gradually loses the ability to learn from the other."[21] Essentially, an effective challenge can produce a symbiotic (mutually beneficial) relationship between old and new, instead of a dialectical (conflictual) one (by, for example, adding alternative, plausible explanations for the same phenomenon).

All three assumption bases are involved in this formulation, since a challenge to any *one* is insufficient. A direct challenge to the peripheral layer (C) in Figure 2.1 is likely to result in an audience reaction of "That's boring!" In contrast, a head-on attack on (A), the fanatically held assumptions (ideological ground), is very threatening and is likely to produce a defensive reaction and draw cries of "That's absurd!" It is only by using the firmly held (generative) assumptions of (B) as a springboard to penetrate the limits established by prior thinkers that the birth of an interesting theory occurs, acknowledged by the comment, "That's interesting!"

While the major thrust of the new thinking involves firmly held (generative) assumptions, a "spillover" or "leakage" trickles into the other two areas. A successful challenge to (B) almost automatically ensures a reformulation of the peripheral weakly held assumptions (C). The seeds might well also be planted to enable growth inward to the fanatically held assumptions of the ideological layer; that is, in order to accept and integrate (B), (C), and (X) into a total framework, revisions in (A) thinking must ultimately occur. If the ideological center is focused on its integrative function rather than its threat system, such movement can take place. Otherwise, a breakdown in communication is likely.

How the "pie" shown in Figure 2.1 can be "sliced" depends upon many factors, such as the size of the theoretical knowledge base in existence at the time, and the researcher's combination of economic, psychological, and intellectual resources. The center dot represents the beginning, with the expansion of the circle being the cumulative accretion of scientific knowledge. In one sense, disturbance of any of the parts of the pie affects the whole; as Boulding notes, "A scientific theory is a Gestalt, not a mere collection or dictionary."[22]

Keep in mind that the aggregate audience is under consideration here. Obviously, there are individual differences. Some persons feel comfortable only when firmly ensconced within the circle. Others, such as those who are very high in arousal needs or are extreme innovators, would eagerly welcome a direct challenge to (A) as well as to (B) and (C).

An alternative depiction of this same phenomenon can be made in terms of the familiar normal curve (see Figure 2.2). If our world of "interesting" ideas can be depicted as a challenge to this routine world, we can attempt to position ourselves along this curve, choosing, for example, to operate at one standard deviation on either side of an average value of intensity of all the assumptions we view as routine for our specified research issue/problem. Indeed, the curve may be skewed in one direction or another. A well-established area of inquiry may

[21]*Ibid.*, p. 62.
[22]*Ibid.*, p. 60.

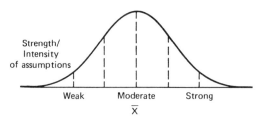

**Figure 2.2.** Composition of the routine assumption ground.

contain many strongly held assumptions, making our task both potentially more interesting and also more difficult. Or, in a relatively new area (such as the sociology of consumption), the curve may be skewed in the other direction. In the latter case, all three areas (B, then C, then A) can be effectively challenged. Therefore, the rate at which boundary expansion occurs can be seen to be more rapid in areas of inquiry not yet firmly established. The frontiers of knowledge are pushed forward until the curve assumes its normal shape and eventually becomes skewed more heavily in the other direction.

Because we are dealing with a methodology for thinking, an analogy from psychology may help to clarify the distinction between the conceptual space within which the interesting theorist operates as contrasted to that of the noninteresting theorist. A rapidly developing area of interest in psychology is transpersonal psychotherapy, a nondirective process of expanding consciousness in which the main focus is on the inner work of the psyche reaching toward transcendence and self-realization. Transpersonal therapy stands in contrast to other Western approaches, which stress specific techniques and seek to solve particular ego problems. This perspective is evident in the work of Carl Jung, who stressed transpersonal experience in therapy rather than the treatment of neurosis. In relation to Figure 2.1, we may conceive of the traditional approaches as being contained within the circle, whereas the transpersonal moves into the triangle. The process of awakening to a new state of consciousness, or transpersonal identity, is depicted in Figure 2.1 by the arrows moving upward, breaking through the boundaries of conventional thought. Three distinct stages are involved in this process: identification, disidentification, and self-transcendence.

### Identification

Identification is a stage characterized by the growth of self-awareness, insight and a new sense of understanding, and an increase in tension and discomfort.[23]

[23] Frances V. Clark, "Transpersonal Perspectives in Psychotherapy," *Journal of Humanistic Psychology*, 17, no. 2 (Spring 1977), 76.

The initial examination of accepted beliefs in theory building may involve similar experiences. The interesting theorist must be sufficiently in touch with self to risk challenging the accepted way of viewing the world. Ability to handle the conflict which occurs when one attempts to break out of the circle of conventional thought and acceptance of responsibility for the consequences are also important characteristics at this stage.

## Disidentification

The second stage is characterized by disidentification with roles, relationships, activities, and so forth: "When [the client] comes to the basic experience of *I Am*, no longer deriving identity from the usual definitions of the self as object, and recognizing the essential no-thingness of the self as experiencer, there is no longer the same investment in preserving self-image or problem solving in terms of ego gratification.[24] According to many Eastern philosophies, attachment forms the basis of all suffering and problems.

For the interesting theorist, disidentification is essential. Going against the tide of popular opinion involves a greater risk if one's ego is heavily invested in acceptance of the new position. One achieves the freedom to think creatively only to the extent that such freedom is granted by the self.

## Self-Transcendence

The third stage, self-transcendence, is characterized by "the emergence of wisdom" or the ability to play with opposites. An increased awareness and appreciation of ambiguity is attained. The theorist who reaches this third stage has solved the mystery of how to realize his or her potential. Frederick Perls, originator of Gestalt therapy, provides an excellent summary statement for this section.[25]

The average person of our time, believe it or not, lives only 5% to 15% of his potential at the highest. A person who has even 25% of his potential available is already considered to be a genius. So 85% to 95% or our potential is lost, is unused, is not at our disposal. Sounds tragic, doesn't it? And the reason for this is very simple: we live in cliches. We live in patterned behavior. We are playing the same roles over and over again. So if you find out how you prevent yourself from growing, from using your potential, you have a way of increasing this, making you more and more capable of mobilizing yourself. And our potential is based upon a very peculiar attitude: to live and review every second afresh.

Self-transcendence may make available at least some of the 85% to 95% of our lost potential.

---

[24] *Ibid.*, p. 77.
[25] Frederick S. Perls, *Gestalt Therapy Verbatim* (New York: Bantam, 1974), pp. 31-32.

In summary, the theorist who desires to be interesting keeps the following suggestions in mind:

1. Know the "taken-for-granted" assumption base of the audience.

2. Know the intensity of the assumptions. Are they (a) held with extreme tenacity or even fanaticism, (b) firmly held, or (c) weakly held?

3. Appeal to a higher state of consciousness of the individual by directly challenging the *firmly held* assumption base through the use of the creative power within.

4. Be sure that the theory has a practical value to the audience.


## Thinking Interesting Thoughts

### A Typology of Propositions

How does one go about constructing an interesting theory? A common thread among interesting propositions is that they always seem to involve negation of accepted ones. What seems to be X is in reality non-X. However, as noted earlier, reliance on a dialectical approach could be misleading. Tables 2.2 and 2.3 do express a dialectical orientation and thus we caution the reader: rather than focusing on the negation of current knowledge, one should create additional propositions which may or may not require negating current thinking. The categories in Tables 2.2 and 2.3 are simply helpful to start the idea generation process.

How can the theorist use the schema in Tables 2.2 and 2.3 in theory construction? First, the appropriate category for the problem being studied must be located. Then the assumption ground currently accepted as "truth" in that area must be specified. Finally, it must be shown that what was thought to be true might, in reality, not be true at all. It could be entirely false *or* it could simply not be truly important. A classic nonmarketing illustration relates to category 9 in Table 2.3, Co-Existence, subtype B: What seem to be phenomena that cannot exist together are in reality phenomena that can exist together. This category is illustrated by Sigmund Freud's assertion that love and hate, which were considered at the time he wrote to be incompatible, are in fact compatible (in the psychological state of "ambivalence"). In other words, what was thought to be X (love and hate are never compatible) turned out to be non-X (love and hate are compatible, under some circumstances). Similarly, the use of crucial experiments may not be an appropriate methodology for understanding complex phenomena (see Table 2.2, Methodology). The position that theory and practice are separate activities has been strongly challenged by persons advocating theory-in-use approaches for developing social theory as a substitute for conventional research approaches (see Table 2.2, Separation). Category 1–B in Table 2.2 is illustrated

### Table 2.2
### Categories for Studying the Interestingness of Propositions

1. Form
   A. What appears to be a multidimensional phenomenon is in reality a unidimensional one.
   B. What appears to be a unidimensional phenomenon is in reality a multidimensional one.
2. Measurement
   A. What appears to measure a concept well does not.
   B. What does not appear to measure a concept well does.
3. Evidence
   A. What was considered evidential support for a position is not.
   B. What was not considered evidential support for a position is.
4. Methodology
   A. What seems to be appropriate methodology is not.
   B. What seems to be inappropriate methodology is appropriate.
5. Assertion
   A. What seems to be an underlying rationale for an act is not.
   B. What seems not to be an underlying rationale for an act is.
6. Values
   A. What seems to be an objective assessment of a phenomenon is in fact a highly value-laden assessment.
   B. What seems to be a highly value-laden assessment of a phenomenon is in fact an objective assessment.
7. Separation
   A. What appear to be inseparable are separable.
   B. What appear to be separable are inseparable.
8. Supply
   A. What appears to be a fixed resource is not.
   B. What does not appear to be a fixed resource is.

by the assertion of Paul Lazarsfeld *et al*. in *The People's Choice*[26] that the flow of mass communications, which was assumed at the time to be direct, is in fact indirect, flowing in two steps through opinion leaders who pass on information to those whom they influence.

The marketing literature also contains numerous examples of Table 2.3 categories. For instance, category 1–A is illustrated by the following proposition: Pierre Martineau's assertion in "Social Classes and Spending Behavior" that the consumption patterns of individuals, who were considered to be unaware of a formal class structure in America at the time he wrote (1958), can in fact be organized according to Warner's six-class system,[27] which ranges from the

---

[26] Paul F. Lazarsfeld, Bernard Berelson, and Hazel Gaudet, *The People's Choice* (New York: Columbia, 1948).

[27] Pierre Martineau, "Social Classes and Spending Behavior," in Louis E. Boon (Ed.), *Classics in Consumer Behavior* (Tulsa, OK: Petroleum Publishing, 1977).

*Table 2.3*
**Additional Categories for Studying the Interestingness of Propositions**

| *Single Phenomenon* |
| --- |

1. Organization
   A. What seems to be a disorganized (unstructured) phenomenon is in reality an organized (structure) phenomenon.
   B. What seems to be an organized (structured) phenomenon is in reality a disorganized (unstructured) phenomenon.
2. Composition
   A. What seems to be assorted heterogeneous phenomena are in reality composed of a single element.
   B. What seems to be a single phenomenon is in reality composed of assorted heterogeneous elements.
3. Abstraction
   A. What seems to be an individual phenomenon is in reality a holistic phenomenon.
   B. What seems to be a holistic phenomenon is in reality an individual phenomenon.
4. Generalization
   A. What seems to be a local phenomenon is in reality a general phenomenon.
   B. What seems to be a general phenomenon is in reality a local phenomenon.
5. Stabilization
   A. What seems to be a stable and unchanging phenomenon is in reality an unstable and changing phenomenon.
   B. What seems to be an unstable and changing phenomenon is in reality a stable and unchanging phenomenon.
6. Function
   A. What seems to be a phenomenon that functions ineffectively as a means for the attainment of an end is in reality a phenomenon that functions effectively.
   B. What seems to be a phenomenon that functions effectively as a means for the attainment of an end is in reality a phenomenon that functions ineffectively.
7. Evaluation
   A. What seems to be a bad phenomenon is in reality a good phenomenon.
   B. What seems to be a good phenomenon is in reality a bad phenomenon.

| *Multiple Phenomena* |
| --- |

8. Co-Relation
   A. What seem to be unrelated (independent) phenomena are in reality correlated (interdependent).
   B. What seem to be related (interdependent) phenomena are in reality (independent) phenomena.
9. Co-Existence
   A. What seem to be phenomena that can exist together are in reality phenomena that cannot exist together.
   B. What seem to be phenomena that cannot exist together are in reality phenomena that can exist together.
10. Co-Variation
    A. What seems to be a positive co-variation between phenomena is in reality a negative co-variation between phenomena.

### Table 2.3 (Continued)

B. What seems to be a negative co-variation between phenomena is in reality a positive co-variation between phenomena.

11. Opposition

A. What seem to be similar (nearly identical) phenomena are in reality opposite phenomena.

B. What seem to be opposite phenomena are in reality similar (nearly identical) phenomena.

12. Causation

A. What seems to be the independent phenomenon (variable) in a causal relation is in reality the dependent phenomenon (variable).

B. What seems to be the dependent phenomenon (variable) in a causal relation is in reality the independent phenomenon (variable).

*Source.* Adapted from Murray S. Davis, "*That's Interesting!* Towards a Phenomenology of Sociology and a Sociology of Phenomenology," *Philosophy of the Social Sciences,* 4 (1971).

"upper upper" or old families to the "lower lower" or unskilled laborers. The social class position of the consumer influences the mix of products and services purchased, the stores patronized, and so forth. This proposition refuted several assumptions firmly held at the time:

1. American society is not organized around social class since incomes tend to be distributed fairly evenly.

2. Since marketing is economic exchange, income serves as the major segmentation variable. Warner's thesis is therefore applicable to broad sociological issues, such as macro living patterns, but not to specific types of consumption.

3. "It is assumed that a rich man is simply a poor man with more money and that, given the same income, the poor man would behave exactly like the rich man."[28]

4. According to Veblen, conspicuous consumption applies primarily to the upper social class.

The requirements of category 1–A are met. What appears to be unstructured (a lack of social stratification relevant to consumer behavior) is in reality a structured phenomenon (according to Warner's social class typology).

Martineau's creativity lies in part in his ability to see relationships between ideas that had not been previously connected by researchers. He saw the applicability of a sociological thesis to consumer behavior. Social mobility was shown to have a strong impact on spending versus saving patterns: "Whereas the stable individual would emphasize saving and security, the behavior of the mobile individual is characterized by spending for various symbols of upward movement."[29] Lower-class persons accumulated material artifacts, such as

[28]*Ibid.,* p. 305.
[29]*Ibid.,* p. 308.

appliances and cars. Middle-class acquisitions went beyond this level and focused on the consumption of "experiences"—through recreation, travel, and education. Travel was considered to be almost solely the aspiration of the middle class. Consumption patterns therefore served as symbolic separators of class membership.

Assuming that the proposition is now part of the assumption ground of marketers, how would one go about forming a new proposition that would be judged interesting today? Is social class as relevant a concept today as it was a couple of decades ago? Have social changes taken place that make any of the assumptions in the 1958 article obsolete? Is stratification, with its implied rank ordering, applicable to consumption (and, if so, what are the relevant dimensions), or are there alternatives to stratification that are more promising?

Historically, social change has taken place vertically, primarily from the top down (the "trickle down" effect). Lower social classes have adopted fashions popular with the upper classes. Recently, however, horizontal or bottom-up change has become evident. Deviant groups such as the hippies have been initiators of changes in lifestyles and fashions. The principles of humanistic psychology have generated diverse lifestyles, with a consequent blurring of distinctions formerly used to designate social class. Ballet and opera, once considered to be an upper-class experience, now draw attendees from diverse segments of society. Prestigious universities have a more varied enrollment; some Ivy League graduates have rural or ghetto backgrounds instead of Park Avenue addresses. Some middle-class persons are questioning the "success ethic," which involves a high degree of mobility, and are striving instead to build an integrated family life. Persons from all classes are packing tents and bicycles and traveling across country.

How can these trends change the assumption base apparent in the Martineau article? One possible proposition would be the following, suggested by Mayer:[30] "The consumption patterns of individuals, which were considered to be organized along social class lines, are actually organized along several political dimensions, independent of income or occupation." Consumers whose lifestyle includes night baseball games, frequent automobile trips, and other resource-intensive consumption may have quite different political interests from those who prefer pollution-free consumption. The empirical question is whether these are correlated with economic considerations.

Now that the basic process of generating interesting propositions has been described, here are brief examples of some of the other categories from Table 2.3.

*Category 2-B.* The market, which was once considered to be homogeneous, is in fact composed of target markets, differentiated on the basis of such dimensions as demographics and psychological and sociological variables.

---

[30]Robert N. Mayer, "Exploring Sociological Theories by Studying Consumers," Faculty Working Paper, Family and Consumer Studies, University of Utah, September 1977.

*Category 5-A*. Lawrence Wortzel asserts, in "Young Adults: Single People and Single-Person Households," that the concept of stable stages of the life cycle, based on marriage and the family as commonly accepted in the marketing literature, is in fact about to be transformed by the evolution of the young adult life cycle stage from one of marriage preparation to one of personal growth, including alternative living arrangements such as cohabitation.[31]

*Category 5-B*. What appears to be changing behavior on the part of the consumer who continually switches brands, as perceived by the manufacturer interested in obtaining brand loyalty, is actually stable, unchanging behavior as perceived by the consumer. The marketer sees the brand as being differentiated from other brands, while the consumer sees all brands as being the same.

*Category 6-A*. Selective distribution, which was once considered to be an inefficient way of obtaining sales response, is in fact an efficient method for promoting prestige items.

*Category 6-B*. John Dickson and Philip Albaum assert, in "A Method for Developing Tailormade Semantic Differentials for Specific Marketing Content Areas," that the widespread use of the original semantic differential scales developed by Osgood *et al.* for the measurement of attitudes may in fact be ineffective when the scales have not been tested in the actual context of the particular problem being researched.[32]

*Category 7-A*. The assertion that selling less, which has been considered to be a bad thing, may in fact be a good thing and the basis for actual strategy. (In demarketing, for example, to preserve the natural beauty of an area, tourists may be discouraged from visiting there.)

*Category 8-A*. Philip Kotler and Gerald Zaltman assert, in "Social Marketing: An Approach to Planned Social Change," that the art of selling such commodities as steel and soap, and the art of selling social objectives such as family planning, which were considered at the time to be uncorrelated, are in fact correlated.[33]

*Category 10-A*. David Caplovitz's assertion in *The Poor Pay More* that expenditures for many goods and services, which were considered at the time he wrote to decrease at the lower income levels, in fact increase at the lower income level.[34]

*Category 10-B*. The assertion that an increase in price, which was once considered to lead to a reduction in sales, in fact leads to an increase in sales in the case of some prestige items.

---

[31] Lawrence H. Wortzel, "Young Adults: Single People and Single Person Households," Paper presented at 1976 Conference, Association for Consumer Research, 1976.

[32] John Dickson and Philip Albaum, "A Method for Developing Tailormade Semantic Differentials for Specific Marketing Content Areas," *Journal of Marketing Research*, vol. 14 (February 1977).

[33] Philip Kotler and Gerald Zaltman, "Social Marketing: An Approach to Planned Social Change," *Journal of Marketing*, vol. 35 (July 1971).

[34] David Caplovitz, *The Poor Pay More* (New York: Free Press, 1963).

## Some Prescriptions

Being interesting is very idiosyncratic. We do not suggest that there is only one way to be interesting or that any one style is preferable to another. What are presented below are some prescriptions which could be useful. These prescriptions relate primarily to the *generation* of interesting ideas and not to the process of having them accepted.

1. Identify favored tools or concepts and try to understand the viewing constraints these might pose. What might your perspective cause you to exclude as ideas or relevant data? For example, if you tend to favor the use of cross-sectional survey data, what might be missing by not using laboratory experiments? Or vice versa? If you tend to use concepts from one particular discipline to explain market behavior what might you be missing by not using concepts from a very different discipline?

2. Adopt a devil's advocate role concerning your own school of thought. This is perhaps the most difficult prescription. Tables 2.2 and 2.3 are helpful, but before they or other aids may be used, it is necessary to first identify or map out your own assumptions. Which ideas or knowledge are you not questioning, or which are you assuming are so convincing that they need not be tested?

3. Specify the type or magnitude of evidence necessary for you personally to question an assumption. What would you need to be shown? Substantial information exists, discussed elsewhere in this book, indicating a very marked tendency among people to avoid disconfirming evidence. Is such evidence available? Have you allowed for it? Have you specifically not allowed for it? (Initially, this evidence need not be adequate to convince others to challenge their assumptions.)

4. Consider every potential description/explanation of a phenomenon as equally plausible, especially those that contradict one another.

5. Be mischievous. Would many people have to suffer intellectual discomfort by adding or deleting substantial bodies of information from their current inventory of knowledge if what you are proposing is true? Have you something surprising? Does your theory require an audience to widen their comfort zones?

6. Favor those interesting scientific or intellectual findings or assertions that rate a high evangelical quotient. Do you feel strongly, even insistent, about your newly found challenge to firmly held assumptions?

7. Don't stop at being interesting. Being interesting does not necessarily require being creative. However, creativity in developing an explanation of your challenge is necessary if others are to pay continued serious attention to your challenge.

## Some Important Caveats

It has been suggested that theories be built that challenge firmly held (as opposed to weakly or fanatically held) assumptions. Such theories are most likely to be greeted as interesting. However, several qualifications need to be kept in mind when you are considering this suggestion. These qualifications or caveats are discussed below.

An interesting theory is not necessarily an important theory simply because it challenges firmly held assumptions. A theory that challenges weakly or fanatically held assumptions may have very significant consequences and hence be very important. Similarly, a theory that does not challenge any assumptions may be very important as well. Thus, posing a theory that gains attention is not the same as posing an important theory.

Being interesting is not a substitute for conventional tests of validity and reliability. In fact, establishing statistical validity and reliability may be an important part of the process of gaining attention. The presence of statistical validity makes it more difficult for someone quickly to dismiss a set of ideas as absurd. Even when empirical verification is not possible or not yet obtained, the various "truth" tests to be discussed in Chapters 7 and 8 should still be applied.

Theories may be relevant for purposes of explanation, prediction, and control. Being interesting does not guarantee the relevance of a theory for any of these purposes. A theory that is interesting because it challenges the assumptions of an audience concerned with explaining market behavior may be of very limited value or relevance to an audience that wants to control or influence market behavior. The latter audience may not have particularly firm assumptions as to why a market behaves as it does; the question of being interesting is not important. On the other hand, this audience would find interesting a demonstration that an intervention strategy that has been assumed effective is actually ineffective. For example, the apparent success of a strategy could be shown to be the result of other actions or a result of bias in the interpretation of data.

As just indicated, not everyone for whom a theory might be relevant will hold even weak assumptions about the phenomena of the theory. For example, a manager or a student unfamiliar with theories of information processing may upon first exposure find them very relevant to his or her interest in consumer behavior. However, because this is an area that is new to the student, he or she may not yet have developed assumptions that could be challenged. The theories encountered are interesting because of their relevance to some task, not because of any challenge they provide to existing assumptions. Thus the notion of familiarity with an area or problem becomes an important mediating factor. A certain degree of familiarity and involvement with an issue is necessary in order for one to establish a groundwork of firmly held assumptions. In fact, we often find interesting those matters about which we have no prior knowledge. For reasons quite unrelated to any preexisting assumptions, they catch our fancy.

## *Summary*

This chapter has developed one particular definition of being interesting—the degree to which firmly held assumptions are challenged. Several important caveats about relying exclusively on this criterion were also presented, even though just briefly. It is most important that assumptions be challenged. Only by challenging assumptions can we reassert our confidence in them. The need to challenge existing assumptions is especially high in a field such as marketing, where many phenomena change over time. Thus a set of assumptions may have been correct at the time they were established, but because of changes in the marketplace, perhaps resulting from actions based on those once correct assumptions, the assumptions may be less valid.

# THREE

# CAUSALITY

*The notion of causality is a central one in the philosophy of science. Some scholars view causality as it applies to social behavior with considerable skepticism whereas others view it as integral to our thought processes. Here we consider a sample of the ideas concerning causality with a bias in favor of causal thinking as a central phenomenon in theory construction. The student familiar with the treatment of causality in the social and philosophical sciences might wish simply to skim this chapter.*

Life is lived forward but understood backwards.

**Kierkegaard**

Although it is all too easy to do, let us not lose sight that causal laws in the social sciences refer to people.

**David A. Kenny**[1]

Only a true adventurer can enjoy a journey into Causality.[2] Hungry for explanation of happenings the causes of which we can only imagine, we undertake a journey with crude maps in hand, hoping to chart the unknown waters and construct understanding from what we discover.

The mind serves as our laboratory, and the maps metaphorically enable us to model perceived reality so that actuality can be better understood. The consideration of causality forces us to break the limits of current knowledge, and therefore of time and space. To do so requires curiosity and courage. Theories serve as the material manifestations of what the mind envisions. Theories, rich in explanatory power, and presumably "true" in their representation of reality, are the desired destination and fruition of our search.

The journey starts with a very simple question: "Why?" From the rookie reporter on the high school newspaper to pros like Barbara Walters and F. Lee Bailey, the ways of asking questions serve as tools of the trade. Table 3.1 lists the standard queries that any good journalist (or, for that matter, any scientist with an inquiring mind) automatically uses.

What are the appropriate labels for the left-hand and right-hand sides of the table? Most of us have had the opportunity to interact with small children. Think about the nature of these conversations. The following example is typical.

*Table 3.1*
*The Art of Asking Questions*

| ? | ? |
|---|---|
| WHO? | WHY? |
| WHAT? | |
| WHERE? | |
| WHEN? | |
| HOW? | |

[1] David A. Kenny, *Correlation and Causality* (New York: Wiley, 1979), p. 11.
[2] Discussion in this chapter reflects the thinking found in: Ackoff (1953); Asher (1976); Bagozzi (1980); Blalock (1964); Bloom (1975); Bunge (1963); Burr (1973); Cook and Campbell (1979); Gibbs (1972); Kenny (1979); Lave and March (1975); Nagel (1961); Stinchcombe (1968); and Von Wright (1974). See full references at end of chapter.

*David,* age 3½:   *Who* was that man at the front door?
*Mother:*          A door-to-door salesman.
*David:*           *What* did he want?
*Mother:*          He wanted to sell us a vacuum cleaner.
*David:*           *Where* did he go?
*Mother:*          Next door to the Miller's.
*David:*           *When* did he start selling vacuum cleaners?
*Mother:*          He started last week, he said.
*David:*           *Why* did he look so tired?
*Mother:*          (Visions of Willie Loman . . . ) Oh, he probably had a long day; maybe he wasn't making many sales; it's cold out and slippery; his arm was bandaged—he must have had an accident; selling is hard work; oh, I don't know. Why don't you go out and play?
*David:*           Because . . .

Now the labels can be inserted. On the left side goes "Finite," and on the right, "Infinite." The first four questions take relatively little time to answer, given the proper information. But, the "Why" question calls into play a causal chain that can go forward and backward ad infinitum; the visit at the door is an arbitrary resting place in what essentially is a continuum of experience.

One of the thorniest issues in the philosophy of science as it applies to a social science such as marketing is the notion of causality. Often we do know with a high certainty that one social-psychological event causes another. The issuance of an invitation to a private party is the cause for people at the party to be present. We cannot say with total certainty that none of these people would be here without an invitation unless a person was checking invitations at the entrance to the ballroom where the party was being held. Even then the person in possession of an invitation might have it illegally. Hence the person doing the checking would have to recognize the persons invited for us to be totally sure that those present were legitimately in possession of an invitation. (If this were a masquerade ball, there would be a serious screening problem and thus this "test" would not be very effective.) It is likely that not everyone to whom an invitation was issued came. In fact, there may be powerful reasons for people receiving an invitation not to come and powerful reasons for persons to go to great lengths to ensure receipt of an invitation. Thus we know that the issuance of an invitation is not a sufficient cause for people to be present. It is a necessary cause—but only for certain categories of people. Others present, such as the host, the guest of honor if there is one, the catering staff, and persons representing the rented ballroom would not likely have received invitations. Thus a different set of causes must be addressed to account for all persons present. However, as just indicated, certain factors may predispose people not to come whether or not in fact they do attend. These factors too must be understood. Thus what appears at first glance to be at least a sufficient if not necessary cause for someone to be in attendance (a formal invitation) may be one of the least important or at any rate least interesting reasons causing people to attend or not attend the party.

Is it ever really possible to specify with reasonable certainty that one social phenomenon causes another? The term "reasonable" in this question is critical. Technically, there can always be either a phenomenon we didn't think about which could cause what we observe or a phenomenon we did think about but couldn't adequately take into account. Thus, we can never be sure that one thing precipitates another, especially in the complex world of events usually present in marketing. Causality is an assumption or an inference rather than a verifiable phenomenon. On the other hand, it is possible to establish rough subjective likelihoods which represent how reasonable it is to think that one thing causes another. This premise is fundamental to all marketing planning and strategy. What constitutes a "reasonable" certainty will vary from person to person and from circumstance to circumstance. This issue is addressed from the perspective of reality tests discussed in Chapter 7. Exhibit 3.1 concerning salt passage research expresses an interesting view as well.

## Exhibit 3.1

*Salt Passage Research: The State of the Art*

*Conclusive evidence on the*
*effects of the utterance*
*"Please pass the salt" is*
*found to be sadly lacking.*

Strongly rooted in the English speech community is the belief that the utterance, "Please pass the salt," is efficacious in causing salt to move from one end of a table to the source of the utterance. In his *Canterbury Tales*, Chaucer notes:

*Shee I askked*
*The salde to passe.*
*Ne surprissed was I*
*Tha shee didde* (4, p. 318).[1]

Similarly, Dickens writes:

*Old Heep did not become disgruntled at my obstinence. "Please pass the salt,*
*Davey," he repeated coldly. I vacillated for a moment longer. Then I passed the*
*salt, just as he knew I would.* (5. p. 278)

The question of whether the movement of salt is causally dependent on the utterance of the phrase, "Please pass the salt," has occupied the attention of numerous philosophers (3, 9, 20). Empirical resolution of the validity of this belief, however, was not undertaken until the classic work of Hovland, Lumsdaine, and Sheffield (8) on the American soldier. Since then, numerous social scientists have explored the antecedent conditions that give rise to

---

[1] I asked her to pass the salt. I was not surprised that she did.

*Source.* Reprinted from Michael Pacanowsky, *Journal of Communications,* 26(4), 31–36 (Autumn 1976).

this apparent regularity. In this article, we will summarize those efforts that shed some light on the complex phenomenon known as salt passage.

Many social observers have noticed the apparent regularity with which salt travels from one end of the table to the source of the utterance "Please pass the salt." Hovland, Lumsdaine, and Sheffield (8), however, were the first to demonstrate empirically that the salt passage phenomenon was mediated by the presence of other people at the table. In a comparison of "others present" with "no others present" conditions, they found that when there were other people present at the table, there was a greater likelihood that the utterance, "Please pass the salt," would result in salt movement toward the source of the utterance. When there were *no other people* at the table, the utterance, "Please pass the salt," had no apparent effect. To test the possibility of a time delay involved in the "no others present" condition, Hovland *et al.* arranged for 112 Army recruits, each sitting alone at one end of a table with salt at the other end, to repeat the utterance, "Please pass the salt," every five minutes for 12 hours. The average distance the salt traveled was .5 inch, which the experimenters explained was due to measurement error. The result of these two studies was, therefore, to demonstrate the importance of the presence of other people in the salt passage phenomenon.

Once the presence of other people was established as a necessary condition for salt passage as a consistent response to the utterance, "Please pass the salt," researchers began focusing on source and receiver characteristics that would affect salt passing behavior. Osgood and Tannenbaum (16) predicted greater compliance with salt passage utterances by high credible sources than by low credible sources. Newcomb (14) predicted greater compliance with sources who were perceived to have similar, rather than dissimilar, attitudes. Rokeach (17) predicted greater compliance for low dogmatic, rather than high dogmatic, people. McClelland (12) predicted greater compliance for high N achievers than low N achievers. Surprisingly, no significant differences were found along any of these dimensions. Differences due to race were found, however, in the original Hovland *et al.* study (8). Black soldiers were more likely to pass the salt to white soldiers, while white soldiers were less likely to pass the salt to black soldiers.[2]

> *Because source and receiver characteristics seemed to have little effect on the extent of salt passage, research attention turned its focus to the effects of message variables as the causal mechanism underlying this phenomenon.*

Janis and Feshbach (10) found that other utterances were just as effective as "Please pass the salt" in achieving salt passage compliance. No significant differences in the extent of compliance were found due to the utterances, "Please pass the salt," "Would you mind passing the salt?" "Could I have the salt down here, buddy?" and "Salt!" Janis and Feshbach noted that in every successful utterance, the word "salt" was found. They concluded that the frequency of the sound waves associated with the phonemes in "salt" was in fact the causal mechanism underlying the salt passage phenomenon.

Zimbardo (21) subjected this hypothesis to an explicit test. He had students from an introductory psychology class sit at a table near a salt shaker while a confederate would say either "Salt!" or "Assault!" He hypothesized that compliance would be as great in the "Salt!" as in the "Assault!" condition. Zimbardo found, however, that the utterance

[2] However, in a replication of the original Hovland *et al.* study, Triandis (19) uncovered the opposite tendency due to race. That is, Triandis found that white soldiers were more likely to pass the salt to black soldiers, while black soldiers were more likely to tell the white soldiers to get the salt themselves.

"Assault!" was met with more calls for clarification than the utterance "Salt!" and the utterance "Assault!" had to be repeated more frequently before the salt would move.[3]

*The search for the source of regularity*
*in salt passing behavior was*
*extended to situational variables.*

Asch (1) tested the effects of pressure to conform on salt passage. In an experiment, a subject was seated at a table with seven confederates. The subject and six of the confederates had salt shakers in front of them; one confederate did not. The confederate without the salt shaker said, "Please pass the salt." Asch found that, when one confederate passed the salt, the subject was more likely not to pass the salt; but when all the confederates passed the salt, the subject was more likely to conform to peer pressure and also pass the salt. Asch concluded that conformity was an essential aspect of salt passage.

Festinger (6) tested the effects of substance uncertainty on salt passage. Subjects were placed at a table where salt was loosely piled on a napkin, while sugar was placed in a salt shaker. When a confederate said, "Please pass the salt," the overwhelming number of subjects passed the sugar. From this study, Festinger concluded that the salt shaker, not the salt itself, was the crucial factor in salt passage.

Bem (2) extended Festinger's study by placing two shakers on the table, both clearly marked with the word "SALT." One shaker had salt in it; the other, however, was filled with pepper. Bem reasoned that, if the salt *shaker* were the crucial factor, both the pepper and salt should be passed about an equal number of times. Surprisingly, Bem found that when prompted with the utterance, "Please pass the salt," people more frequently passed the shaker with salt in it than passed the shaker with pepper in it. Bem concluded that, in salt passage, there is an interaction effect between substance in the shaker and the shaker itself.

Festinger (7) tested the effects of payment on subject evaluation of salt passage. In a "high reward" condition, subjects were given $20 for passing the salt. In a "low reward" condition, subjects were given $1 for passing the salt. Subjects' evaluations of how much they liked salt passing were then obtained. No significant differences in salt passage liking were found between the two groups. Subjects paid $20, however, expressed more interest in participating in another session of the experiment than did their $1 counterparts. Festinger concluded that subjects in the $1 condition were probably more trustworthy than subjects in the $20 condition.

Milgram (13) tested the effects of threats on salt passage. In a "no threat" condition, subjects were not forewarned about any consequences of passing salt to a confederate. In a "high threat" condition, subjects were told that if they passed the salt, they would be struck by lightning. Subjects were seated in metal chairs attached to lightning rods. Thunder in the distance was simulated. Significant differences were found in salt passage compliance between "no threat" and "high threat" groups. Interestingly, in the "high threat" group, there was differential response to the threat of lightning. For golfers and persons who had previously undergone electroshock therapy, there was less reluctance to exposure to

---

[3] In a replication and extension of the Zimbardo experiment, Kelley (11) found that if the confederate had a steak in front of him. "Assault!" was just as effective as "Salt!" in causing salt passage. Kelley concluded that receivers make attributions as to the meaning of utterances based on environmental cues that they perceive.

possible lightning bolts. Milgram concluded that, for most people, salt passage is contingent on a supportive environment.

> *In a descriptive study Schramm (18) reported that the utterance, "Please pass the salt," was more efficacious in England, Canada, and the United States, than it was in Argentina, Pakistan, and Korea.*

Schramm noted the high correlation between the countries where "Please pass the salt" was effective and the degree of exposure of the populace to mass media. He concluded that salt passage is related to an index of the number of color television sets, tape cassettes, and mood synthesizers in a country. Schramm, however, made no claims about the causal ordering of the variables.

Orne (15) studied the motivations to comply among salt passers. After exposing subjects to the treatments of typical salt passage studies, he asked them for their motivations in salt passage. Options were

a. I passed the salt because I thought I would be rewarded.

b. I passed the salt to reduce cognitive dissonance.

c. I passed the salt because the behavior was consistent with previously made public commitments to salt passing.

d. I passed the salt because that's what I thought I was supposed to do.

Over 90 percent of all subjects chose response d, strong evidence of the presence of high demand characteristics in the situation. Responses a, b, and c were more popular among students with social science backgrounds. Orne cautioned, nonetheless, that the high demand characteristics of these situations may call into question the findings of previous research.

> *Why does salt move from one end of a table to another when someone says, "Please pass the salt?"*

Through the efforts of social science researchers, we are able to offer some educated guesses as to the causes of salt passage. Unfortunately, we do not yet have a complete understanding of this complex phenomenon. Findings tend to be inconclusive or inconsistent. Clearly, more research is needed.

Future research must be more systematic. Three directions especially warrant pursuit. First, although research to date has uncovered no personality correlates of salt passage compliance, this is probably due to the few numbers of personality traits that have been examined. There are still numerous personality traits left to investigate: Machiavellianism, authoritarianism, social desirability, tendency to embarrass easily, and so on. Possible interaction effects between source and receiver personality characteristics suggest that there are years of necessary research yet to be done in this area.

Second, future research needs to be concerned with the effects of demographic variables. The importance of race differences found by Hovland *et al.* and Triandis cannot be overlooked. (The fact that the Triandis findings conflict with the findings of Hovland *et al.* should not discourage us, but sensitize us to the complexity of the phenomenon under investigation.) Crucial demographic variables—like sex, age, preferred side of bed for arising in the morning, religion, and others—have yet to be examined.

Third, future research needs to be concerned with the effects of situational variables on salt passage. Kelley's "presence of steak" variable and Milgram's "high threat" variable are suggestive. Effects of information-rich environments, overcrowding, presence of armed conflict, and so on would seem to mediate the salt passage phenomenon.

Finally, given the complexity of salt passage, social scientists must be willing to abandon their traditional two-variables approach. More sophisticated methodologies are needed. Consideration must be given to using variables from all three research areas to construct elaborated non-recursive path models permitting both correlated and uncorrelated error terms. Until our methods match the complexity of our phenomena, we are apt to be left with more questions than answers.

In summary, then, we find that at present social science has not found firm evidence to support the validity of the folk belief that the utterance, "Please pass the salt," is causally linked to the movement of salt from one end of a table to another. Salt passage is a complex phenomenon and systematic research on the impact of personality traits, demographics, and situational variables must be assessed. The question of why the utterance, "Please pass the salt," should be associated with salt passage continues to be a source of puzzlement and intrigue for social scientists.

### References

1. Asch, R. "Conformity as the Cause of Everything." *Journal of Unique Social Findings* 13, 1952, pp. 62–69.
2. Bem, R. *Beliefs, Attitudes, Values, Mores, Ethics, Existential Concerns, World Views, Notions of Reincarnation and Human Affairs.* Belmont, Cal.: Wadsworth, 1969.
3. Berkeley, R. *It's All in Your Head.* London: Oxford University Press, 1730.
4. Chaucer, R. "The Salt Merchant's Tale," in R. Chaucer (Ed.) *The Canterbury Tales.* London: Cambridge University Press, 1384.
5. Dickens, R. *David Saltmine.* London: Oxford University Press, 1857.
6. Festinger, R. "Let's Take the Salt out of the Salt Shaker and See What Happens." *Journal for Predictions Contrary to Common Sense* 10, 1956, pp. 1–20.
7. Festinger, R. "Let's Give Some Subjects $20 and Some Subjects $1 and See What Happens." *Journal for Predictions Contrary to Common Sense* 18, 1964, pp. 1–20.
8. Hovland, R., R. Lumsdaine, and R. Sheffield. "Praise the Lord and Pass the Salt." *Proceedings of the Academy of Wartime Chaplains* 5, 1949, pp. 13–23.
9. Hume, R. "A Refutation of Berkeley: An Empirical Approach to Salt Passing." *Philosophical Discourse* 278, 1770, pp. 284–296.
10. Janis, R., and R. Feshbach. "Vocal Utterances and Salt Passage: The Importance of the Phonemes in 'Salt'." *Linguistika* 18, 1954. pp. 112–118.
11. Kelley, R. "Attributions Based on Perceived Environmental Cues in Situations of Uncertainty: The Effects of Steak Presence on Salt Passage." *Journal of Pepper and Salt Psychology* 32, 1968, pp. 1–5.
12. McClelland, R. "Brown-nosing and Salt-passing." *Journal for Managerial and Applied Psychology* 18, 1961, pp. 353–362.
13. Milgram, R. "An Electrician's Wiring Guide to Social Science Experiments." *Popular Mechanics* 23, 1969, pp. 74–87.

14. Newcomb, R. "The ABS Model: When S is Salt." *Journal for Emeritus Ideas* 12, 1958, pp. 10–18.
15. Orne, R. "Salt on Demand: Levels of Moral Reasoning in Salt Passing Behavior." Forthcoming unpublished manuscript.
16. Osgood, R., and R. Tannenbaum. "Taking Requests with a Grain of Salt: Effects of Source Credibility on Salt Passage." *Morton Salt Newsletter* 42, 1953, pp. 2–3.
17. Rokeach, R. A. *Whole Earth Catalog of Personality Correlates for the Social Sciences.* New York: It's Academic Press, 1960.
18. Schramm, R. *Process and Effects of Mass Media Extend to Everything.* Frankfurt, Germany: Gutenburg Press, 1970.
19. Triandis, R. "Salt and Pepper: Racial Differences in Salt Passing Behavior." *Journal of Social Findings for Improved Social Relations* 110, 1973, pp. 16–61.
20. Whitehead, R. "A Refutation of Berkeley and Hume: The Need for a Process Perspective of Salt Passage." *Journal of Static Philosophy* 1, 1920, pp. 318–350.
21. Zimbardo, R. "Salt by Any Other Name Is Not Quite So Salty." *Reader's Digest* 38, 1964, pp. 86–114.

David A. Kenny summarizes a perspective and posture we suggest the reader adopt. "Modern epistemology tells us that proof is a good that is never achieved by social scientists or any scientist for that matter. As the ancient Hebrews felt about their God, the scientist should never speak the words truth or proof but always keep them in mind."[3]

The position taken in this chapter is that through a better understanding of some of the issues involved in dealing with causality, we can arrive at more certain estimates of how reasonable a particular causal relationship is. Behind this position lies the assumption that marketing management will be more effective if marketing managers think in terms of causation.

A causal statement is one that asserts that a change in the value of one variable produces a change in the value of another variable. An example would be: the higher the commission paid to sales personnel for new accounts, the greater the effort they will expend in seeking new accounts. This example will be elaborated upon in a later section examining the nature of causal statements within a marketing context. Before this elaboration can take place, however, it is worthwhile to examine briefly the historical evolution of the concept of causality so that it can be placed in its proper perspective as part of the science of marketing.

## The Philosopher's View of Causality

David Hume was the first philosopher to reject the view that universal laws could be derived from the patterns of our past experiences. Hume's assertion that we

---

[3] Kenny, *op. cit.*, p. 2.

know only that which we learn from immediate sense impressions set the scientific world in turmoil.

Hume investigated how people arrived at subjective feelings from their immediate impressions. He found three categories:[4]

1. Resemblance and contrast, which are necessary for the development of logic and mathematics.

2. Continuity in time and space, used in experimental and descriptive studies.

3. Causal connection, which is a truth that has permanence and involves more than observation.

Philosophers then proceeded to debate whether it was meaningful to search for universal, abstract laws in the study of human behavior. Weber took the position that it is valid to have an interest in thinking at the abstract level as a means to an end. In discovering the universal generalities, we can better understand how the concrete individual functions.[5] Abraham Kaplan states:

Neither means nor ends are absolute. The end sought is not an ultimate destination but a temporary resting place; the means to it is not something merely to be traversed but itself partakes of the value in the journey. A scientist may well be interested in coming to know a generalization so that he can understand particulars; but equally, the particular may be of scientific significance to him because of the contribution it makes to his quest for generality.[6]

The marketing manager is interested in identifying those individuals or groups of individuals who are most relevant as potential consumers of the firm's product offering. However, without knowledge of human nature in general—the things that people have in common—segmentation decisions are made with only superficial information. Individual consumers are unique; however, they also share much in common. We function not only as individuals, but also in groups, both formal (such as buyers' cooperatives and fraternal associations) and informal (such as "cliques" at work or school which share information with one another).

If we assume that patterns do exist in human behavior, we can think in terms of causal sequences. The discovery of every variable that causes another variable to change is usually impossible. However, by thinking in causal terms, we can at least eliminate some alternative explanations and include others that seem to fit into the particular sequence under consideration. For example, most of us are familiar with a classic marketing failure, the Edsel. Consider this scenario in the aftermath of this "bomb" in Ford's corporate headquarters. The salespeople deny responsibility: "If those ivory tower research and development people had

---

[4]Charles Ramond, *The Art of Using Science in Marketing* (New York: Harper, 1974), p. 23.

[5]Max Weber, *The Methodology of the Social Sciences* (Glencoe, IL: Free Press, 1949), pp. 78–79.

[6]Abraham Kaplan, *The Conduct on Inquiry: Methodology for Behavioral Science* (New York: Chandler, 1964), p. 115.

any touch with the real world, they would have known that we couldn't sell a car with that radical a design." The head of the design department retaliates: "It's marketing research's fault. They didn't get a good reading on the market. We based our design on the results they gave us." And so forth, ad infinitum. An estimated four thousand individual decisions were made just on styling considerations for the Edsel.[7] Obviously, no one of these decisions alone caused the final failure. The task for the manager in this case is to deal with the particulars that seem relevant, disregard those that are insignificant or unrelated, and construct a "means-end chain" to show causality. Understanding the role of styling in the Edsel's failure may involve selecting only three or four of the four thousand decisions to study. Such effort takes time and patience. Failure to make the effort, however, can be far more painful in the long run.

Making causality explicit is therefore important in clarifying our thinking about events of importance. Knowing that variables are related or associated with each other is essential. Going beyond this level and investigating *how* they are related adds significantly to the utility of the results: "There should be a clear statement of the nature of the mechanism whereby one variable affects another."[8] In this way, the tracing of the chain of events is clarified, enabling the marketing manager to make his or her decisions in a more logical, precise way.

Those persons who reject the use of causation do so for a number of reasons. We shall briefly discuss some of these alternative viewpoints.

### Free Will

Some scholars argue that since individuals have freedom of choice or "free will," we cannot make generalizations about them. Causality is therefore presumed to exist outside our domain. However, "a free choice is not uncaused, but one whose causes include in significant measure the aspirations and knowledge of the man who is choosing."[9] While it may be true that the consumer is free to choose whichever brand he or she wants on a particular shopping trip, the marketer does not have to stand helplessly on the sidelines, merely observing the process. Marketing researchers can provide information, not about the particular consumer, but presumably about others with similar attitudes, interests, and opinions. Creative advertising people can design effective campaigns that appeal to the aspirations of these consumers. Sales promotion specialists can arrange attention-getting point-of-purchase displays. Well-trained salespersons can interact effectively with customers, role taking and empathizing with their needs. The marketing mix variables are within the control of the marketing manager.

[7]Thomas L. Berg, *Mismarketing: Case Histories of Marketing Misfires* (Garden City, NY: Doubleday, 1971), p. 228.
[8]Gerald Zaltman, Christian Pinson, and Reinhard A. Anglemar, *Metatheory and Consumer Research* (New York: Holt, Rinehart & Winston, 1973), p. 125.
[9]Kaplan, *op. cit.*, p. 121.

The stimuli in the marketing environment can have measurable effects on the internal psychological states of the consumer (such as knowledge and feelings) which in turn determine choice behavior.

## Determinism

Another point of view is what might be termed "apocalyptic determinism." According to this view, our lives are so completely determined that, in general, we have no control over the inevitable events in our future.[10] Indeed, our choices are limited by circumstances but this does not mean that present circumstances were foreordained with no viable alternative present along the way. Geriatrics may not be able to prevent our eventual deaths; however, measures can be taken to slow the process of aging and make old age a more productive and fulfilling stage in the life cycle. Likewise, as marketing managers, we may frequently be unable to halt the eventual obsolescence of our product. We can, however, use the controllable "Four Ps" to slow the product's decline. For example, we can conduct research into the characteristics of those persons termed "laggards" and redesign promotional strategies to reach these persons more effectively and to encourage them to adopt the declining product and remain loyal to it after others have forsaken it for newer, more innovative offerings.

### Strict Empiricism

A major theoretical orientation of social scientists seeking alternatives to causation is that of strict empiricism. These researchers stress only the strict statistical associations among variables. They are concerned, for example, with the magnitude of association, which we will deal with later in this chapter. "Theoretical abstractions," such as causation, are considered to have no scientific value.[11]

The empiricist approach is also evident in marketing. Bagozzi, in a discussion of the inductive statistical (IS) model, recognizes the value of such an approach in terms of prediction but questions its explanatory power: "Events that are intrinsically improbable deserve explanation, yet the IS model is limited, by definition, to accounting for phenomena which can be represented as occurring 'with very high likelihood.' The IS model, for instance, cannot easily explain such marketing phenomena as the emergence of consumer movements, consumption of fads and fashions, impulse buying, consumer fetishes, and other unusual or infrequent behaviors in the marketplace."[12]

At least two problems are encountered with this approach. First, without a

[10]*Ibid.*
[11]George A. Theodorson, "The Use of Causation in Sociology, " in Llewellyn Gross (Ed.), *Sociological Theory: Inquiries and Paradigms* (New York: Harper, 1967), p. 132.
[12]Richard Bagozzi, *Causal Models in Marketing* (New York: Wiley, 1980), pp. 24–25.

theoretical basis for establishing a relationship between two variables, the scientist may be associating factors that have no *logical* relationship. Becoming excited at discovering a high $R^2$ statistic when relating the number of dog bites in a rural community to retail sales at Macy's hardly advances scientific knowledge. Statistics alone can be quite misleading. One can readily increase $R^2$ with no corresponding increases in theoretical insight by simply using an alternative measure, a lagged value of the same phenomena, and by aggregation of units of analysis.[13] Causal modeling does not seek to maximize $R^2$. In fact, when developing understanding of complicated social phenomena such as exchange relations between salespersons and customers, advertising effects on behavior, or major purchase decisions in complex organizations an $R^2$ above .50 is suspect.[14] The reason for being suspect is simply that it is usually very difficult to *successfully* identify, measure, and express interrelationships among the diverse factors affecting complex social phenomena. This is especially the case when we are examining a neglected area or taking a fresh approach to an area that has had a long tradition of study.

### Relational Terms

Some sociologists, notably Gibbs, advocate the statement of theory in relational terms rather than causal ones. Gibbs contends that when causality is made explicit in theory, one encounters certain issues and problems. For example, how large must a coefficient of correlation be before causality can be inferred? Different data sets might produce varying results. Also, how much evidence does one need in order to conclude that it is sufficiently consistent?[15]

Gibbs therefore argues for the use of symmetrical relational terms: "The greater X, the less Y"; "The greater X, the greater Y." Why state a theory in causal terms if it is not tested that way?[16] Is causation capable of being expressed in space–time relations?

That caution should be used in defining sequences in causal terms can be further emphasized with a quotation from Alan Watts:

[Consider] someone who has never seen a cat. He is looking through a narrow slit in a fence, and, on the other side, a cat walks by. He sees first the head, then the less distinctly shaped furry trunk, and then the tail. Extraordinary! The cat turns round and walks back, and again he sees the head, and a little later the tail. This sequence begins to look like something regular and reliable. Yet again, the cat turns round, and

---

[13] Kenny, *op. cit.*, p. 262.

[14] Kenny, *op. cit.*, p. 9; K. G. Jöreskog and D. Söreborn, "Statistical Models and Methods for the Analysis of Longitudinal Data," in D. J. Aignerad and A. S. Goldberger (Eds.), *Latent Variables in Socioeconomic Models* (Amsterdam: North-Holland, 1977); P. A. Suppes, *A Probablistic Theory of Causation* (Amsterdam: North-Holland, 1970).

[15] Jack Gibbs, *Sociological Theory Construction* (Hinsdale, IL: Dryden, 1972), p. 26.

[16] *Ibid.*

he witnesses the same regular sequence: first the head, and later the tail. Thereupon he reasons that the event *head* is the invariable and necessary cause of the event *tail*, which is the head's effect. This absurd and confusing gobbledy gook comes from his failure to see that head and tail go together: they are all one cat.[17]

Therefore, not all events we consider are of a cause–effect nature. To consider them as such would amount to reducing human behavior to a stimuli–response model, a Newtonian world view that has been successfully challenged by modern thinkers in many fields, notably, physics[18] and psychology. The "old school" in physics dealt solely with the "particle" nature of matter, whereas the "new physics" recognizes that what appears to be a subatomic particle at a particular time may manifest in its "wave" nature a moment later.[19] While the particle nature is essentially deterministic, our wave nature is revealed primarily through free will or free choice. It is this wave nature that is difficult to capture through traditional survey or experimental research methods.

Valle[20] develops the following argument: our wave side operates through volition, in a vector consisting of intensity *plus* direction. Just as physicists resolved the particle versus wave controversy by demonstrating that both of these properties exist together (co-constitute one another), so free will and determinism can be viewed as co-existing in any individual. We might perceive therefore of the consumer who is completely determined—totally lacking in intensity (the motivation to seek information about a product, such as a new car, or to act in any way toward a purchase or choice decision), and also in direction or focus. Such an individual is completely predictable so long as he or she stays within this particle nature.

However, if the intensity and direction of volition change, the wave nature increases proportionately. For example, if the reliable old Chevy that can be counted on to go in rain, sleet, or snow suddenly refuses to budge and requires expensive repairs, the volition toward purchasing a new car changes. The energy formerly contained in the particle nature becomes focused, or wavelike. At this point, the consumer becomes relatively less predictable and controllable. Our research methodology, survey or experimental, does not capture this volitional side of the respondent. As Valle states:

*human behavior can never be predicted with certainty* because of its intrinsic "wave" nature. In fact, one can now see that the variance, the error that is evident in all experimental data, *is* the ignored volitional side of the human subject. Our "wave" side

[17]A. W. Watts, *The Book on the Taboo Against Knowing Who You Are* (New York: Collier, 1966), p. 26.

[18]Fritjof, Capra, *The Tao of Physics* (New York: Bantam, 1975).

[19]Ronald S. Valle, "Relativistic Quantum Psychology: A Re-Conceptualization of What We Thought We Knew," in Ronald S. Valle and Rolf von Eckartsberg (Eds.), *The Metaphors of Consciousness* (New York: Plenum Press, 1981), pp. 419–436.

[20]*Ibid.*

is the reason there is a "built-in" variability that can *never* be accounted for in the purely "particle" approach of an objective social science as psychology is presently conceived.[21]

An integration of both views, determinism *and* free will, is therefore appropriate. We cannot separate the particle and wave nature and emerge with "a consumer." Consumer behavior can be viewed only in terms of relations, since energy or volition must be directed toward another (the salesperson in the purchase of a new car). Marketing involves complex socioeconomic interactions that go beyond basic cause–effect mechanisms. While causality has its place, theory development that concentrates *solely* on this suffers from oversimplification, ad hoc operationalization of variables, and reduction of the individual to only his or her particle nature.

Given this framework, let us turn to some uses of causality in marketing.

## Causal Statements

In this section we shall explore issues of causality with an illustration. The causal statement, "The higher the commission paid to sales personnel for new accounts, the greater the effort they will expend seeking new accounts," will be elaborated upon in order that causality be better understood.

### Association

First consider the notion of *association*. An association between changes in commissions for new accounts and changes in the seeking of new accounts (called *prospecting*) must exist. Without changes in the two events, we cannot establish an association. A sales manager cannot observe a single rate of commission for new accounts and a single measure of prospecting and make a statement that there is or is not a relationship between the two phenomena. Thus, it is necessary to establish co-variation.

The sales manager may establish co-variation in one of two ways. First, an experiment may be conducted. The sales manager may randomly assign individual sales personnel into two groups, an experimental group and a control group (although the problems of conducting this experiment may make it unrealistic to implement). The experimental group would receive a higher (or lower) than normal commission on sales to first-time accounts, while the control group would receive their normal commission. The number of new accounts and possibly the level of sales to new accounts of each group would be compared after some predetermined time period elapsed. The difference between the two groups

[21] *Ibid.*, p. 433.

would then be attributed to' the difference in commissions related to new customers. A more feasible alternative would be to let the sales force as a whole serve as its own control group. In this case, sales to new customers associated with the regular commission would be noted and compared with new customer sales after a different commission is put into effect. The difference in sales at the two time periods is attributed to the difference in two commission schemes. Either experiment assumes that nothing else is happening to affect sales during the experiment, at least nothing that can't be taken into account and controlled for.

Another approach would be to examine natural or nondeliberate differences among sales commission plans. If such data were available, the sales manager would compare the commission plans of firms that differentiate between new customer and present customer sales. The amount of prospecting done by the sales force of the various firms would also be noted. The sales manager would try to determine whether, for example, firms that pay higher commissions for new customers than for old also have more prospecting done by their sales force.

There are two important considerations with respect to observing association or co-variation. One consideration is the magnitude of the changes observed. The second is the consistency of co-variation. We shall look at the magnitude issue first. Ordinarily, the more the level of prospecting changes with a change in commission for finding new customers, the more reasonable it is to assume a causal relationship. This can be illustrated by conditions 1 and 2 in Table 3.2. Under condition 1 the magnitude of the effect of a differentiated commission is greater than in condition 2. Thus, we would feel more certain that a differentiated commission plan influences prospecting if our research data were closer to condition 1 and less certain if they were closer to condition 2. However, we must be very careful. While condition 2 makes us less certain, we cannot rule out the possibility that a differentiated plan does make a difference, albeit a small difference. There may be very many factors none of which alone makes much difference. This implies a very different approach to motivating sales personnel to seek new customers (use many techniques) than when only one or a few factors

### Table 3.2
### Effects of Differentiated Commission Plan

|  | Percent of Salesperson's Time Spent Prospecting | |
|---|---|---|
|  | Condition 1 | Condition 2 |
| Differentiated (higher) commission for new customers | 30% | 12% |
| No differentiated (higher) commission for new customers | 10% | 10% |

have substantiated impact (use few techniques). Magnitude of association is only a guide to causation.

The sales manager should also look for consistency in the findings about differentiated commission plans and prospecting. In general, the more frequently an association is noted, the more confident he or she can be that the association is a true one. Moreover, the more varied the situations in which the observation is made, the greater the level of certainty that can be placed in the association. Thus, consistency has two dimensions: simple frequency of occurrence and variety in contexts of occurrence. These are good guidelines—but only guidelines—for establishing causality.

## Causal Direction

Establishing which of two variables causes the other (holding aside for the moment the issue of mutual causation) is more difficult than establishing association. Causal analysis assumes a time priority: a change in a variable in the present will produce a change in another variable in the future. A future change cannot cause a change in another variable earlier in time. Of course, an anticipated future event may cause us to take a particular action in advance of that event; however, the *anticipation* of that future event (in contrast to the event itself) is a present experience.

First, if we know there is a strong association between two variables, that is, if magnitude and consistency are high, and we know variable A does not cause variable B, then we might assume with some confidence that variable B causes variable A. If changes in commissions on new customer sales have a strong *positive* correlation with changes in amount of prospecting and we know that an *increase* in the amount of prospecting does not cause a *higher* commission rate on new customer sales, then we would conclude that the reverse causal order holds.

In the case of the experiment, the sales manager knew the cause (his own action) of the change in the causal variable (differentiated commissions). This enabled him to rule out with some degree of confidence the possibility that another variable was operating which happened to influence both the use of a differentiated commission plan and time spent prospecting, thereby making it seem like the differentiated plan was the true causal factor. Being in control of the causal factor may thus be helpful in determining causal direction.

Causal direction may also be inferred through the use of statistical techniques, such as cross-lagged correlations. For example, the positive correlation between the use of a differentiated commission plan and subsequent prospecting efforts should be greater than the positive correlation between the use of the plan and prospecting efforts prior to the use of the plan. In effect, there would be no variation in the prior prospecting activity to correlate with the subsequent variation in commission schemes if our supposed causal direction was correct.

(We shall return later to the issue of low prospecting leading to the use of a differentiated commission plan, which in turn leads to high prospecting.)

In many instances it is possible to determine through observation that a change in one variable preceded a change in another variable. In gathering data about commission plans and level of prospecting, the sales manager would want a record of the date at which the differentiated plans went into effect. Presumably, these dates would all be earlier than the recorded dates for the increases in prospecting activity.

Perhaps the reader has already thought about certain arguments. For example:

1. The low levels of prospecting may be thought of as causing the use of differentiated commission plans. It could be that sales personnel, for some reason, begin spending less time prospecting. This drop-off in prospecting worries management, who then institute the new commission plan. In a real sense, the change in prospecting activity does precede the initiation of the new compensation plan. (This does not, of course, mean that the causal direction we have been discussing up to this point is invalid.) However, some differences may exist. The likelihood of a drop in prospecting causing the use of a differentiated compensation scheme may be less (or conceivably more) than the likelihood of the new compensation plan causing an increase in prospecting. It is also probable that a rise in prospecting (for whatever reasons) by sales personnel in a given firm would not cause the initiation of differentiated compensation plans in that firm. Also, if a firm initiates the kind of plan we have been discussing, experiences an increase in prospecting, and then drops the plan, it could experience:

(a) A decrease in prospecting, but not as low as previous levels.

(b) A decrease to previous levels.

(c) A decrease below previous levels (sales personnel becoming angry and avoiding new clients if the opportunity cost were not significant).

(d) A still greater increase (as they discover and continue to develop a new class of customer who may be better or easier to obtain but who would not have been approached initially in the absence of the incentives offered by the new compensation plan).

2. The causal relationships may be broken down almost endlessly. For example:

(a) Initiation of new compensation plan → increase in prospecting.

(b) Initiation of new compensation plan → higher earning potential → increase in prospecting.

(c) Initiation of new compensation plan → higher earning potential → arousal of latent comsumption preferences among sales personnel → increase in prospecting; and so on.

(d) Decrease in prospecting → initiation of new compensation scheme.

(e) Decrease in prospecting → increased concern among sales management → decision to use a new compensation plan.
(f) Decrease in prospecting → drop in sales → increased concern among sales management → decision to use a new compensation plan, and so on.

It is in the process of further specifying causal relationships that we are able to explain a phenomenon known as the self-fulfilling prophecy. It is sometimes argued that the very forecast of an event can cause it to occur. If a shortage of food is predicted because of a crop failure or strike, people may rush out to purchase food stocks beyond what they would normally purchase. This in turn "causes" a food shortage. It is not, however, the forecast which caused the shortage, but the expectations of a shortage which produced behavior resulting in a shortage. The initial forecast was predicted on the basis of one phenomenon, say a strike or crop failure, as the causal force, but it became true as a result of another or different causal phenomenon. Only on the surface was there a self-fulfilling prophecy. In our example of the sales personnel, we might find prospecting levels to rise prior to the actual implementation of the new plan. Sales personnel, in anticipation of the new plan, might begin lining up new customers so that when it comes into effect, they would be able to benefit more quickly. In a special sense, the forecast of the new plan has an impact even prior to its initiation. It is important to know whether this is happening. An increase in prospecting would seem to be the cause of the new plan, but the causal connection would probably be specified thus:

Decision to initiate new plan → anticipation of benefits of the plan --→ early prospecting so that sales to new customers will occur as early as possible after the beginning of the plan --→ increase in level of prospecting --→ initiation of plan (the anticipatory behavior of sales personnel would further justify its initiation) --→ increase in prospecting.

.The reader may readily generate alternative specifications.

## Nonspuriousness

Nonspuriousness means that the relationship between the causal and caused variables is not the result of their relationship to a common third variable. Sometimes two variables appear to be related to each other because they are each influenced by the same third variable. The example of spuriousness often used is that twin brothers may resemble each other, not because one brother caused the other, but because they share the same parents. The relationship between the use of a differentiated compensation plan and increased prospecting is nonspurious, although other factors may be present, each of which influences both variables. However, when these other factors are controlled for, that is, when their effects are eliminated or suspended, the relationship still holds.

There are various ways of determining nonspuriousness. One approach is simply to manipulate the third variable. Assume that at the time the new compensation plan was put into effect, a new product line was also introduced which would be purchased primarily by firms or persons not currently using the company's present products. The key relationships are shown below. Conceivably, the new product line alone could have caused sales management to decide to offer the new compensation plan because they felt the plan was necessary to motivate sales personnel even though in truth the plan would have no impact. The new product line could also itself cause increased prospecting because the new set of potential customers happened to be easily located and to be eager customers. (The student familiar with the statistical technique of partial correlation will recognize the suitability of this technique for controlling for the effect of third variables.) The firm could have conducted an experiment whereby the sales force would be randomly assigned to different groups, one of which had the new product line without the new compensation plan, one of which had the new compensation plan without the new product line, one of which had both the new product line and the new compensation plan, and one of which had neither the new plan nor the new product line. We won't go into the details of this experiment but simply indicate that comparisons among these four groups would permit conclusions about the relative and joint effects of the new plan and new product line. It might even be found that the relationship between the new product line and prospecting is spurious.

It should be evident now that in a very real sense causal statements cannot be tested fully. We can only say with total certainty that A causes B if there are no other relevant variables operating in ways we do not know or cannot take into account. As Blalock puts it, "The basic difficulty is a fundamental one: there seems to be no systematic way of knowing for sure whether or not one has located all the relevant variables. Nor do we have any foolproof procedures for deciding which variables to use."[22]

## Mapping

The concept of mapping presented in Chapter 6 is directly related to the causality issue. The selection of variables and their interrelationships depend upon the

[22]Hubert Blalock, Jr., *Causal Inferences in Nonexperimental Research* (New York: Norton, 1964), p. 14.

experienced reality of the observer and how he or she structures or maps that experienced reality. Maps differ among individuals in terms of their degree of specification. It may be helpful to use a distinction developed by Cook and Campbell:[23] *molar* refers to the level at which causal laws are posed in terms of complex and large objects; *micromediation* is the process of specifying causal connections at the micro level of the particles composing the molar objects. Micromediation is illustrated in the pendulum drawing, Figure 3.1.

As Lewis points out, " . . . the so-called effect immediately becomes only an intermediary step, a part of a sequence itself, leading up to a still further end or effect. Thus, there are some effects of which we have knowledge that may appear to us as being the end of a concatenation of causes. Actually, the causes are but a series of changes which we observe leading to an *arbitrary resting point*. It is *our minds* which have established these resting points—these *effects*."[24] Cook and Campbell acknowledge that multiple causes may account for any effect, a fact recognized by researchers when we conduct factorial experiments. Causal statements at the molar level are meaningful in that they potentially can be tested even when the entire micromediation is not specified. Such molar statements can be verified as being either largely right or largely wrong.

In terms of mapping, the traveler who wishes to go from New York to Chicago is obviously better off having a map of the world in which major cities are noted than in having no map at all. Some estimate can be made of the expected distance between the two cities and the general direction in which to travel. A more detailed map of the United States would reduce the error considerably. Micromediation would be improved through specification of highways, their numbers, distances between points, and so forth.

As one moves away from road maps to more abstract mapping of reality within a marketing context, the causal network obviously grows in complexity. Complexity varies according to the requirements of the situation and the makeup of individuals. For example, one recent study suggests that, given identical product information, persons having simple causal arrays and those having more

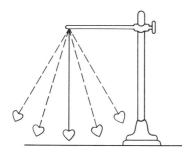

**Figure 3.1.** Micromediation.

*Source.* Ralph M. Lewis, *The Conscious Interlude* (Kingsport, TN: Kingsport Press, 1977), p. 167.

[23] Thomas D. Cook and Donald T. Campbell, *Quasi-Experimentation: Design and Analysis Issues for Field Settings* (Chicago: Rand McNally, 1979), p. 32.
[24] Ralph M. Lewis, *The Conscious Interlude* (Kingsport, TN: Kingsport Press, 1977), p. 166.

complex causal arrays (over a range of "causes" including the product itself and the influence of others' opinions) differed significantly in terms of their beliefs, attitudes, and attributions toward the product.[25] Causally simple individuals, who tended to consider only one cause, formed more extreme beliefs toward the product. Thus, if a causally simple individual received a favorable message toward a particular brand of automobile, he or she would be likely to adopt an extremely favorable belief compared with a causally complex person. The latter would consider more causes and thus display less confidence in the causal allocations. Causal complexity may indicate which strategy the individual will use in processing information, and it has a number of applications in the marketing area.

## A Framework for the Relevance of Causality to Marketing

A useful framework for marketers to consider has been developed by Cook and Campbell.[26] Their eight major points are listed below, with an example of their relevance for marketing.

1. Causal assertions are meaningful at the molar level even when the ultimate micromediation is not known.

For example, in tracking the New York City sales of a medicated vapor salve, it is meaningful to say that on a molar level the consumer selecting Brand X from the retail shelf causes the sale of the product. Furthermore, we might find it meaningful to link the various elements in our marketing strategy to sales of the salve. The new advertising campaign, the free supermarket samples, the temporary price reduction, the bright blue and silver package design—all of these causal assertions are testable and imply ways of controlling the marketing environment. Research of this nature may turn up unexpected causal links. For example, one cause of high volume sales of a leading brand of salve in the New York market was the usage of the product by Hispanic consumers for a variety of ailments, including arthritis. The existence of Spanish language media gives the marketer a means of following through on this cause–effect relationship.

2. Molar causal laws, because they are contingent on many other conditions and causal laws, are fallible and hence probabilistic.

In marketing, the clearest illustration of this is the low correlation between consumer intentions to buy and actual purchase. Major companies spend millions of dollars annually conducting research with consumers before rolling products into regional or national markets. Consumers may respond favorably

[25] Richard W. Mizerski, "Causal Complexity: A Measure of Consumer Causal Attribution," *Journal of Marketing Research* (May 1978), 220–228.
[26] Cook and Campbell, *op. cit.*, pp. 32–36.

to concept boards, taste tests, and in-home use tests. Initial purchase rates may encourage further penetration. Yet, frequently the necessary loyalty or re-purchase behavior does not develop. Perhaps the consumer's economic situation changes, with a tightening of the purse strings. A child may arrive, with a consequent change in lifestyle. The price of the product may not be perceived as a relevant factor to a consumer who has been given the product for an in-home test or given a coupon for the initial purchase. A premium-priced soup currently being test marketed in Atlanta and Phoenix is encountering strong consumer resistance on repurchase because of the differential cost involved. Although first-period sales (with heavy use of coupons) were encouraging, the company is now trying to reach a decision on whether to test the product in additional markets or sell it for salvage immediately.

3. The effects in molar causal laws can be the result of multiple causes.

As mentioned earlier, it is realistic to assert that any effect may be the result of many different causal factors. In research concerning the effectiveness of advertising, for example, the marketer may be interested in isolating the impact of a particular magazine ad on consumer awareness of the product. Therefore, agencies such as Daniel Starch ascertain how many readers recall having seen the ad, how many remember its content, and so forth. However, it is reasonable to assert that this particular ad (or, in fact, the entire advertising effort of the firm) is only one in an entire array of causes of sales.

4. While it is easiest for molar causal laws to be detected in closed systems with controlled conditions, field research involves mostly open systems.

Marketing, as an applied social science, essentially involves research done in open systems. Therefore, great care must be taken in making sure that those factors that *are* under the control of the researcher be clearly specified and manipulated. Failure to do so often leads to inaccurate (and expensive) results. For example, a leading paper towel manufacturer wanted to be first to successfully market a disposable baby diaper. Top secrecy dominated manage-ment's thinking as R & D perfected the product and strategy was formulated. To maintain this confidentiality, the diaper was tested only on new arrivals among the company's executive families. Unfortunately, no use instructions accom-panied the product, and since this was a new concept, no guidelines were available. Some of the test families used as many as four or five liners at a time.

Looking at aggregate volume figures, the company was extremely encouraged and proceeded immediately into several test markets, only to find that volume was much lower than expected. Armed with proper instructions, real customers were using only one liner per change, which depressed demand considerably. The field research had not been carefully designed and monitored and had produced misleading data.

5. Dependable intermediate mediational units are involved in most strong molar laws.

Dependable units are much more readily accessible in the physical sciences than in the behavioral sciences. The normal, healthy individual can depend upon the vital life forces' regulation of breathing, the beating of the heart, digestion of food, and so forth. In marketing, the consumer is a considerably less dependable unit. So much of marketing involves symbolism and individual psychological processes. However, certain *patterns* of behavior can be isolated and studied, particularly when a market segmentation study has reduced the units of analysis to a subset with some common characteristics.

Industrial selling is an area in which more stable units exist. While not entirely "rational," industrial selling offers a somewhat more controlled situation than does the consumer buying process. The salesperson is a powerful mediating factor in the buying process of some industrial products and services, particularly complex and technical ones. By taking a theory-in-use approach, one may determine what causal factors are present (and absent) in the unit of the successful industrial salesperson.

6. Effects follow causes in time, even though they may be instantaneous at the level of ultimate micromediation.

With the possible exception of pure impulse buying, consumer decision processes occur over a period of time. For example, at time period 1 the consumer becomes aware of the product through an ad on TV. At time 2 a friend is observed using the product and replies favorably to an inquiry about it. Time 3 finds the consumer comparing the product's price to those of similar brands on the supermarket shelf and finding it 10 cents higher. At time 4, 5, and 6 the consumer clips a 40-cent coupon from the newspaper, purchases the product, and likes it. Time 7 finds a repurchase and a brand-loyal customer. How consumers store, process, and retrieve the information that leads to the purchase (or nonpurchase) of products and services is an important area of current research in the field of marketing.

7. Some causal laws can be reversed, with cause and effect interchangeable.

Although sales and advertising may be correlated, it is often difficult to determine whether the company's advertising influenced sales, or whether the relationship resulted from management's taking into account expected sales when setting the ad budget. Methodologically, the possibility of simultaneous or bidirectional causality does not fit well into traditional estimation models, in which a false model may go undetected. Bass found a temporal distinction between the sales-to-advertising and advertising-to-sales relationships.[27] Although two-way causality was apparent in data aggregated on an annual basis, the

---

[27] Frank M. Bass, "Advertising Spending Levels and Promotion Policies: Profit Potential for the Application of Management Science," The Eleventh Annual Albert Wesley Frey Lecture, Graduate School of Business, University of Pittsburgh, April 1979, p. 4.

sales-to-advertising direction tended to disappear in bi-monthly data. Therefore Bass suggests the need for mixed multiple equation models, so that the sales-to-advertising relationship can be modeled using annual data and the advertising-to-sales modeled for a briefer (bimonthly) time period.

8. The paradigmatic assertion in causal relationships is that the manipulation of a cause will result in the manipulation of an effect.

For marketers, the determination of a cause is most useful if it can be manipulated to achieve a desired outcome, commonly the sale of a product or service. Many areas of scientific inquiry are researched in both basic and applied ways. In contrast, marketing research is essentially of an applied nature. Marketing managers demand "actionable" research, which means that the seemingly abstract concepts of marketing theories must be translated into managerial or policy implications. For example, a 1976 national telephone survey of attitudes of recent purchasers of new cars revealed that, overall, new car buyers were optimistic about oil and gas supplies in the future and that these opinions were directly related to their intention to buy an additional car. However, the majority did not expect to buy the same size car again. The managerial implication drawn from this survey was that a well-developed ad campaign could persuade consumers to purchase either a larger or smaller car. Auto manufacturers with short-term profits in mind might choose to promote larger cars; those with a longer time horizon would be more likely to promote energy-conserving models.[28] The energy situation is a key causal factor, with attitude change and subsequent faltering demand for large cars resulting. The variable of car size is controllable, but existing production facilities, lead time required to change models, company image, dealer network, and numerous other factors modify that control.

## Summary

Much discussion and debate have accompanied the evolution of the concept of causality. Through a better understanding of the issues involved in dealing with causality, more certain estimates of how reasonable a particular causal relationship is can be made. However, consumer behavior involves complex interrelationships, reflecting both in the particle and wave nature of individuals. Our wave nature eludes capture by the researcher solely concerned with cause and effect. The recognition that both natures can exist side by side presents some interesting challenges to consumer researchers.

[28] Charles C. Lehman, "The Ambiguity of 'Actionable Research,'" *Journal of Marketing*, October 1977, pp. 21–23.

## References

Ackoff, Russell, *The Design of Social Research*. Chicago: University of Chicago Press, 1953.

Asher, Herbert B., *Causal Modeling*. Beverly Hills, CA: Sage, 1976.

Bagozzi, Richard, *Causal Models in Marketing*. New York: Wiley, 1980.

Blalock, Hubert, Jr., *Causal Inferences in Nonexperimental Research*. New York: Norton, 1964.

Bloom, Martin, *The Paradox of Helping*: *An Introduction to the Philosophy of Scientific Practice*. New York: Wiley, 1975.

Bunge, Mario, *Causality*: *The Place of the Causal Principle in Modern Science*. New York: Meridian, 1963.

Burr, Wesley, *Theory Construction and the Sociology of the Family*. New York: Wiley—Interscience, 1973.

Cook, Thomas D., and Donald T. Campbell, *Quasi-Experimentation*: *Design and Analysis Issues for Field Settings*. Chicago: Rand McNally, 1979.

Gibbs, Jack, *Sociological Theory Construction*. Hinsdale, IL: Dryden, 1972.

Kenny, David A., *Correlation and Causality*. New York: Wiley, 1979.

Lave, Charles A., and James G. March, *An Introduction to Models in the Social Sciences*. New York: Harper, 1975.

Nagel, Ernest, *The Structure of Science*. New York: Harcourt, 1961.

Stinchcombe, Arthur, L., *Constructing Social Theories*. New York: Harcourt, 1968.

Von Wright, George Henrik, *Causality and Determinism*. New York: Columbia, 1974.

# FOUR

# THINKER TOYS: CONCEPTS, PROPOSITIONS, AND THEORIES

*This chapter, like the preceding chapter, is intended primarily for the reader who has not previously been exposed to a discussion of concepts, propositions, and theories. Most attention is given to concepts, which are the building blocks of theories. Theories are defined as explanations—as opposed to descriptions—of events in terms of a set of at least partially interrelated propositions. The propositions consist of a stated relationship between two or more concepts. Thus a theory may also be viewed as a system for ordering concepts in a way that produces understanding or insight.*

Physical concepts are free creations of the human mind, and are not, however it may seem, uniquely determined by the external world. In our endeavor to understand reality we are somewhat like a man trying to understand the mechanics of a closed watch. He sees the face and the moving hands, even hears it tick, but he has no way of opening the case. If he is ingenious he may form some picture of a mechanism which could be responsible for all the things he observes, but he may never be quite sure his picture is the only one which could explain his observations. He will never be able to compare his picture with the real mechanism and he cannot even imagine the possibility of the meaning of such a comparison.

**Albert Einstein**[1]

The construction of theory has certain similarities to the construction of a home. The theory's foundation is composed of building blocks, or *concepts*. The formation of *propositions* from these concepts proceeds as does the mortaring of blocks together, each related to certain of the others to form the whole. The result is a model home, one that should be capable of being remodeled, with areas added or deleted as a body of knowledge (or a family) evolves. As a home acquires its meaning or purpose through the personality of the family living there, it grows in richness and becomes a theory. It is more than just a set of blueprints or a full-scale expression of the blueprints. Theories differ from models in that they explain rather than simply reflect or replicate (as a model does).

The analogy can be carried further. For example, just as a decision must be made as to the suitable location for the home (rural area, suburbs, central city), so the theory builder must position the marketing theory within its proper context. The quality of materials must also be carefully considered: Are the concepts "rich" in terms of the inferences that can be drawn from them and in their practical implications for the marketing manager?

The basic evolution of the plan is significant. Does the designing of the home progress from the exterior style inward to the electrical and heating systems that support the operation, or from the interior out? In theory construction, does the underlying reasoning move through a chain of logically sequenced points toward a conclusion, or backward to a cause? The former process sometimes termed *deductive*, and the latter, *inductive*.

Sole reliance upon deductive reasoning could potentially result in many action-oriented implications; however, a failure to analyze causes can lead to a fallacious marketing strategy. A manager acting on the basis of such a model may move forward with a marketing program built upon faulty assumptions and a lack of awareness of the causes of the predicted behavior. Such a thinking methodology resembles the engineering of a fast moving train, with signals being ignored along the way and an inability to return to the origin if the need arises.

On the other hand, total reliance on inductive reasoning may lead to a

---

[1] Albert Einstein and Leopold Infeld, *The Evolution of Physics* (New York: S. and S., 1938), p. 31.

continual analysis and questioning of causes, with little or no action taken. A combination of the two methodologies (found, for example, in syllogistical reasoning) is more useful. Such reasoning is based on a premise, a statement, and a conclusion. The premise is a particularly important part of this trilogy. If the assumption base upon which conclusions are made is in error, the validity of the theory is brought into question. Consider the proposition illustrated in Figure 4.1.

The proposition is based on the premise that the time involved in decision making is a function of the number of people present. The statement that many persons are in attendance at a meeting would therefore lead to the conclusion that consensus would be obtained only at great length. Obviously, this conclusion is oversimplified and does not take into account important factors such as the cohesiveness of the group and the presence or absence of key decision makers who wield influence within the network. One proposition is as good as another, if sound reasoning does not make the difference.

Because of the importance of understanding modes of reasoning, considerable space will be devoted to them in subsequent chapters. It is our purpose in this chapter to examine the tool kit that the theoretician uses in constructing a theory.

**Figure 4.1.** The fewer the participants, the earlier the agreement. In all meetings, keep the number to a minimum. . . . You'll go home much earlier.

*Source.* Royce A. Coffin, *The Negotiator: A Manual for Winners* (New York: AMACOM, 1973), p. 29.

## The Basic Tools

Figure 4.2 illustrates the inner workings of a model—the relative position of concepts, propositions, and theories to one another.

Three theories are depicted, including the one under construction, theory I. It contains a concept, D, which has been used in theory III. Here, however, D is being used differently because it is being related to concept A, which was not a part of theory III.

The relationship between concepts B and C appeared in the same propositional form in theory II. However, theory II was very specific and dealt with only one context, whereas theory I is general, covering several marketing contexts.

The propositions in our theory are specific as to direction of relationship and the nature of the relationship (that is, positive or negative). Some concepts are not related (such as C and D).

A theory is therefore comparable to the human organism. The nerve centers and organs form basic units but must be joined (via the spinal cord and circulatory system) to contribute toward the organism's purpose. Basic cells exist in positive and negative polarities. However, whether the theory has life depends largely upon the competence and creativity of the builder.

### An Illustration

A brief example of the use of concepts and propositions will be given. Special emphasis will be given to concepts since they are so basic to theory construction.

In marketing, we are interested in developing theory that aids in the

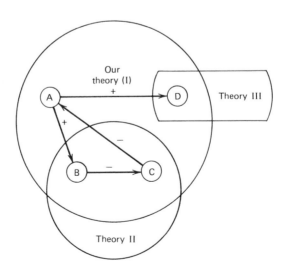

**Figure 4.2.** The anatomy of a marketing theory.

explanation, prediction, and/or control of marketplace behavior. For example, the rise in consumerism has prompted marketers to seek out causes of the dissatisfaction expressed by consumers. One set of questions relating to this issue revolves around consumer complaint behavior: "Are complainers different from noncomplainers?"; "How do the situational and individual differences affect complaint behavior?"

We have a choice to make between two distinct approaches to developing a theory of consumer complaint behavior. The first option is to develop at the outset a global theory, including all those variables thought to be relevant. The well-known Howard-Sheth model is one such attempt at building a comprehensive theory of buyer behavior. The second option is to begin with a "small component part" theory and proceed to gradually add other variables. The beginnings of such a simple theory are depicted in Figure 4.3.[2]

With either option, concepts must be first defined and then put into a form by which they can be measured (discussed later as "operationism"). For example, interpersonal trust, the individual difference variable in this first fragment of a theory of complaint behavior, is defined by the psychologist Rotter as "an expectancy held by an individual or a group that the word, promise, verbal, or written statement of another individual or group can be relied upon."[3] A scale developed by Rotter from social learning theory and used extensively in psychology operationalized this concept.

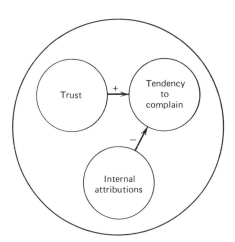

**Figure 4.3.** The embryo of a theory of complaint behavior.

[2]Valerie A. Valle and Karen Lawther, "Interpersonal Trust and Attribution of Responsibility: Determinants of Elderly Consumer Complaining," Paper presented at the Annual Convention of the American Psychological Association, Toronto, August 1978.
[3]Julian B. Rotter, "Generalized Expectancies for Interpersonal Trust," *American Psychologist*, 26 (1971), 443–452.

The second concept, attribution of responsibility, is the situational variable in the theory. If a person perceives that others are responsible for the situation (such as an unsatisfactory buying experience), an external attribution is made. When blame is attributed to oneself, the attribution is internal.

Why were these concepts chosen, and how are they related to complaint behavior?

Since marketing is an exchange process, a central element is trust between buyer and seller. When dissatisfied with a marketplace experience, a consumer would be unlikely to complain if the seller could not be trusted to respond and to take some action. The relationship of trust and the tendency to complain is posited in the following proposition: "As the degree of trust increases, the tendency to take a complaint action increases. That is, those low in trust should complain less than those high in trust."[4]

The second proposition relates attributions and complaint behavior, with an inverse relationship specified between an internal attribution and the tendency to complain. If a consumer feels personally responsible for a problem with a product, complaint action is less likely.

Obviously, the next step is to extend the theory by evolving other concepts and propositions, and to test these propositions empirically. Subjecting marketing theory to "real world" tests is essential. Even well-established (or dominant) paradigms need to be tested in a variety of contexts. Such paradigms have a way of persisting (until an "interesting theorist" comes along). The established theory may be abruptly reminded that it has become somewhat smug and could stand an "awakening" (of which the "rude" variety is illustrated in Figure 4.4).

The dominant thought in marketing, for example, has centered around a unit, or individual, paradigm. As will be noted later, theorists are now advancing toward a view which considers the interrelatedness of the buyer and seller. The choice of the trust concept in the preceding complaint behavior example illustrates this emphasis on interdependencies.

**Figure 4.4.** A real world awakening shakes a dominant paradigm.

*Source.* Charles Schultz, Pittsburgh Press, April 17, 1979. Copyright © 1979 United Feature Syndicate.

[4] Valle and Lawther, *op. cit.,* p. 2.

# Concepts

As noted earlier, concepts are the groups of characteristics upon which theories are constructed. An additional way of depicting their basic role appears in Figure 4.5.

Concepts have been subject to a debate among philosophers, similar to the controversy over causality discussed earlier. It is not usually difficult to state what a concept *does*; it represents, identifies, and recognizes. For example, innovativeness represents "the degree to which an individual is relatively earlier in adopting new ideas than other members of his social system."[5] Knowing what a concept *is*, or where it exists, is more elusive. The innovator exists, but only in relation to others in the social system. This functional interrelatedness of concepts is what gives them significance and allows them to be communicated. Concepts reside in the world of thought and enable us to make sense of a complex universe filled with nonrecurring experiences. To raise a question about the concept "innovativeness" is important in terms of clarifying and refining the concept. However, as Caws points out, ". . . this is a metascientific activity, having much the same relation to science proper as a piece of scaffolding has to a building which is under construction, so that the interest in concepts is an intermittent one."[6]

## Functions of Concepts

The position known as *instrumentalism* examines concepts in light of the types of problems with which they commonly deal and the ways they contribute to solving these problems. Language is viewed as an instrument used in performing

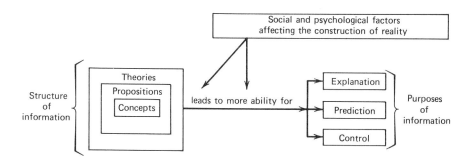

**Figure 4.5.** The structure of science.

[5]Everett M. Rogers and F. Floyd Shoemaker, *Communication of Innovations: A Cross-Cultural Approach* (New York: Free Press, 1971), p. 88.
[6]Peter Caws, *The Philosophy of Science: A Systematic Account* (Princeton, NJ: Van Nostrand, 1965), p. 28.

an action. Therefore, a concept is determined by the context in which the action is to be taken.[7]

We can examine this position by discussing the marketing concept of "product class." The marketer needs to know whether the consumer has a well-defined product class concept to accommodate the product.[8] The product class involves more than a grouping of brands. For example, a new company entering the wine market must position its brand among those currently being offered. Its rosé must be positioned in relation to a relatively lower-priced Gallo Vin Rose and a relatively higher-priced Mateus, among others. However, this is only part of the buyer's conceptual structure. At a more general level are product class concepts and the definition of the broad category that subsumes wine. This higher level of the hierarchy, depicted as level (d) in Figures 4.6 and 4.7, is affected by many variables. Figure 4.6 represents a possible conceptual structure for a wine consumer in California, where wines are purchased at the supermarket and are physically positioned on shelves near soft drinks and other beverages. The buyer from Pennsylvania, on the other hand, might have the conceptual structure depicted in Figure 4.7. Wine in this case must be purchased in a state-controlled liquor store. Thus, the meaning, or conceptualization, of wine in a product class may be quite different, affecting frequency of purchase, quantity bought, and attitudes toward the product (and thus having implications for marketing strategy).

Therefore, while a concept is stated in basic terms, it should be abstract and general enough to fit many different contexts. The innovativeness concept mentioned earlier, for example, has relevance not only for various marketing situations, but also across many disciplines (for example, innovativeness has been studied in rural sociology, in education, in medicine, and among primitive tribes).

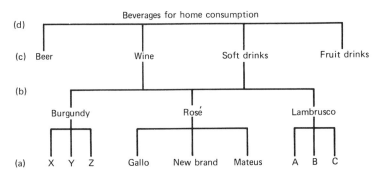

**Figure 4.6.** Conceptual structure for wine.

[7]Abraham Kaplan, *The Conduct of Inquiry: Methodology for Behavioral Science* (New York: Chandler, 1964), p. 46.
[8]John A. Howard and Jagdish N. Sheth, *The Theory of Buyer Behavior* (New York: Wiley, 1969), p. 279.

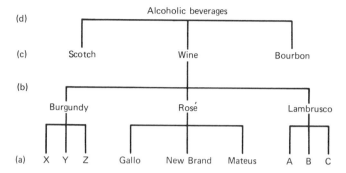

**Figure 4.7.** Alternative conceptual structure for wine.

## Terminology

Concepts are stated in scientific terms. Kaplan distinguishes three types of terms: notational, substantive, and auxiliary. *Notational terms* serve as a shorthand method of expressing concepts. Such terms both precede and follow the process of conceptualization.[9] By stating "Let $y = f(x)$," we facilitate the communication of a concept and provide direction for its use (e.g., taking derivatives). However, notational terms are basically abbreviations and can be replaced. On the other hand, *substantive terms* are those which "cannot be eliminated without loss of conceptual content."[10] They are fundamental to the concept. For example, if we eliminated the term "adopting" from the definition of innovativeness (page 77), it would lose its meaning. Or if we eliminated the term "expectation" from a definition of consumer satisfaction, the concept would assume a very different meaning.[11] *Auxiliary terms* are those which make the grammatical meaning of the language clear or play a minor role in notation.

Among the substantive terms, important differences exist. *Observational terms* are those which can be directly observed. "Brand choice" is an example of a term that is easily verified. One can observe the shopper in the supermarket selecting "Brand X" rather than "Brand Y" and paying for it at the checkout counter.

*Indirect observables* require inferences or indirect observations. Why did the consumer select that particular brand? If we ask the buyer to reconstruct his or her information processes leading to the selection, will we obtain an accurate report? We may be able only to infer a memory search when no observable sources (such as point-of-purchase displays, unit price information, and label information) are consulted. Similarly we may only infer levels of expectation

[9] Kaplan, *op. cit.,* p. 49.
[10] *Ibid.*
[11] Richard Oliver, "A Cognitive Model of the Antecedents and Consequences of Satisfaction Decision," *Journal of Marketing Research,* November 1980.

and post purchase satisfaction based on the degree of hesitancy a consumer displays in selecting a given brand.

*Constructs* are terms that cannot be observed through either direct or indirect means but that can be applied on the basis of observables. Nagel's discussion of ideal or "limiting" concepts is relevant here. For example, the notion of *perfect elasticity* may be suggested by empirical subject matter. It is not amenable to experimental observation since it may not accurately describe an event. However, by using limiting concepts, we can formulate theories in a relatively simple fashion that can be tested by mathematical analysis: "Despite the fact that a theory may employ simplifying concepts, it will in general be preferred to another theory using more 'realistic' notions if the former answers to the purposes of a given inquiry and can be handled more conveniently than the latter."[12]

In reference to any theory, it is the *relationship* of its constructs that is significant. "A theoretical term has *systemic meaning*: to discover what it is up to we must be prepared to send not a single spy but whole battalions."[13] In areas such as marketing, which do not have well-developed paradigms, the systemic relevance or meaning of concepts leads to Catch-23 or the paradox of conceptualization. Charles O. Jones has cleverly described this situation:

Yossarian looked at the professor soberly and tried another approach. "Does Orr have a theory?"

"He sure does," Professor Daneek responded.

"Then can you approve his dissertation?"

"I sure can. But first he has to make his concepts explicit. That's part of the rule and we follow it scrupulously."

"Then why doesn't he?"

"Because he has a theory," Daneek said calmly, "and you can't start with a theory."

"I see. He should have started with a set of concepts."

"That's right. As Abraham Kaplan puts it: 'Proper concepts are needed to formulate a good theory.'"

"Well," Yossarian sighed, "all he has to do is turn things around and then you can approve his dissertation."

"No. Then I can't approve his dissertation."

"You mean there is a catch."

"Sure there is a catch," the professor replied. "Catch-23. Anyone needs a good theory to arrive at the proper concepts."

The paradox of needing to develop good concepts in order to develop good theories which are needed to develop good concepts is solved by the process of approximation: "The better our concepts, the better the theory we can formulate

---

[12] Ernest Nagel, *The Structure of Science: Problems in the Logic of Scientific Explanation* (New York: Harcourt, 1961), p. 132.

[13] Kaplan, *op. cit.*, p. 57.

with them, and in turn, the better the concepts available for the next, improved theory."[14] Concept development is very important in marketing. It is also very risky in that it requires "doing before knowing," that is, plunging into the intellectual or substantive problems of the marketing discipline as if we really know what we are doing and, in so doing, improving what we know.

We shall now turn to some methodological problems concerning marketing concepts.

***The Locus Problem.*** The locus problem is that of choosing the subject matter for inquiry in marketing and the conceptual structure within which to formulate hypotheses.

The issue of selecting subject matter is generally a personal one. We choose a subject that is intriguing to us. Or a client may present a problem whose solution requires the kind of skills we find rewarding to apply. Different people differ greatly in what they find intriguing and rewarding. It is sometimes useful to distinguish between process-oriented interests and context-oriented interests. For example, some individuals are primarily interested in such processes as the diffusion of innovations, interpersonal exchange, socialization, communication, and so forth independently of what innovations are involved, who is participating in an exchange relation, who is becoming socialized into what groups, what communication content and function are, and so forth. What is of primary interest is that the process is occurring. The context in which it occurs is of considerable importance for understanding the process, but for the process-oriented person the context is not quite as intellectually intriguing as the process itself.

The context-oriented person may be primarily concerned with industrial marketing, the aviation industry, fashion, health care marketing, and so forth. Where the process-oriented person may examine these subject areas for manifestations of a particular process, the context-oriented person will often focus on several different processes as a way of understanding better how firms purchase major pieces of equipment, why consumers reject particular fashions, how consumers evaluate and select among alternative health plans, and so forth.

The distinction made here between process- and context-oriented people is one of convenience only. Few individuals are concerned only with a given process and have no favorite contexts in which to pursue this process. Similarly, few people are committed exclusively to a single context without any favorite process for guidance in understanding that context. In fact, many individuals have one or more processes *and* contexts that especially intrigue them. The subject matter they select will tend to be where the joint challenge and payoff are greatest. For example a person may be equally interested in the petrochemical industry and grain industry as well in the process of organizational buying and corporate

---

[14] Charles O. Jones, "Doing Before Knowing: Concept Development in Political Research," *American Journal of Political Science,* February 1974, pp. 215–228.

policy formulation. A variety of circumstances such as an energy crisis, a Supreme Court decision on patent rights, and access to boards of directors may result in a high priority being given to the study of corporate policy formulation in the petrochemical industry.

The choice of conceptual structure within which to formulate hypotheses is affected in part by our favored subject matter. There is likely to be a prevailing set of ideas or way of viewing different subject matter such as corporate policy formulation or apparel innovation diffusion or attitude change among health care professionals. We may feel comfortable with the prevailing set of ideas and use them to help formulate our hypotheses, or we may find it appropriate to be "interesting" and deliberately challenge these ideas. In either case we are influenced by prevailing ways of viewing processes and contexts.

Often, too, as we work with different processes and contexts, we find conceptual structures developed in one setting which may be useful in another setting. For example, a conceptual structure originally developed for understanding innovation diffusion in agriculture has been found useful in the study of innovation diffusion in such contexts as the apparel industry and steel industry. Persons outside of marketing are finding the concepts and tools of marketing useful in their contexts. Similarly, the exchange paradigm developed in sociology and social psychology has had a considerable impact on recent thinking about marketing phenomena.[15] How conceptual structures for dealing with issues in one subject area may eventually influence the conceptual structure used for dealing with other subject areas, either quite by accident or through deliberate broadening efforts, is an interesting topic in the sociology of knowledge which goes beyond our immediate concerns here.

The conceptual structures within which we formulate hypotheses will be a function of several factors. In no special order of importance, these factors include the following.

1. The discipline we are trained in: an anthropologist may be quite unlikely to use conceptual frameworks developed in biophysics and social biology despite possible benefits these areas may offer.

2. The conceptual structures considered legitimate by peers who will evaluate our work: although certain theories in high energy physics may offer useful analogies for the study of population change and hence be of concern to business chains locating new retail sites, a board of directors or journal referee might be reluctant to accept research findings that were guided by an unfamiliar framework.

[15] Cf. S. J. Levy and Gerald Zaltman, *Marketing, Society and Conflict* (Englewood Cliffs, NJ: Prentice-Hall, 1975); Gerald Zaltman, Tom Bonoma, and Wesley Johnston, *Industrial Buying Behavior* (Cambridge, MA: Marketing Science Institute, 1978); Richard P. Bagozzi, *Causal Models in Marketing* (New York: Wiley, 1980).

3. What we are aware of or knowledgeable about outside our own discipline: only if we are aware of research or agenda setting in state legislatures can we use conceptual and methodological frameworks developed in that area to facilitate our understanding of corporate decision making, stockholder meetings, or even family decision making.

4. What has worked for us in the past: even when confronted with a new situation, say a new context in which to work, we quite naturally at first apply frameworks that have been fruitful in our prior work.

The reader should be able to extend this list considerably. In fact, doing this is suggested as an exercise.

*Level of Abstraction.* Concepts can be expressed in very general or in very specific terms. Table 4.1 illustrates the problem of specifying concepts. The researcher must carefully define at what level of abstraction a concept is formulated. If a scale worded in a general way is used to measure opinion leadership in fashion, and a specific scale is used for opinion leadership in culinary matters, methodological problems could result from noncomparability of data.

**Ideal Types**. An ideal type is a concept that does not function as either a directly or indirectly observable term. Weber notes, however: "If one perceives that concepts are primarily analytical instruments for the intellectual mastery of empirical data and can be only that, the fact that [certain] concepts are necessarily ideal types will not cause him to desist from constructing them.[16] Rogers' conceptualization of the norms of the social system relevant to diffusion consists of two ideal types: traditional and modern. These types provide a framework for analysis and are not to be construed as depicting what "ought" to be. Individuals in a social system characterized by modern norms are more cosmopolitan, oriented toward change, scientific, rational, technologically developed, and empathetic. A traditional social system consists of individuals with the opposite attributes. Rogers and Shoemaker do advise caution in dealing with these conceptualizations as dichotomies, however; actual occurrences will lie somewhere on a continuum between these two types.[17]

*Operationism.* Operationism refers to the requirement that each concept correspond to operations that define its application and give it scientific meaning. The classic example is intelligence, a concept that is measured throughout the application of intelligence tests.[18] In the physical sciences, concepts can often

---

[16]Max Weber, *The Methodology of the Social Sciences* (Glencoe, IL: Free Press 1949), p. 106.

[17]Rogers and Shoemaker, *op. cit.*, p. 33.

[18]Kaplan, *op. cit.*, p. 40.

**Table 4.1**

**Measures Illustrating the General–Specific Continuum of Psychographic Constructs**

| General | | Specific |
|---|---|---|
| Self-Designated Opinion Leader | Self-Designated Fashion Opinion Leader | Self-Designated Midi Opinion Leader |
| 1. My friends or neighbors often come to me for advice. | 1. My friends and neighbors often ask my advice about clothing fashions. | 1. Several of my friends asked my advice about whether the midi would become a fashion or not. |
| 2. I sometimes influence what my friends buy. | 2. I sometimes influence the types of clothes my friends buy. | 2. I told my friends that the midi was a recurrent style from yesteryear and that it would be unflattering and make most women look older. |
| 3. People come to me more often than I go to them for information about brands. | 3. My friends come to me more often than I go to them for information about clothes. | 3. At coffee breaks my friends tended to ask my opinion of the midi more often than I initiated the conversation about it. |
|  | 4. I feel that I am generally regarded by my friends and neighbors as a good source of advice about clothing fashions. |  |
|  | 5. I can think of at least two people whom I have told about some clothing fashion in the past six months. |  |

Source. W. Darden and F. Reynolds, in *Construing Life Style and Psychographics*, W. D. Wells (Ed.), (New York: American Marketing Association, 1974). Reprinted with permission.

be readily operationalized. The measurement of temperature or tensile strength can be done directly. However, how does one go about measuring concepts that do not have clear physical manifestations? Opinion leadership, for example, represents the degree to which an individual is able to informally influence other individuals' attitudes or overt behavior in a desired way with relative frequency. The most frequently used measurement of this concept has been the self-designated opinion leadership scale illustrated earlier in Table 4.1. Consider the three questions in column one: (1) "My friends or neighbors often come to me for advice"; a positive response to this question indicates that the person is sought out for advice, for example, playing a reactive role in communication; (2) "I sometimes influence what my friends buy" may indicate performance of a proactive role; for example, the person gives advice which may not have been solicited by his or her friends; and (3) "People come to me more often than I go to them for information about brands" measures the proportion of reactivity as compared to proactivity. Thus, the questions display a bias regarding which aspect of the concept is being emphasized. The researcher must be aware of this bias and use the measures most relevant to the hypotheses.

Likewise the measurement of age, a commonly used demographic, is not so straightforward as one might suppose. Typically, age is measured chrono-logically, with persons in various age groups expected to show some differences in consumer behavior (for a variety of physical, social, and psychological reasons). However, what would happen if we measured age another way, by asking questions such as those in Table 4.2? The results obtained from this measure of nonchronological age may or may not correspond to those from chronological age. Using this measure, a 92-year-old great-grandmother might score "younger" than her 60-year old son. This relationship is meaningful in that it improves our ability to explain and predict consumer behavior.

The difficulties involved in operationalizing marketing concepts are evident as one surveys the literature. For example, in operationalizing opinion leadership, researchers have relied on various sociometric classifications; personality inventories; the Wells and Tigert Activities, Interests and Opinion Scale; mass media exposure measurements; the Rogers-Cartano Scale, and numerous other techniques—all designed to measure one concept! Consumer satisfaction and dissatisfaction have also been subjected to a variety of measurements. It is unclear, for example, whether (or when) satisfaction and dissatisfaction are two end points of one continuous scale, or are in fact two different concepts (requiring separate measurement). This diversity serves to illustrate the com-plexity of many of the concepts we deal with in marketing and the need for substantive research to improve methodology, concepts, and, thereby, theory.

Even when empirical referents have been found for concepts, one must be careful not to misuse them by framing them into scientific questions that are incorrect. A classic example can be found in the psychology literature published at a time when researchers sought the answer to "What causes human behavior?"

### Table 4.2
### *An Alternative Way to View the Phenomenon of Age*

Through experience, the decisions I make tend to be:

Considerably better than those made by people with less experience
than I have had
Somewhat better
Neither better nor worse
Somewhat worse than those made by people with less experience
Considerably worse

Compared to the average person, my approach to problems and new
situations is:

Considerably more open-minded and adaptable
Somewhat more open-minded and adaptable
Neither more nor less open-minded and adaptable
Somewhat less open-minded and adaptable
Considerably less open-minded and adaptable

Compared to the average person, I feel that I am able to get things done:

Extremely well
Fairly well
About as well as others
Not as well
Far less well

Compared to people in general, I would say I am:

Considerably more physically active
Somewhat more physically active
About as physically active as they are
Somewhat less physically active
Considerably less physically active

Compared to people around my age, I make:

A much better appearance
A somewhat better appearance
About as good an appearance as they do
A somewhat worse appearance
A much worse appearance

Compared to people around my own age, I am:

Much more involved with life
Somewhat more involved with life
About as involved with life as they are
Somewhat less involved with life
Much less involved with life

**Table 4.2 (*Continued*)**

Compared to how people around my own age feel about life in general, I am:

Much more optimistic
Somewhat more optimistic
About as optimistic as they are
Somewhat less optimistic
Much less optimistic

The things that I do now are:

Much more interesting than they were in the past
Somewhat more interesting than they were in the past
About as interesting as they have been in the past
Somewhat less interesting than they were in the past
Far less interesting than they were in the past

As I grow older, things seem:

Much better than I thought they'd be
Somewhat better than I thought they'd be
No better nor worse than I thought they'd be
Somewhat worse than I thought they'd be
Much worse than I thought they'd be

Most of the things I do are:

Very boring and monotonous
Somewhat boring and monotonous
So-so
Somewhat exciting and varied
Very exciting and varied

I tend to make plans for things I'll be doing:

A few months from now
A month from now
A week or so from now
A few days from now
Today or tomorrow

The lot of the average person is:

Much better now than it has ever been
Somewhat better than it has ever been
About the same now as it has been
Somewhat worse now than it has been
Much worse now than it has ever been

*Source*. Gerald Zaltman, Robert Perloff, and Valerie A. Valle, *The Elderly as Victims of Consumer Deception*, A Final Report to the Administration on Aging, April, 1980.

in terms of environment *versus* heredity. While both concepts are valuable, the error in terms of theory occurs by one's considering them separately; that is, when environment is determined as the "cause" of a behavior, heredity is ruled out (or vice versa). The research psychologists who made this false assumption—work spanning a 30-year period—has therefore been discarded. Traces of this thinking still permeate modern psychology. Rose states that psychologists:[19]

. . . tend to pose questions about the sources of human behavior in terms of combinations of discrete hereditary and environmental influences. That is, to use an analogy from chemistry, they unwittingly conceive of concrete human behaviors as *mixtures* of forces from hereditary and environmental sources, whereas they might often be more accurately conceived of as *compounds* of such forces. Mixtures retain the characteristics of their constituent elements, whereas compounds usually exhibit entirely new characteristics and properties.

For example, social class has been and often still is considered to be a mixture having *three* component parts: level of education, type of occupation, and financial status. Certainly the use of this concept in the marketing literature has reflected a mixture image of social class. When viewed as a compound, social class would be construed as a group of people sharing similar levels of prestige and similar and related beliefs, attitudes and values.[20] All of these may be strongly influenced by level of education, occupation, and wealth, but social class is not a combination of these factors but rather a fusion of effects resulting from these and other factors. This fusion becomes a unique entity with its own character which does not resemble any of its contributory factors.

***Pragmatism***. A pragmatist, as opposed to an operationist, looks for meaning in statements in terms of what they signify: "what counts is not origins, but outcomes, not the connections with experience antecedently given but those which are yet to be instituted."[21] Meaning is interpreted as being a plan of action. Kaplan notes that pragmatists have been severely misunderstood because of the narrow definition given to the word "action." Critics of pragmatism have contrasted action with contemplation, and practice with theory. Kaplan states:[22]

The "usefulness" that pragmatism associates with truth is as much at home in the laboratory and study as in the shop and factory, if not more so. If we are to continue to speak with William James of the "cash value" of an idea, we must be careful to have in mind a universally negotiable currency, and especially one that circulates freely in the world of science itself.

Marketing research is recognized as producing actionable results. The combination of this quality with well-grounded theories from the behavioral

---

[19]Arnold M. Rose, "The Relation of Theory and Method," in Llewellyn Gross (Ed.), *Sociological Theory: Inquiries and Paradigms* (New York: Harper, 1967), p. 216.

[20]Gerald Zaltman and Melanie Wallendorf, *Consumer Behavior: Basic Findings and Management Implications* (New York: Wiley, 1979), p. 84.

[21]Kaplan, *op. cit.*, p. 42.

[22]*Ibid.*, p. 44.

sciences provides a framework for substantive, creative, and meaningful theory development.

*Concept Validity.* "Validity" is derived from a term denoting strength. The scales that we use to measure concepts form one basis for establishing validity. Also, we must determine whether we are actually measuring what we set out to study. Table 4.3 illustrates the various types of concept validity. An extensive treatment of these types may be found elsewhere.[23]

Two major methods are available for assessing convergent and discriminant validity. The multitrait, multimethod approach developed by Campbell and Fiske represents pioneering work in this area.[24] Using this method, the researcher analyzes the pattern of correlations among two or more traits (empathy with others, love for self, and regard for others could be traits of the concept "compassion") measured by two or more methods (Likert, Guttmann, and Thurstone scaling). Several criteria are used to establish convergent and discriminant validity. Bagozzi notes some problems inherent in the method, however, including the lack of criteria to determine the extent to which the operationalization of the concept measures it (that is how well do these measures of compassion "get at" what compassion *really* is), the adequacy of the whole trait-method matrix, and the magnitude of variance caused by trait versus method.[25]

The causal modeling approach takes the above criteria into account. Solutions of a system of structural equations allows determination of convergent and discriminant validity. Bagozzi asserts:

Not only can it be used to perform a traditional multi-trait multi-method matrix analysis, but it does this in a more rigorous and less ambiguous way. Moreover, causal modeling furnishes one with a versatile means to investigate other forms of validity such as criterion-related, predictive, and nomological validities. An important point to note is that causal modeling offers the advantage over traditional methods that measurement error is taken into account explicitly.[26]

The reader is encouraged to consult these and other references for additional information on the critically important subject of validity assessment.[27]

---

[23]Cf. Gerald Zaltman, C. Pinson, and R. Angelmar, *Metatheory in Consumer Research* (New York: Holt, Rinehart & Winston, 1973).

[24]Donald T. Campbell and D. W. Fiske, "Convergent and Discriminant Validation by the Multi Trait-Multi Method Matrix," *Psychology Bulletin*, 56, 81–105.

[25]Richard P. Bagozzi, "Causal Modeling: A General Method for Developing and Testing Theories in Consumer Research," *Association for Consumer Research*, Kent B. Monroe (Ed.), Vol. 8, 1981.

[26]*Ibid.*, p. 133.

[27]Cf. Edward G. Carmines and Richard A. Zeller, *Reliability and Validity Assessment* (Beverly Hills, CA: Sage, 1979); and John L. Sullivan and Stanley Feldman, *Multiple Indicators: An Introduction* (Beverly Hills, CA: Sage, 1979).

### Table 4.3
### Types of Concept Validity

| | |
|---|---|
| 1. Observational validity | The degree to which a concept is reducible to observations. |
| 2. Content validity | The degree to which an operationalization represents the concept about which generalizations are to be made. |
| 3. Criterion-related validity | The degree to which the concept under consideration enables one to predict the value of some other concept that constitutes the criterion. |
|    3a. Predictive validity | A subtype of criterion-related validity in which the criterion measured is separated in time from the predictor concept. |
|    3b. Concurrent validity | A subtype of criterion-related validity in which the criterion and the predictor concepts are measured at the same time. |
| 4. Construct validity | The extent to which an operationalization measures the concept which it purports to measure. |
|    4a. Convergent validity | The degree to which two attempts to measure the same concept through maximally different methods are convergent. It is generally represented by the correlation between the two attempts. |
|    4b. Discriminant validity | The extent to which a concept differs from other concepts. |
|    4c. Nomological validity | The extent to which predictions based on the concept which an instrument purports to measure are confirmed. |
| 5. Systemic validity | The degree to which a concept enables the integration of previously unconnected concepts and/or the generation of a new conceptual system. |
| 6. Semantic validity | The degree to which a concept has a uniform semantic usage. |
| 7. Control validity | The degree to which a concept is manipulable and capable of influencing other variables of influence. |

*Source.* G. Zaltman, C. Pinson, and R. Angelmar, *Metatheory in Consumer Research* (New York: Holt, Rinehart & Winston, 1973), p. 104.

In summary, concepts are the groups of characteristics upon which theories are constructed; they have significance through their functional interrelatedness. They are stated formally and are subject to several methodological considerations. The concepts give shape to the theory (its morphology), whereas the relationships specify the underlying process, or mechanism, through which the theory becomes a living organism. This brings us to the topic of propositions.

## Propositions

Propositions are functional relationships between or among concepts. They appear in every model or theory, in a variety of forms. Propositions may be explicit or implicit, general or specific, of practical import (that is, useful to the marketing manager in decision making) or not directly applicable but possibly of value because a necessary linkage is formed in the overall model. The following hypothetical example illustrates the role of proposition formation in theory building.

***Creative Consultants, Inc.***   Creative Consultants, Inc., a firm composed of persons with expertise in promoting the fine arts, has been retained by the Rochester Museum Association. A meeting is in progress in the Board Room, with directors from five museums present. Lydia Fuller, the dynamic "mastermind" behind the meeting, is presenting her purpose for inviting Herb Kaplan, head of Creative Consultants, to advise them:

"The success of the King Tut exhibit has shown us that there are a lot of ways to make fine arts profitable. We've asked you here to explore these. We've seen the museums in other cities capitalize on this tour. Although we can't attempt anything on that scale, there are some excellent smaller foreign exhibits available. We're hoping you can suggest some ways we can develop similar programs on a more limited scale to meet our needs."

Herb Kaplan responded by first demonstrating to the group some slides of an African art exhibit currently touring the United States. The exhibit was not doing well, but he attributed the lack of patronage to the absence of a "good system" (theory) upon which appropriate promotional plans could be based. He indicated that he had, however, isolated some interrelated ideas (propositions). Just as Kaplan placed his first transparency, labeled "Marketing Concepts," on the overhead projector, a disgruntled voice from the back of the room boomed out:

"Wait a minute, what does marketing have to do with a service like ours? We function for those who appreciate art—why should we go out and try to attract crowds of people? If the art's good, people recognize it and come anyway. How will our regular patrons react when they see us trying to push Rembrandt in the same way the latest rock star might be promoted?"

Ripples of somewhat uncertain laughter permeated the room. Obviously most of the participants felt a little uncomfortable at mixing art and marketing, even though it was an inevitable part of their lofty role.

Herb Kaplan had encountered the "temperamental artist" (or the aspirant thereof) many times since Creative Consultants' formation. He explained how art satisfies an important consumer desire for aesthetic pleasure, culture, and "experience." A sound marketing program served as the link between the two interested parties.

Myra Feldsen, a museum director from Indianapolis, agreed that marketing was needed. She said that she had noted that special exhibits, especially those open at night, seemed to draw a lot of businessmen and professionals. Mel Blank, from Buffalo, agreed with Myra and noted that such persons were typically too busy to spend much time at museums but might show up for a program that really caught their attention.

Herb Kaplan responded, "Myra and Mel, what you've just said are really propositions that can form the building blocks for describing your market. Once you have this market described, you'll have the basis for selecting media. Myra, you've defined several of your needs for information—who are your target markets? What factors in the Indianapolis market are most related to museum patronage of special events? Your working proposition seems to be that special exhibits would appeal to professionals and managers who wouldn't otherwise frequent the museum. And Mel, you've added an explanatory note to Myra's proposition—that time constraints and a heavy activity schedule would keep such persons away unless a special stimulus got them into the museum."

Participants continued to state concepts and propositons worth investigating. Kaplan noted each carefully, and a second meeting was scheduled to discuss the theory thus constructed and to assign responsibility for various phases of the project.

The Creative Consultants, Inc., case demonstrates that propositions are used by practitioners whether or not they are recognized as such, and that empirical testing is essential if any reliance is to be placed on the marketing theory formed from these statements of interrelationships. The locus problem, or proper context for marketing strategy based on theory, is also illustrated.

## Propositions as Elements of Theory

Propositions, then, represent an advancement beyond concepts toward theory formation and testing. A marketing example would be Bagozzi's study of performance and satisfaction among industrial salespersons.[28] The interrelation-

---

[28]Richard P. Bagozzi, "Performance and Satisfaction in an Industrial Sales Force: An Examination of Their Antecedents and Simultaneity," *Journal of Marketing*, 44 (Spring 1980), 65–77.

ship between two concepts—performance and satisfaction—is explored. Bagozzi outlines four possible ways of viewing the nature of this relationship: (1) performance causes satisfaction; (2) satisfaction causes performance; (3) the two are reciprocally related; and (4) performance and satisfaction are not related causally, so any empirical association is spurious. In order for managers to effectively motivate and understand their sales forces, they should know the nature of this relationship. Based upon previous research and the logic of balance theory, Bagozzi hypothesizes that job performance influences job satisfaction (relationship 1 above), but not vice versa (relationship 2), and selects three individual difference variables to use as co-variates (to test possibility 3 above). Figure 4.8 shows the causal model.

Hypotheses are stated as follows:

H1: Job performance will be positively associated with job satisfaction.

H2: The greater the value placed on specific tangible and nontangible rewards associated with the job, the higher the performance of activities leading to these rewards and the greater the satisfaction with subsequent attainment of these rewards.

H3: The greater the task-specific self-esteem, the higher the performance of activities leading to valued outcomes and the greater the subsequent satisfaction with achievement of these outcomes.

H4: Verbal intelligence will be positively associated with performance.

Table 4.4 shows how the variables were operationalized or measured. The first three hypotheses were supported by the data. Further tests should

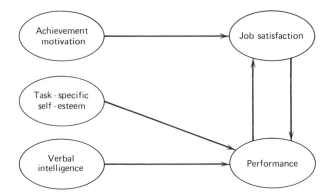

**Figure 4.8.** A causal model showing hypothesized relationships and predicting outcomes.

*Source.* Richard P. Bagozzi, "Performance and Satisfaction in an Industrial Sales Force: An Examination of Their Antecedents and Simultaneity." *Journal of Marketing*, 44 (Spring 1980), 68–69. Reprinted with permission. Published by the American Marketing Association.

**Table 4.4**
**Data Collection Instruments and Reliabilities**

| Variable | Measurement | Cronbach Alpha Reliability of Composite[a] |
|---|---|---|
| Performance | Dollar volume of sales each person achieved for the year | — |
| Job Satisfaction | Measure 1—four six-point Likert items (Do you feel promotion opportunities are wider in jobs other than yours? Would you advise a friend looking for a new job to take one similar to yours? Do you feel your pay is as high in comparison with what others get for similar work in other companies? How satisfied are you with your general work situation?) Measure 2—four six-point Likert items (Do you feel it is as easy to demonstrate ability and initiative in your job as in others? Do you think that there is as much a feeling of security in your job as in others? Do you find your work challenging, exciting, and giving you a sense of accomplishment? How much control do you feel you have over your work activities such as number of calls required in a week, etc.?) | 0.78 |
| Task-Specific Self-Esteem | Measure 1—two nine-point and one five-point Likert items Measure 2—three nine-point items | 0.77 |
| Achievement Motivation | Measure 1—four five-point Likert items Measure 2—four five-point Likert items | 0.60 |
| Verbal Intelligence | Thirty-item matched response scale | — |

[a]Cronbach Alpha values were computed from the following formula (see Lord and Novick 1968): $\alpha = [n/(n-1)][1 - (\Sigma\, \sigma_i^2/\sigma_T^2)]$, where n = number of items, $\sigma_T^2$ = variance of the total index, and $\Sigma\, \sigma_i^2$ = sum of item variances.

*Source.* Richard P. Bagozzi, "Performance and Satisfaction in an Industrial Sales Force: An Examination of Their Antecedents and Simultaneity," *Journal of Marketing*, 44 (Spring 1980), 68–69. Reprinted with permission. Published by the American Marketing Association.

then be made (using partial correlations) to determine whether the correlations are spurious. That is, are there antecedents that affect both the cause and effect? 

The validity of such findings can be strengthened by one's eliminating rival hypotheses and by further specifying the model. For example, if task-specific self-esteem is related to job performance, and job performance is related to job satisfaction, then what is the relationship (if any) between self-esteem and satisfaction? Replication of findings is important, but it is also important to test a large variety of possible relationships. As Stinchcombe notes: "As the number of *similar* tests to the theory increases, *the number of alternative theories each new test eliminates* becomes much smaller."[29]

## Commentary on Theory

A theory is an interrelated set of concepts which explains an event or phenomenon. Technically, a simple proposition relating two concepts should be a theory. In practice, a theory is usually considered to be a collection of two or more interrelated propositions which either partially or fully explains an event. While a model may *describe* an event, a theory provides substantive explanation and understanding. Thus a theory contains a model. When a model goes beyond statistical or mathematical explanation and provides substantive explanation and understanding, it becomes a theory. Thus theorizing is the mental process of "acquiring explanations about why certain variations occur and why they do not. It is not merely a matter of finding empirical relationships that happen to occur in the real world, but rather of learning the circumstances under which variation in variables brings about variation in other variables in a way that acquires multiple levels of generality."[30]

A theory contains a good deal of speculation. However confident we may feel about a theory, ultimate proof is often elusive. There are sources of error in the measurement of concepts (variables) and our models of complex phenomena are often incomplete. When we add to these problems the fact that there always lurks the possibility of an alternative explanation we didn't think of, then the idea of ultimate proof of a theory doesn't make sense. Yet at the same time we do develop and use theories (see Chapter 6, for example), make judgments about their truthfulness or validity (see Chapters 7 and 8), and act upon these judgments.

Theories are as diverse in style and personality as the people who fashion them. The visitor to the Palace of Versailles can well imagine the grand theory of France in relation to the rest of the world that Louis xiv must have held. Other personalities weave middle-range theories or historical theories. History is rich in

[29] Arthur L. Stinchcombe, *Constructing Social Theories* (New York: Harcourt, 1968), p. 21.
[30] Wesley R. Burr, *Theory Construction and the Sociology of the Family* (New York: Wiley-Interscience, 1973), p. 23.

theory, as is drama. For example, Arthur Miller vividly portrays alienation through the character of Willie Loman in *Death of a Salesman*. The fabric of this play is as much a theoretical statement as Bagozzi's structural equation model or Durkheim's famous sociological theory of egoistic suicide.[31] Miller depicts the salesman's sense of alienation in an individualistic, competitive world; Bagozzi relates self-esteem to job performance; Durkheim relates individualism and commercial employment to higher rates of egoistic suicide.

As theory evolves, the expression becomes clearer and more complete. One way of viewing the evolution is as an upward spiral, with each movement upward being an expansion of consciousness or increased awareness of the total set of forces involved in explaining a particular phenomenon. The laws, or general-izations, that result from this process can be viewed symbolically. The apparently complex world of marketing (or physics, engineering, philosophy) can be analyzed through the laws which are its ingredients. Just as the universe manifests in geometric patterns with nature following a system of order, so too can any problem be viewed geometrically, as, for example, a triangle: with only two elements or conditions, the problem is incomplete; the third point completes the problem. For example, in reproduction, the male and female unite to form offspring. In electricity, the positive and negative poles of the battery unite to produce the spark. In marketing, the buyer and seller unite to form the exchange transaction or sale. Proposition formation serves as a completion of the triangle in which two concepts are related to form the third point; alone, they would have no power. When we recognize the universal nature of things and realize what we already know, then we can speak in terms of laws. By thinking symbolically at the conceptual level, we are more likely to evolve laws or generalizations.

## Summary

Most of this chapter has been devoted to the topic of concepts, which are the basic building blocks of theories. These blocks are united to form propositions, which in turn are connected to form theories or explanations. Concepts, and whatever is subsequently done with them, are, in Albert Einstein's words, "free creations of the human mind." This is perhaps the single most important thing to consider while reading subsequent chapters. A wide variety of social or professional conventions exist for the development, testing, and use of concepts. These are simply guidelines for tinkering.

[31]Emile Durkheim, *Suicide* (New York: Free Press, 1951).

# FIVE

# DEDUCTIVE AND INDUCTIVE THINKING

*In this chapter we suggest that much creative thinking is the result of the nearly simultaneous use of both deductive and inductive thinking, although the deductive approach is often used to present the results of our thinking to others. By deemphasizing the role of inductive thinking, there is a substantial risk of losing creativity. This is especially true with respect to creative insights which may be derived from practical experience.*

People do not get married or divorced, commit murder or suicide, or lay down their lives for freedom upon detailed cognitive analysis of the pros and cons of their actions.

**R. B. Zajonc**[1]

He who hesitates is lost.

**Old proverb**

Look before you leap.

**Old proverb**

Before exploring the notion of theory-in-use, a central theme in this book, it is necessary to understand the predominant *espoused* approach used in theory construction—the logical or hypothetical deductive method.

The theory-in-use approach focuses on generating concepts, propositions, and theories by observing multiple subjects or cases where theories are in apparent use. It involves both inductive and deductive logic. Often, however, we find one or the other mode of logic being advocated. The logical deductive approach *starts* with a set of concepts and propositions and then deduces that, if these propositions are true, and if certain other conditions are met, certain specific and observable events will occur. The goal of this method of theory construction is to "gradually eliminate invalid propositions and increase the number of useful valid ones."[2] The inductive mode stresses the formal or informal accumulation of data, which may lead to a tentative theory.

The benefits of each approach have been argued for decades, as indicated by this early statement by Francis Bacon:[3]

There are and can only be two ways of searching into and discovering truth. The one flies from the senses and particulars to the most general axioms, and from these principles, the truth of which it takes for settled and immovable, proceeds to judgement and to discovery of middle axioms. And this way is now in fashion (deduction). The other derives from the senses and particulars, rising by gradual and unbroken ascent, so that it arrives at the most general axioms last of all (induction). This is the true way, but as yet untried.

[1] R. B. Zajonc, "Feeling and Thinking: Preferences Need No Inferences," *American Psychologist*, 35, no. 2 (1980), 172.
[2] Wesley R. Burr, *Theory Construction and the Sociology of the Family* (New York: Wiley-Interscience, 1973), p. 3.
[3] Francis Bacon, Aphorism XIX, Novum Organum, 1620.

Reynolds takes the argument further and identifies the steps in each strategy and their underlying assumptions:[4]

| INDUCTIVE APPROACH | LOGICAL DEDUCTIVE APPROACH |
|---|---|
| (research then Theory) | (theory then Research) |
| Step 1: Select a phenomenon and list all the characteristics of the phenomenon. | Step 1: Develop an explicit theory in either axiomatic or process description form. |
| Step 2: Measure all the characteristics of the phenomenon in a variety of situations (as many as possible). | Step 2: Select a statement generated by the theory for comparison with the results of empirical research. |
| Step 3: Analyze the resulting data carefully to determine if there are any systematic patterns among the data "worthy" of further attention. | Step 3: Design a research project to "test" the chosen statement's correspondence with empirical research. |
| Step 4: Once significant patterns have been found in the data, formalization of these patterns as theoretical statements constitutes the "laws" of nature. | Step 4: If the statement derived from the theory does *not* correspond with the research results, make appropriate changes in the theory or research design and continue. |
|  | Step 5: If the statement from the theory *does* correspond with the results of the research, select further statements for testing or attempt to determine the limitations of the theory (situations where the theory does not apply). |

It should be emphasized that although the extremes are presented here as ideal

---

[4] Paul D. Reynolds, *A Primer in Theory Construction* (New York: Bobbs-Merrill, 1971).

types, these approaches are not mutually exclusive. In fact, it is essential to realize that they are often used simultaneously. We shall rely on two different representations to convey this important idea.

George E. P. Box, an eminent statistician, remarks that "science is a means whereby learning is achieved, not by mere theoretical speculations on the one hand, nor by the undirected accumulation of practical facts on the other, but rather by a motivated iteration between theory and practice."[5] He continues to observe, with reference to Figure 5.1, that "Matters of fact can lead to a tentative theory. Deductions from this tentative theory may be found to be discrepant with certain known or specially acquired facts. These discrepancies can then induce a modified, or in some cases a different theory. Deductions made from the modified theory may or may not be in conflict with fact, and so on. In reality this main iteration is accompanied by many simultaneous subiterations."[6] Box's thinking is displayed in Figure 5.1 and in somewhat more detail in Figure 5.2.

Seymour Fine presents a very interesting perspective on the same process. Drawing on John Dewey's classic book *How We Think*, Fine describes the reasoning process as "a two-way movement from partial, fragmentary, and often confused facts to an idea, and then back again to facts (not merely the original facts but new particulars). The first leg of the trip is heuristic, intuitive, inductive. The second leg reinforces, orders, and synthesizes the original data by connecting them with one another and with additional facts to which the data have brought attention. The trip is never back and forth just once, but continuous. With each

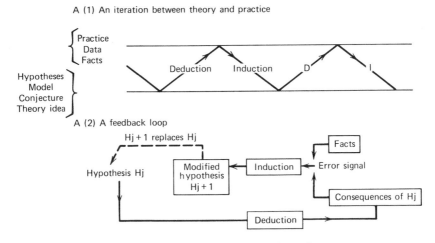

**Figure 5.1.** The advancement of learning.

[5]George E. P. Box, "Science and Statistics," *Journal of the American Statistical Association*, 71, no. 356, (December 1976), 791.
[6]*Ibid.*, p. 791.

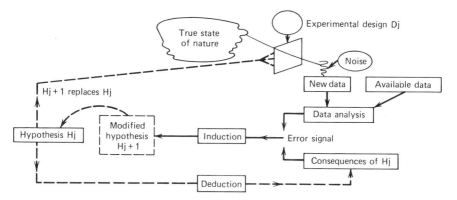

**Figure 5.2.** Data analysis and data getting in the process of scientific investigation. The experimental design is here shown as a movable window looking onto the true state of nature. Its positioning at each stage is motivated by current beliefs, hopes, and ideas.

circuit, the original facts and the inferred ideas are strengthened into *premises* and in turn, into final *beliefs* or conclusions."[7] Figure 5.3 summarizes these ideas.

When fact and idea or intellect and intuition are not allowed to interact, at least one usually suffers and it is generally the realm of fact or intellect which does. We think Exhibit 5.1 expresses this as well as any long narrative might.

## Inductive (Research then Theory) Approach

Despite the iterative and perhaps even simultaneous nature of inductive-deductive reasoning, it will be useful at this point to stop and examine further the

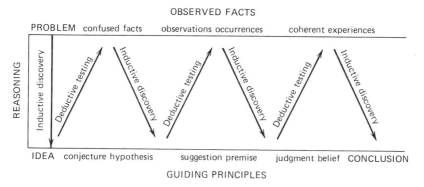

**Figure 5.3.** The idea within the context of the problem-solving process.

*Source.* Seymour H. Fine, *The Marketing of Ideas and Social Issues.* Praeger Social Studies Series, (New York: Praeger, 1981), p. 9.

[7] Seymour H. Fine, *The Marketing of Ideas and Social Issues* (New York: Praeger, 1981).

**Exhibit 5.1**

*Source.* From Russell Myers, Broom Hilda Cartoon. Reprinted by permission of Tribune Co. Syndicate, Inc.

differences in these two approaches or ideal types of theorizing. An example will facilitate discussion.

***Example.*** A men's clothing store manager has seen sales decline consistently over the past six months, despite a recent large budget "prestige" advertising campaign and point of sales promotion. The manager is very concerned since this is usually the best six-month sales period.

An inductive approach would involve listing as many characteristics of the phenomenon as possible: competitive behavior; sales trends among different types of clothing; sales trends in prior periods; sales trends among specific groups of customers (defined geographically, demographically, by lifestyle, by social structure, and so on); changes in fashion trends; customer complaints; advertising impact; and so forth.

The manager could generate other characterisitcs but suffice it to say that he tries to be fairly comprehensive and include characteristics that will generate *very different* explanations of the sales decline.

In Step 2 the manager would gather information concerning the characteristics developed in Step 1. He might generate secondary information from the store's records and from trade sources. For example, sales figures could be compared with those of the same time span in previous months. Drastic fashion changes would be monitored by the leading trade publications. Primary marketing research, in the form of a survey, would be necessary to ascertain changes in the customer mix. Demographics and lifestyle dimensions could be researched through mail questionnaires or personal interviews. The manager would seek data for as many different situations as possible. For example, data could be broken down by specific product lines and time periods, as well as certain geographical areas and target groups. Data on other stores in the same line of business would also be useful but much more difficult to obtain.

Step 3 would entail analyzing the data to determine if any systematic patterns can be identified. This might involve generating frequencies and cross-tabulation. If sample sizes are small, nonparametric statistics could be used. With larger samples, a host of multivariate methods are available. Any statistical analysis used must go hand in hand with the manager's intuitive judgment as to the validity of the findings.

The manager and research department systematically ruled out a number of explanations, but one pattern consistently came out: sales had been decreasing proportionally to the number of regular "big buy" customers who had *not* been coming in since the advertising compaign had started. He looked closely at the advertising campaign and how it might have affected his regular customers. Although he had always had a "high-value" image (good price, good quality) the recent campaign had attempted to add a little more prestige to the store, since he was hoping to broaden his market a little. He reasoned that the higher-prestige advertising had resulted in a lower acceptance of his store by regular customers (it didn't fit their image anymore).

Step 4 would focus on generalizing this pattern and presenting it as a theoretical statement. In this case the manager concluded that a store patronage problem was present. People who are regular shoppers may develop an attachment to a store that matches their self-image. The greater the compatability of shopper and store "personalities," the greater the store patronage. Conversely, a lower compatibility leads to lower store patronage.

The general theoretical statement derived above has implications for the manager in future advertising and promotion efforts. However, one must estimate how "good" the explanation is that he came up with and how much confidence one would place in making a decision based upon it.

## Deductive (Theory then Research) Approach

A manager faced with the same problem could have approached it in a more deductive manner. After discussing the problem with a consultant, a general approach was developed to explain the problem, which could be represented by the diagram in Figure 5.4. We'll assume the consultant had encountered this representation in a professional journal and had found it to be a useful framework.

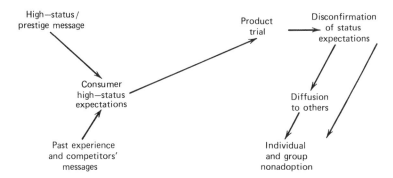

**Figure 5.4.** Deductive approach.

The technical name they gave this explanation was the "diffused disconfirmed expectations" theory. Essentially it means that the advertisements developed a high-status image for the store (relative to competition and among new as well as old customers) which was not confirmed when they actually visited the store. These people did not purchase and subsequently told their friends not to go to this store for "high-status" clothing.

According to Step 2 the manager would select one aspect of the diagram and see if it is true for his particular situation. One aspect might be that high-status advertising creates an impression/expectation of high-price/high-status products and personnel. They also might deduce that this would be more predominant among people who were occasional customers and who had a large number of clothing store alternatives. Another aspect could be that people whose expectations are *not* confirmed actively tell others in their social circle who in turn do not purchase at this store.

It might be further deduced that this would occur among those customers who had a large number of social contacts spread over a large number of groups.

Step 3 would entail actually operationalizing the previous statement and testing it to determine its validity. Specifically, the hypothesis might be tested that the more an expectation is disconfirmed, the greater the tendency to tell others in one's immediate social circle. When this is operationalized as an empirical statement, one would expect to find that customers whose expectations were disconfirmed had told more people about their experience than customers whose expectations were *not* disconfirmed. The test of the hypothesis would have to hold the customer's number and type of social contacts constant or controlled so the result would not be confounded. Thus, people with higher disconfirmation scores would also have higher social diffusion scores than people with lower disconfirmation scores.

If support for the statement were found, an effort also might be made to develop instances where it does not apply (Step 5). Also, is the reverse true—does higher confirmation result in a customer *not* telling friends? If so, what is the implication for the manager? If the test "disproved" the statement, then that *aspect* of the theory might be reformulated or a different type of research design or measurement procedure might be adopted.[8]

## Induction and Deduction:
## Parts of the Same Wheel

Both approaches represent a different *process* of developing and testing theories. Also, both can result in different theories being developed for what appears to be the "same" problem. There have been great arguments concerning which approach is "best" and which approach is *actually* practiced by researchers and scientists.[9] But are the two approaches completely incompatible?

Wallace[10] would suggest that although they reflect different assumptions about theorizing, they do in fact represent different *stages* of the overall process of developing and testing theories. Rather than choosing between theories or theory strategies, why not combine them into an ongoing process? The "Wallace Wheel," shown in Figure 5.5 represents such a process.

Given the two approaches stated earlier, the logical inductive approach (research then theory) stresses the *left* half of the wheel (starting with observations), while the logical deductive approach stresses the *right* half of the wheel

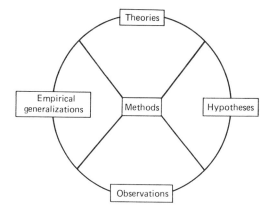

**Figure 5.5.** Wallace wheel.

[8] This is the process that deductive reasoning follows. It provides explanation by having a set of propositions and then deducing that, if these propositions are true and certain other conditions are met, certain specific and observable events occur.

[9] Phillip E. Hammond, *Sociologists at Work* (New York: Basic Books, 1964).

[10] Walter L. Wallace, *Sociological Theory* (Chicago: Aldine, 1969), p. ix.

(starting with theories). The difficulty with this traditional approach to reconciling the issue is that it underplays the iterative nature of the thinking process.

Recently, a large sports car distributor was faced with a problem of low sales for a new model. It had been six months since the introduction of the car and, despite heavy promotional efforts at both the national and local levels, sales were lower than expected. The distributor's first reaction to the problem stressed the left half of the wheel. He had compared the car to other new models that he had introduced in the past and, on the basis of his experience, felt it was too much money for the type of features that were offered. He transmitted this explanation to the national sales manager for the car company, who quickly rejected it, suggesting that their research had indicated that consumers felt the features offered were above average for a car in that price range.

Somewhat unsure of his first reaction now, the distributor talked to his salespeople and the service personnel for alternative explanations. Rather than receiving a common response, he received no fewer than twelve different reasons why they thought the car wasn't selling well. Some of these included the following: the ads were directed at the wrong people; the advertising theme was inappropriate; the product was "too different" compared with past models; competitive models were more exciting; the car cost too much; and the car had received mediocre reviews from car magazines. Given the diversity and experience of the people involved, he reasoned that all might have some truth to them but each was only a partial explanation.

Unsure of how to fit all the pieces together, the distributor talked to an automotive research and consulting firm. The consultant's first response was to ask the distributor if he had reviewed the sales figures of competitive cars to see if the same trend existed. The distributor had not but promised to review them. The review showed that the trend in competitive cars was one of increasing sales.

Subsequent to this, the consultant proposed that they do an in-depth analysis of current owners of the car as well as people who had considered the car but had not purchased it. To guide the research, he suggested they do focus group interviews with each type of person to better develop a conceptual model of the buying process for this type of car, then test the model out in a broader-based sample using telephone interviews. (Note: In essence they are using the focus interviews to tap the left side of the wheel and the telephone interviews to tap the right side of the wheel.)

The focus interviews were carried out and revealed a number of problems, the most common of which was a "product image compatibility" problem. That is, the image of the new model was highly incompatible with the image of the models that had preceded it. This factor was reinforced by the use of a high-profile advertising campaign that was directed at past owners of that brand of car.

To test the pervasiveness of this problem, telephone interviews were used to see if the same conditions held for people with diverse demographic as well as car ownership characteristics. The results showed that the problem existed more strongly among past owners but was also pervasive among people who were car enthusiasts but had not reached the income level where they could afford the car.

When reviewing the situation, keep in mind that this was not always a linear process as the distributor moved around the wheel. There was short-circuiting as different explanations, concepts, and facts were considered, evaluated, and accepted or rejected. There was a constant interplay between inductive and deductive thinking, with each playing a different but important role.

## Logical Deduction: Problems and Prospects

There are a number of issues that must be raised when one is developing deductive explanations of marketing phenomena. These include causality, establishing tests for a theory, and getting the theory in the first place.

## Causality

The issue of causality has long been debated in the social sciences. In our wheel example developed earlier, can we really say that higher perceived "store-customer" compatibility *causes* higher store patronage? Since this is a key area in both the deductive as well as inductive approaches to theory construction, Chapter 3 dealt with it in extensive detail.

## Testing Theories in the Deductive Mode

Once a general *theoretical* statement has been made, the next step is to make a deduction and translate it into an *empirical* statement so that observations can be made and the "truth" of the statement tested. This testability of a statement is of extreme importance to logical deductive analysis.

Poyla[11] and Stinchcombe[12] outline the general logic of testing theories in the deductive mode. Referring back to the clothing store example, two situations could have developed when the perceived store-image-compatibility (SIC)/store-patronage (SP) relationship was tested.

[11] G. Poyla, *Patterns of Plausible Inference* (Princeton, NJ: Princeton University Press, 1968).
[12] A. L. Stinchcombe, *Constructing Social Theories* (New York: Harcourt, 1968).

|          Situation I          |          Situation II          |
|:---:|:---:|
| (A)          (B) | (A)          (B) |
| High SIC =>     High SP | High SIC =>     High SP |
| High SP is not found in test | High SP is found in test |

|          |          |
|:---:|:---:|
| Therefore reject theory | Theory is more credible |

(*Note.* => represents "implies.")

In Situation I the theory and its empirical consequences imply that customers who have high SIC scores should also have high SP scores and consequently they should, on the average, shop more often at a particular store than people who have low SIC scores. However, suppose the test (i.e. a field experiment) revealed that this was not the case; that people with high SIC scores in fact had *lower* SP scores and shopped less often at a particular store than people with *low* SIC scores. Traditional deductive logic would dictate that the theory be ruled as false. It should be noted that this deduction could be wrong for what Stinchcombe labels "irrelevant" reasons. These might include the following: the concepts involved were not operationalized properly, the method of testing was weak, or the sample size was too small to generate the true SIC and SP scores of customers. This does not mean that we could not remedy these problems and test again; however, the canons of logic demand that, with this test used as a basis, the theory be rejected if it implies something that is false. This follows the traditional deductive view that although there could be no conclusive *verification* of a hypothesis, there could be conclusive *falsification* of a hypothesis.

Since this original approach to science concerning falsification was put forth, philosophers of science (such as Duhem) have argued that this is a gross oversimplification and distortion of science. A scientist never tests a single hypothesis, but rather by necessity tests it against a background of auxiliary hypotheses and assumptions. When a hypothesis is falsified, one is never sure *which* of these auxiliary hypotheses and assumptions is false. Thus, a theory cannot be conclusively falsified.[13] Thus, reference is made to the "falsification fallacy." There is always the possibility that had some other variable been considered in addition to those in the "falsified" hypothesis, the hypothesis might indeed be supported.

That statement takes us to Situation II. In the case of confirmation, deductive logic does not tell conclusively what can be said about the theory. The test indicates something positive has happened, but not conclusively that the theory has been proven. In Stinchcombe's and Poyla's terms the theory is more credible or believable than before the test. However, relating back to the earlier statement

[13] L. Lauden, "On the Impossibility of Crucial Falsifying Experiments," *The Philosophy of Science*, 32 (1965), 39–68; William Sauer, Nancy Nighswonger, and Gerald Zaltman, "Current Issues in the Philosophy of Science: Implications for the Study of Marketing," paper presented at AMA Conference on Marketing Theory, San Antonio, February 1982.

that logical deduction seeks to "gradually eliminate invalid propositions and increase the number of useful, valid ones," there could be *other* explanations for observing that some customers had higher SP scores and shopped at a particular store more often.

*What might some of these alternative explanations be?* One might develop a "restrictive distribution explanation." It may be that people were not aware of or could not get to other clothing stores that carry this line of products. Rather than just a high compatibility of store image, the "real" reason they shopped at that particular store may have been a *perception* that they had no real alternatives. Thus, store patronage was high but this was based on market distribution factors rather than image factors. Sales were going down not because of a store image change but rather because new competition may have opened up in the area *or* new transportation facilities had been developed which allowed this particular target group to frequent previously inaccessible clothing stores.

The reader might try to develop other alternative theories which could explain the observations generated in the test. From your own intuition and knowledge, categorize them from most likely to least likely. That is, which of the theories you developed is *the most likely alternative* to our initial store image/diffusion theory?

This approach includes two related yet distinctive strategies: *multiple tests* of theories and testing *different theories*.

## Multiple Tests

The strategy of multiple tests suggests that although we may never completely prove a theory, it can be made increasingly more credible by our testing the *same* theory in a variety of different situations:

| Situation I | Situation II | Situation III | Situation IV |
|---|---|---|---|
| $A = B$ | $A = B$ | $A = B_1, B_2, B_3$ | $A = B_1, B_2, B_3$ |
| B false | B true | $B_1, B_2, B_3$ similar | $B_1, B_2, B_3$ different |
| A false | A more credible | A substantially more credible | A much more credible |

*Source.* A. Stinchcombe, *Constructing Social Theories* (New York: Harcourt, Brace, 1968), p. 20.

Situation III would be described by testing the theory in a number of similar situations. For example, higher SIC scores might be associated with higher SP scores in a particular clothing store in a particular city ($B_1$), but we could also deduce that this relationship might be true for different clothing stores in the same city ($B_2$) or different clothing stores in different cities ($B_3$). *What other tests are similar in nature that you can think of to test this theory?*

Situation IV generalizes the theory not only to different target populations but gives a broader interpretation to the concept of store image and store patronage. On what different populations or products and services might you test this relationship? For example, a stronger test would be to observe this relationship in sports and automotive stores. A stronger test still would suggest that this theory covers other areas such as choice of colleges or political candidates. That is, students choose a college campus based on the perceived image compatibility of the school and themselves, which they also report to others close to them. Similarly, a person "patronizes" a particular political candidate based on the perceived image compatibility of the candidate and himself. Think of other tests that suggest quite different situations than those mentioned in Situation III.

The logic of stating that Situation IV gives a stronger test than Situation III is as follows: If you could make only one more observation to test a theory, you would choose one that is quite *different* from the prior one you made. In the examples just mentioned, the value of observing the political candidate choice is much greater than another observation of clothing stores. If we can deduce empirical observations in a number of *different* situations, the theory is more powerful than if we deduce observations only in *similar* situations.

## The Most Likely Alternative Theory

Rather than focusing on the same theory and deducing observations in similar and different situations, we could test the same theory against an *alternative* theory. The "restricted distribution" theory was an example of such a theory. That alternative theories should be generated is not only a logical but a natural step to take. For example, given any particular business or marketing problem, how likely is it that the interested parties will agree on the same theory? Chapter 7, on reality tests, will show in greater detail that what different people will or will not regard as true varies. Different people are likely to have a different theory-in-use for the same business or marketing problem.

Faced with this situation, there are a number of strategies that can be used to eliminate alternative theories using deductive logic. The first derives from the following logic: if we say our theory implies higher SP scores and an alternative theory implies lower SP scores, then if higher SP scores are observed the alternative theory is falsified. In fact, what you could do is develop a *number* of likely alternative theories, all of which imply lower SP scores.

- A (our theory) and (F, G, H . . . other theories) imply higher SP scores.
- (C, D, E . . . likely alternative theories) imply lower SP scores.
- If we observe higher SP scores, then by classical logic C, D, E . . . are false and A (our theory) is more credible.

Thus, this test eliminates several possible alternative theories. However, there were other theories that also implied high SP scores—including the "restricted distribution" theory—that were made more credible by the test. How are these evaluated and tested?

The next step is to develop implications of these remaining theories that are very *different* from one another—different in the sense that "there is almost no overlap between the theories that imply the one empirical and the theories that imply the other.[14] For example, the "restricted distribution" theory would not only imply higher SP scores but also imply that people were *not* aware of or could not visit other stores. The store image compatibility theory implies that people *are* aware of and could have visited other competitors' stores. Therefore, if we observe that people were aware of and could have visited other stores then we reject the "distribution" theory even though both explanations predict higher SP scores.

The general approach to ruling out alternative likely theories is the following:

- A (a theory) implies certain empirical observations $B_1$, $B_2$.
- C and D are alternative theories that imply that either or both $B_1$, $B_2$ will *not* occur.
- e.g., C = $B_1$ but not $B_2$.
    D = $B_2$ but not $B_1$.
- Therefore if $B_1$ and $B_2$ do occur, then C and D are false and A is substantially more credible.

To summarize, the basic approach of the logical deductive mode is "the elimination of alternative theories by investigating as many of the empirical consequences as is practical, always trying for the greatest possible variety in the implications tested."[15]

The elimination of rival or competing alternative hypotheses is an important strategy. However, a serious risk is encountered where this approach is followed automatically. Many hypotheses considered to be rival hypotheses may actually be quite compatible were a previously unspecified variable considered. Certain values of this variable may make one hypothesis correct and another incorrect while other values of the variable may result in the opposite. *The failure to be imaginative in locating such variables or at least the failure to ask whether apparent competing hypotheses cannot both be correct under certain conditions not only prevents the enrichment of an explanation by adding concepts but may impoverish explanations by eliminating some hypotheses which might have validity.* The rather partisan nature of science encourages us to prove our theories while disproving other people's theories. This is not necessarily unhealthy or inappropriate. However, neither should it be undertaken without first determining whether possible compatibility exists.

[14] Stinchcombe, *op. cit.*, p. 21.
[15] *Ibid.*, p. 22.

## Summary

This chapter has attempted to show the differences between deductive and inductive logic, while stressing that, although these approaches to theory construction are different, they can be seen as part of the same theory construction "wheel."

Approaches to using deductive logic must place particular emphasis on the tests that can be used in verifying and falsifying alternative explanations as well as generalizing a particular explanation.

# SIX
# CONSTRUCTING THEORIES-IN-USE

*Throughout this book we have been urging an eclectic approach to the creation of theories about marketing phenomena. Different approaches have their own advantages. No single approach is inherently superior. However, in this chapter we feature one particular approach, not because it produces inherently more valid and more reliable information than any other—it is not at all clear that it does. Instead, we feature the theory-in-use approach partly because it produces different kinds of insights than more conventional approaches and partly because it is an approach the reader is not likely to encounter in a formal sense. The basic message we want to convey is that people's "theories" about their own behavior may offer special insights to the researcher that other approaches do not yield. A theory-in-use approach might fruitfully be added to but not substituted for other approaches.*

I hear and I forget
I see and I remember
I do and I understand.

**Confucius**

The argument goes that applied research is radically different from basic scientific work. . . . This implies a false comparison with the natural sciences. It is true that technical engineers could not succeed without the knowledge provided by abstract research in mathematics and laboratory experiments of the 'pure' sciences. But it is misleading to draw an analogy between the natural and social sciences. Nowhere in the social realm are there unconditional laws and basic theories already well established. Quite to the contrary, it is the study of concrete and circumscribed practical problem-areas that has contributed a part of present-day general sociological knowledge.

**Lazarsfeld and Reitz[1]**

Religion rests its case on revelation, science on method, ideology on moral passion; but common sense rests its assertion that it is not a case at all, just life in a nutshell. The world is its authority.

**Clifford Geertz[2]**

The theory-in-use approach is a rather different approach to theory development. It may be described as a more inductive, inferential process of thinking about phenomena. The basic idea is simple: if you want a good theory of, say, selling, you should understand what a successful salesperson thinks and does. Underlying this idea is another simple notion: people often think in if–then statements. That is, individuals often think and behave in terms of "If I do this, then that may happen." These thoughts may not be very conscious or explicit, and generally the observer or theory builder can only assume that such if–then thoughts underlie particular behaviors. "Putative theory" may thus be an equally valid term for the approach described in this chapter.

Let us use personal selling as an illustration. An effective salesperson employs a number of ideas or concepts in his or her interactions with customers. A highly successful office furniture salesman will be used as an illustration here. A basic principle this salesman has described is: *initially be a consultant about a problem rather than an advocate of particular equipment or furniture.* What ideas or concepts does this particular salesman have as reflected in the principle he espouses? One idea is that of being consumer-problem oriented. A second idea is being a consultant or advisor. Implicit in this idea is that a consultant role may be

---

[1] P. F. Lazarsfeld and J. G. Reitz, *An Introduction To Applied Sociology* (New York: Elsevier, 1975), p. 10.
[2] Clifford Geertz, "Common Sense as a Cultural System," *The Antioch Review*, no. 1, 1975, p. 5.

perceived to be more on the side of a client (the consumer). An advocate in this context would be perceived as being more on the side of another party (i.e., the supplier of office equipment). These ideas, implicit in the principle given to us by the salesman, suggest the following if–then thinking: "If I appear to be concerned with understanding the consumer's problem, and if I offer general advice about solving that problem, then the consumer will perceive me to be on his or her side and thus relatively more objective, and hence is more likely to accept suggestions I make about the office equipment and furniture I represent, and is more likely to order at least some of my equipment to solve his or her problem." It is important to point out that all the salesman gave us was the principle in italics above. The statement just provided in quotes is an elaboration of the kind of if–then thinking on the part of the salesman *we* believe underlies this principle.

It is possible to go a bit further. There are a few propositions implicit in this thinking process. One proposition is: the more oriented a salesperson is to understanding consumer problems, the more likely it is that the consumer will accept his or her advice. A second proposition is that the more a salesperson displays a consulting role (as opposed to an advocacy role), the more likely the consumer is to accept purchase advice. The more advice a consumer accepts, the more likely the salesperson's products are to be used in the solution of the consumer's problems. This may be shown diagrammatically (Diagram 6.1).

This diagram represents a simple theory. The theory, however, is incomplete at least as far as our office equipment salesman is concerned. This salesman also described other principles he follows. Each of these principles could be elaborated upon as we have done above. We shall focus on only one other principle: *always use referrals*. By referrals he meant making reference to other firms that he had worked with and that the consumer knows of and/or could telephone or visit. This particular salesman uses as referrals both firms that purchased his equipment and those that did not purchase his equipment for acceptable reasons (for example, the product line did not match customer needs), but that he felt valued his advice. Use of referrals may be very subtle as well as very explicit. The apparent reasoning behind this principle is: "If I refer to other firms I've helped, then my advice will be taken more seriously, and if I refer to firms who have followed my advice which did not involve my own line of equipment, my role as a consultant will be enhanced and I'll be perceived less as an advocate." Two propositions worth noting here are the following: (1) the larger the number of

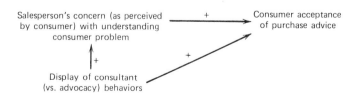

**Diagram 6.1**

other firms advised, the more credible the salesperson's advice; and (2) the more that advice is perceived as not being uniquely linked to the salesperson's line of equipment, the greater his or her overall credibility as a consultant (versus an advocate). Thus, we have in Diagram 6.2 a slightly more elaborate version of Diagram 6.1.

This diagram identifies several interrelated concepts. Undoubtedly, additional concepts and propositions could be developed from the same principles, not to mention those which could be derived from other principles the salesman uses. It is not our purpose to develop this particular salesman's theory, but simply to indicate that he does have one which he apparently uses with considerable success. Had we suggested to our salesman friend that he possessed a rich, complicated, and well-developed theory, he would probably have taken offense. The term "theory" often implies something abstract and perhaps not especially helpful or relevant. The concepts or ideas this salesman uses are hardly abstract; he applies them almost daily. Neither are they unhelpful or irrelevant; they provide him with a very comfortable living and a sense of personal accomplishment. He would also be a bit surprised if we were to enumerate the large number of concepts implicit in the several selling principles he provided, and he would be somewhat puzzled too if we claimed they formed a complicated causal model. This surprise and puzzlement would merely illustrate the fact that few people ever bother or need to bother to identify the "theories" they use in everyday life. Because of this, we are typically not conscious of the richness of our thoughts or the fact that we use theory daily.

The ideas in the preceding paragraph are also reflected by the noted anthropologist Clifford Geertz in his essay, "Common Sense as a Cultural System." Two particular observations in this essay are especially relevant here. The first observation Geertz makes is that common sense is "a relatively organized body of considered thought, rather than just what anyone clothed and in his right mind knows."[3] Thus, there is much more to common sense than ordinarily meets the eye. Common sense represents the most pervasive body of

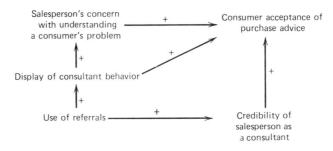

**Diagram 6.2**

[3]*Ibid.*, p. 7.

thought we possess. Of course, there is a tendency (which the reader may be experiencing right now) to discount the intellectual value or profundity of common sense. This is related to Geertz's second observation: "... it is an inherent characteristics of common sense thought precisely to deny [that it is a relatively well-organized body of thought] and to affirm that its tenets are immediate deliverances of experience, not deliberate reflections upon it."[4]

Thus, the old dictum that "there is nothing so applied as a good theory" has considerable truth. Also, the process of creating theories from principles may involve a gradual transfer from conscious to subconscious thought. After much experience, consciously developed principles become embedded in the subconscious as habits. The behaviors these principles give rise to become customary, perhaps even automatic ways of doing things.[5]

Before we discuss the rationale for a theory-in-use approach and outline the specific steps in using a theory-in-use strategy for building theory, the following brief points should be made concerning our illustration.

1. Not every successful salesperson in the same industry dealing with the same customers will rely on the same principles. Other effective salespersons may have different theories that work well for them.

2. Even if basically the same principles were identified, different salespersons might enact or put them into use differently.

3. Other observers might identify concepts and propositions other than those we identified. More than one set of propositions might logically underlie a given principle.

We shall return to these points shortly.


## Why a Theory-in-Use Approach

It is important to understand the rationale for employing a theory-in-use approach in the development of marketing theory. The basic rationale lies in the very definition of knowledge, the pursuit of which is a major reason for building a theory. Perhaps the best definition of knowledge is provided by a well-known sociologist of knowledge, Burkart Holzner:[6]

---

[4]*Ibid.*

[5]The reader who is interested in pursuing this idea further should consult the literature on psychological scripts. A good introduction may be found in R. C. Schank and R. P. Abelson, *Scripts, Plans, Goals and Understanding: On Inquiry Into Human Knowledge Structures* (Hillsdale, NJ: Lawrence Erlbaum, 1977), esp. Chap. 3.

[6]Burkart Holzner, *Reality Construction in Society* (Cambridge, MA: Schenkman, 1968), p. 20.

. . . "knowledge" can only mean the mapping of experienced reality by some observer. It cannot mean the "grasping" of reality itself. In fact, philosophical progress has produced the conclusive insight that there can be no such thing as the direct and "true" apprehension of "reality" itself. More strictly speaking, we are compelled to define "knowledge" as the communicable mapping of some aspect of experienced reality by an observer in symbolic terms.

Knowledge, then, is the mapping of experienced reality. It is our own picture of what we hold to be true. Different salespeople may experience differently the reality of selling the same product to the same customer and hence map out or describe differently what they "know" about selling to that customer. Similarly, different theory builders observing a given salesperson in interaction with his or her customer might describe this selling process differently (i.e., have different maps) and in ways which may not necessarily agree with the way the salesperson or the customer see it. Holzner and Marx state this more abstractly: "Yet all knowledge originates in an observer and retains the stamp of the observer's peculiar relation to the experiential base."[7] Knowledge, and especially theory, is ultimately *personal*. Knowledge may have many ways of being valid,[8] but it is still socially and psychologically construed. This simple but important point is perhaps the one point on which all contemporary philosophers, sociologists, psychologists, and historians of science are in agreement.

If knowledge is the mapping of experienced reality, an important way of uncovering knowledge is to learn about the maps that are held by people with appropriate experiences. A person with an appropriate experience might be an especially successful salesperson if we are concerned with a theory of personal selling, a successful product manager if we are concerned with a theory of product management, and so forth. (The criterion of "success" will be examined shortly.) If we learn what knowledge guides their behavior, we might have a theory which has pragmatic validity: it works for at least one person. One might then look at several cases in search of commonalities of knowledge which seem to underlie effective practice. We emphasize practice because it is practice which provides the reality that people experience and hence is the basis of what constitutes knowledge for them. Because that knowledge carries their unique personal imprint (determined by various social and psychological factors), we might prefer to call that knowledge a "theory" to suggest a degree of tentativeness or caution in its use by others without adequate testing.

A theory-in-use approach is not a substitute for other ways of understanding the world of behavior among managers, distributors, buyers, or whomever it is we want to theorize about. Rather, a theory-in-use approach is necessary to help augment our understanding of the behavioral world as we ordinarily study it

---

[7] Burkart Holzner and John H. Marx, *Knowledge Application: The Knowledge System in Society* (Boston: Allyn & Bacon, 1979), p. 93.
[8] G. Zaltman, C. Pinson, and R. Angelmar, *Metatheory in Consumer Research* (New York: Holt, Rinehart & Winston, 1973).

using focus group interviews, mail surveys, personal interviews, laboratory experiments, and a variety of data analytic techniques. Theories-in-use interact with the behavioral world. The understanding of one requires the understanding of the other. Argyris and Schon make this point very well:[9]

> Theory-building is reality-building, not only because our theories-in-use help to determine what we perceive of the behavioral world but because our theories-in-use determine our actions, which in turn help to determine the characteristics of the behavioral world, which in turn feed into our theories-in-use. Consequently, every theory-in-use is a way of doing something to others (to one's behavioral world), which in turn does something to oneself.

In this chapter, discussion is limited to successful practices as a basis for illustration. *A theory-in-use approach should also include unsuccessful practices.* If, for example, we consistently found the same principle(s) to be used by unsuccessful practitioners, we might conclude that the underlying proposition or theory has been falsified and we can rule it out as a possible explanation of the phenomena we are concerned with. Additionally, if the same principle appears to be used in the same way by both successful and unsuccessful practitioners, we can conclude there are very likely to be important concepts and propositions missing from our theory which, if present, would explain why the principle may be true in both cases but not be associated with the same result. For example, two salespeople working under identical circumstances may both display an identical fashion consultant-like behavior and elicit consumer acceptance of advice. Closer inspection of the situation may reveal certain demographic variables to be relevant. For example, the more years of experience in the industry customers perceive a salesperson as having, the more likely they are to accept the salesperson in a consultant role. Thus we would add perceived relevant years of professional experience as a new variable which influences the impact of consultant-role behavior on the consumer acceptance of purchase advice. Had we not examined cases of unsuccess where the original proposition didn't appear to work, we would not have sought an additional important variable. Had we looked only at unsuccessful instances of the use of the original proposition, we would have discarded it as being untrue.

One very important caveat must be used when one is focusing on successful and unsuccessful practitioners. It is possible to be right (and hence successful) for the wrong reasons. Also it is possible to be wrong (and hence unsuccessful) but have correct reasons. Under certain market conditions (such as very high-quality products, strong demand, an active rule of reciprocity) a salesperson who is very unskilled intellectually and interpersonally might be successful in terms of contracts closed or some other criterion of success. Under very unfavorable market conditions an otherwise highly skilled salesperson might be unsuccessful.

[9] Chris Argyris and Donald A. Schön, *Theory in Practice: Increasing Professional Effectiveness* (San Francisco: Jossey-Bass, 1974).

Thus, degree of success may not always or consistently be a good indicator of the quality of a theory-in-use.

A theory-in-use approach partially reflects two research traditions. One is single-subject research; the other is grounded theory. Single-subject research is a well-established methodology.[10] It is represented both by the case history or case study approach and the single-subject experimental design approach to research. The single "subject" may be a single person, a single family, a single organization, community, and so forth. In fact, many of the major—even classic—contributions to knowledge in the social sciences are based on single-subject research methods. Sigmund Freud, Jean Piaget, Erving Goffman, and Margaret Mead are social scientists whose pioneering work involved single-subject research. Single-subject research is in fact in widespread use. The very use of the case study approach to teaching marketing knowledge assumes that case research or development is a valid way of uncovering knowledge of sufficient validity to warrant its use as a teaching foundation. Donald T. Campbell, once a critic of the case study approach, has since rather strongly endorsed this approach as a means of building theories and both validating and invalidating them.[11] He concludes that: "After all, man is, in his ordinary way, a very competent knower, and qualitative common-sense knowing is not replaced by quantitative knowing. Rather, quantitative knowing has to trust and build on the qualitative including ordinary perception. We methodologists must achieve an applied epistemology which integrates both.[12]

The notion of grounded theory is also relevant to a theory-in-use approach. This notion has been best articulated by Glaser and Strauss.[13] A grounded theory is one which is discovered from data carefully obtained from sound social research. Concepts must be carefully chosen on the basis of their possible relevance to the phenomenon being explored and their level of abstraction must be specified. They must be carefully operationalized, with sampling biases identified and validity and reliability tests performed. The resulting data are subsequently interpreted in light of the patterns they display. Grounded theory is increasingly used in social science research.[14] In certain ways the interpretation of factor scores and the specification of factor labels, especially in survey feedback exercises where respondents or subjects analyze their own data, is an instance of

[10]C. F. Sidman, *Tactics of Scientific Research* (New York: Basic Books, 1960); J. M. Neal and R. M. Liebert, *Science and Behavior* (Englewood Cliffs, NJ: Prentice-Hall, 1973), esp. 8. We particularly encourage the reading of Chris Argyris and Donald A. Schön, *Theory in Practice: Increasing Professional Effectiveness* (San Fransisco: Jossey-Bass, 1974).

[11]Donald T. Campbell, "Qualitative Knowing in Action Research," Kurt Lewin Award Address, Society for the Psychological Study of Social Issues, Meeting with the American Psychological Association, New Orleans, September 1, 1974.

[12]*Ibid.*

[13]Barney G. Glaser and Anselm L. Strauss, *The Discovery of Grounded Theory: Strategies for Qualitative Research* (Chicago: Aldine, 1967).

[14]W. H. Dunn and F. W. Swierczek, "Planned Organizational Change: Toward Grounded Theory," *The Journal of Applied Behavioral Science*, 13, 2 (1977), 135–157.

grounded theory. The investigator uses the multivariate technique of factor analysis to help respondents provide theoretical insights. (Whether factor analysis itself is an instance of grounded theory is a matter of debate which need not be pursued here.)

A somewhat different perspective suggests that a grounded theory approach has always been widely used but that the formal presentation of this work, such as publication in scholarly journals, misrepresents it as having been developed in a logical deductive mode.[15] In fact, it is suggested that the logico-deductive approach has never really been used in the social sciences, and rather little used in the physical and natural sciences.[16]

Using single subjects, be they persons or small- or large-scale organizations, as a source of data and developing theory from these data appear to be both common and fruitful methodology in social science research. This will generally involve qualitative research or a sort of participant observation in which the theory builder acts as both reporter and elaborator.[17] This requires face-to-face interaction with the subject and a closeness with the subject characterized by social intimacy and confidentiality.[18]

A theory-in-use approach involves considerable interaction with individual subjects. For this reason single-subject research methods are relevant. However, it is very important that multiple subjects be used. A sample of a few theory holders is insufficient. It is not possible to specify a particular minimum sample size. However, since a theory-in-use approach is primarily intended as a way of *discovering* theory as opposed to *testing* theory, one rule of thumb is to stop when the ideas you obtain from new subjects begin to get redundant. Redundancy, of course, is important. It is necessary to have enough cases to know that a given idea is not unique to the circumstances of one particular subject. In general the number of cases required for discovering a theory that merits refining and testing is considerably less than that required for actual testing of a formalized theory.

## An Excursus on Mapping

The concept of mapping, introduced in the preceding section, is central to the definition of knowledge and thus central to any approach to theory building.

[15] Ian I. Mitroff and Ralph H. Kilmann, *Methodological Approaches to Social Science: Integrating Divergent Concepts and Theories* (San Francisco: Jossey-Bass, 1978).

[16] Cf. J. E. Douglas, *Understanding Everyday Life* (Chicago: Aldine, 1970); P. Feyerabend, *Against Method: Outline of an Anarchistic Theory of Knowledge* (London: Humanities Press, 1975); Charles E. Lindblom and David K. Cohen, *Usable Knowledge: Social Science and Social Problem Solving* (New Haven, CT: Yale University Press, 1979); Ian I. Mitroff, *The Subjective Side of Science* (New York: Elsevier, 1974); A. Schultz, *The Phenomenology of the Social World* (Evanston, IL: Northwestern University Press, 1967).

[17] Robert Bogdan and Steven J. Taylor, *Introduction to Qualitative Research Methods: A Phenomological Approach to the Social Sciences* (New York: Wiley, 1975).

[18] John Lofland, *Analyzing Social Settings: A Guide to Qualitative Observation and Analysis* (Belmont, CA: Wadsworth, 1971).

Consequently, a short excursus on the nature of maps is in order before we specify various steps involved in mapping theories-in-use.

Webster defines a map as a representation of an area.[19] An area can represent either geographical space or the scope of a particular concept, operation, or activity such as one's area of expertise or academic field of concentration. Maps help us find our way around various areas.[20] They do so by specifying what boundaries exist, where particular places or phenomena are located, and where these places belong. This "belongingness" derives from an overall view of an area that identifies where things *should be* in relation to one another. For example, if a map of the United States were presented to you and the city of Chicago were located in California, the immediate response would be that the map is wrong. Why? Because Chicago *should be* in Illinois, where it *really is* located. It is important to stress that this map has as its boundary the United States. If it were a world map, there could have been three or four places Chicago *could* have been, since more than one city in the world has been called Chicago.

This brings up the importance of specifying the *function* of a map. Why is the map created and how will it be used? Road maps are constructed so that a person wanting to travel from one area to another can do so in an efficient manner. The word "efficient" is used because people might still reach their destination without this particular map although not without considerable trial and error. Maps reduce trial and error because they are constructed on the basis of the past experiences of others; they summarize the experiences of others who had similar intentions (traveling on land from A to B) and have already made the trip. In this sense, the map is both socially constructed and communicated by numerous others. The social construction and communication occur as a number of people travel the same route and agree that the map is an accurate representation. This occurs because the route is of particular significance to these people; a lot of people need to travel this particular route, albeit for many different reasons. Thus, some routes are identified in greater detail than others on any particular map, reflecting both the importance of the problem and the diversity of the people involved.

Maps must be constructed so that they are easily communicated to others. The actual communication of the content of the map reflects the diversity of those using it as well as the social bond that links them. That is, the map must be of a particular form and incorporate symbols that the majority of people can understand and use. Think of the confusion that would result if all road maps were in the form of mathematical formulas or relied on celestial navigation charts! The specificity of the symbols used and their interrelationships should be compatible with the people involved and their intentions. Further, the scale on the map indicates the degree of accuracy required by those using it. Road maps

---

[19] *Webster's New Collegiate Dictionary* (Springfield, MA: Merriman, 1976), p. 701.
[20] S. Toulmin, *The Philosophy of Science* (New York: Harper Torch Books, 1966).

are constructed with fairly broad scales (1 inch = 50 miles), reflecting the fact that general orientation rather than specific direction is the main purpose of these maps. However, city maps use narrower scales since specific direction is required.

Why do maps remain useful over time? They do so because the phenomena they represent are relatively stable. If the road between Pittsburgh and Chicago changed its course every month, most maps would be useless to the majority of people. Maps could be constructed, but they would have to be changed on a regular basis. However you could study these changes and see if regularities existed and construct a new map that is seasonally adjusted. This is what celestial maps, in fact, accomplish. The planets move in a manner that precludes the construction of one map that would tell you at any particular point in time where a planet is located or where you are in a particular ocean. However, since celestial maps are constructed in a manner that concentrates on the *relationship* between planets, if one planet is located, many others can be precisely located even if their absolute position changes over time. Thus, although positions change, the relationship stays the same, as this relationship is relatively enduring over time.

This latter point must be emphasized, since mapping, as the concept is used in this book, follows the celestial rather than the road map course. It is the *dynamic* relationship between objects or ideas that we are attempting to map.

Why do maps change? The fact that maps change over time reflects both the social nature of their construction (such as the people who make them change) and the dynamic nature of the phenomena involved. People don't always follow maps—either intentionally or unintentionally. Unintentional deviation occurs because of miscommunication of the contents of maps; that is, people don't always understand the symbols involved or interpret them in the same manner as those who constructed the map. The result is what we call "getting lost." While some people see this as a great mistake and argue about how to get back on the *right* route, others explore the uncharted area. This exploration can lead to the discovery of better routes between two points or even altogether new points. This is reminiscent of the "aha" experiences of scientists who, while pursuing one goal, find something quite different.[21] Exhibit 6.1 contains a tongue-in-check illustration. The new routes or new points change the content of the map, but change it only within the original boundaries. Similar changes can occur in an intentional manner, as when the early explorers deliberately mapped out the United States or astronomers map out the universe. Again, it is important to note that these maps are constructed with certain boundaries and symbol systems in mind. Changes are seen as filling in the map rather than constructing a whole new map.

Constructing a whole new type of map, such as a topographical versus geographical map, requires changes of a more extreme nature. The old phenomenon is now "seen" and represented in a whole new way, with different

---

[21] This is also called serendipity.

## Exhibit 6.1

### On Experimental Design

I constructed four miniature houses of worship—a Mohammedan mosque, a Hindu temple, a Jewish synagogue, a Christian cathedral—and placed them in a row. I then marked 15 ants with red paint and turned them loose. They made several trips to and fro, glancing in at the places of worship, but not entering.

I then turned loose 15 more painted blue; they acted just as the red ones had done. I now gilded 15 and turned them loose. No change in the result; the 45 traveled back and forth in a hurry persistently and continuously visiting each fane, but never entering. This satisfied me that these ants were without religious prejudices—just what I wished; for under no other conditions would my next and greater experiment be valuable. I now placed a small square of white paper within the door of each fane; and upon the mosque paper I put a pinch of putty, upon the temple paper a dab of tar, upon the synagogue paper a trifle of turpentine, and upon the cathedral paper a small cube of sugar.

First I liberated the red ants. They examined and rejected the putty, the tar and the turpentine, and then took to the sugar with zeal and apparent sincere conviction. I next liberated the blue ants, and they did exactly as the red ones had done. The gilded ants followed. The preceding results were precisely repeated. This seemed to prove that ants destitute of religious prejudice will always prefer Christianity to any other creed.

However, to make sure, I removed the ants and put putty in the cathedral and sugar in the mosque. I now liberated the ants in a body, and they rushed tumultuously to the cathedral. I was very much touched and gratified, and went back in the room to write down the event; but when I came back the ants had all apostatized and had gone over to the Mohammedan communion.

I saw that I had been too hasty in my conclusions, and naturally felt rebuked and humbled. With diminished confidence I went on with the test to the finish. I placed the sugar first in one house of worship, then in another, till I had tried them all.

With this result: whatever Church I put the sugar in, that was the one the ants straightaway joined. This was true beyond a shadow of doubt, that in religious matters the ant is the opposite of man, for man cares for but one thing: to find the only true Church; whereas the ant hunts for the one with the sugar in it.

*Source.* Mark Twain, reprinted in L. L. Cummings and W. E. Scott (Eds.), *Readings in Organizational Behavior and Human Performance* (Homewood, IL: Irwin, 1969), pp. 88–89.

symbol systems and boundaries. This is akin to Kuhn's paradigm shift. From a social standpoint, great effort is expended to justify the need for the "new" map, its accuracy as well as its communication to others. Creating new types of maps is more difficult than filling in current maps, although both are necessary if phenomena are to be adequately mapped. Filling in one map many times leads us to consider a whole new map as it becomes clear that the old map doesn't cover all the points we want to reach.

Let us consider now in the context of marketing some of the issues about socially constructed maps of experienced reality which we have been illustrating primarily in terms of road maps. The reader has undoubtedly encountered several different definitions of the term "marketing." Different definitions reflect the different ways in which the phenomenon of marketing is experienced by different people. The way one person experiences or "sees" marketing is no more or less real to that person because another person experiences the phenomenon differently. The symbols used to communicate about marketing phenomena are generally agreed upon and are usually word symbols such as market segmentation, product line, day-after recall, and cents-off coupons. In fact, the subject matter indices of basic marketing textbooks are all nearly identical in their listing of key words which are symbols of the phenomena they describe. This is not to say that the structure flavor of the books' contents are identical. Each book, while using common symbolism (marketing terms), conveys the unique imprint of each author as a participant–observer.

Maps change as new points are added or new routes are added to correct existing points. Consumerism is an illustration of a relatively new point or area of study in marketing. Discussion of strategic planning is an illustration of a new (to marketing) route for achieving certain goals just as new techniques for evaluating advertising copy or the application of operations research techniques for solving certain logistical problems represent new routes which may have been intentionally or unintentionally discovered.

The shift to a broadened concept of marketing to include both profit and nonprofit agencies and a view of marketing as an exchange or transaction system involved a more extreme change in mapping. As we noted earlier, such paradigm shifts involve the expenditure of great effort from a social standpoint to justify the need for a "new" map. Debates about these "new" maps still persist many years after their initial appearance.

One important point needs to be developed further. We have talked about maps being socially construed. This implies several things. First, how one person views marketing is a function of how he or she learned about marketing initially. We are all influenced in our thinking about marketing by other people—people who taught our courses, people who wrote our reading materials, people we studied with, people who employed us, and people we worked with. What we believe about differences between product marketing and service marketing or between industrial as opposed to ultimate consumer marketing is a function of the particular socialization process we encountered (say, what our academic instructors thought, what our firm's sales training program stressed).

Second, demands for expertise are made of us by clients or customers. A salesperson is thus likely to give special prominence in his or her map to marketing as a selling phenomenon. A person responding to the needs of nonprofit agencies is likely to give greater prominence to marketing as a generic phenomenon, while a person responding to the needs of, say, the shipping industry is likely to display more of an operations research orientation to marketing. Thus, special interest groups that consume marketing expertise may influence what a given marketer sees as prominent in marketing at a given time and thus how he or she experiences marketing.

Third, there are certain systemic influences which are social in nature. People with common interests in the same phenomenon, such as marketing, form professional associations such as the American Marketing Association, Association for Consumer Research, American Association of Advertising Agencies, and so forth. These associations and other interest groups have various cultural artifacts such as magazines, journals, conferences, and research awards programs. The social or cultural artifacts, in turn, shape the further development of the field. That is to say, they influence the mapping activities of people who experience marketing. By these groups' granting or withholding of professional recognition, they encourage or discourage people in marketing with respect to particular activities. And, of course, it is the activities we engage in that set the limits of realities we experience.

What are the limitations of maps? First, the term "map" is an analogy and should be used as such. The term aids in thinking about phenomena but in no way implies that this is the *only* way to understand or experience the world. This brings up the crucial point that maps are *representations* of phenomena and are related to particular functions and groups. Thus, maps are contextual in nature. A road map is useless to an astronomer charting the universe, but useful if the astronomer wants to travel by vehicle across the country to a conference.

Second, maps are limited to certain boundaries; these boundaries, while not immutable, nonetheless define the area within which the map is most likely to be used with predictable results. Airline pilots could use road maps to fly by, but the results, particularly at major airports, would be disastrous.

Third, although maps are related to particular groups and functions, they should be constructed so that they are route-neutral.[22] A map should represent an area in such a way that it is indifferent to starting points and destinations. Users will not all be going the same way nor traveling for the same reason, so maps must accommodate diversity while still providing organization and consistency.

Fourth, the map used determines the routes taken and what is allowed to be on the map. Maps sensitize us to some routes while also systematically diverting our attention from other routes. The "fish net fallacy" makes the point clearer. Suppose an ichthyologist travels the seas using a fish net of two-inch mesh; fish that are less than two inches in length will escape him, and when he pulls up the net he will find only fish two inches or more. An observer may be tempted to generalize that all fish are two inches long or more. Until he analyzes his method of fishing, the conclusion will go unchallenged. Mapping experiences can result in similar problems. Thus your preferred method of mapping should be clearly specified and periodically reviewed to scrutinize which particular routes are being missed.

Finally, the mapping of experiences surfaces the question: Are all experiences mappable? Is there a determinancy to marketing whereby, if we search long enough and develop the right tools, we can map all dimensions of marketing

---

[22]*Ibid*.

activity? This misses the point to some degree. We are not saying the marketplace is a machine that is a well-ordered and logical chain of cause-effect relationships. Rather, mapping allows us to develop representations of marketing activity that are useful within particular contexts and with particular goals in mind. Other representations could be developed with different goals in mind. However, once the context and goal of a particular mapping have been set, then the efficacy of a mapping can be judged along certain dimensions such as reliability, validity, feasibility, and managerial implications. The map, as well as changes in it, becomes a better representation only insofar as it improves along these dimensions, which are developed and changed through social interaction and communication among the various individuals or groups who have a stake in its ultimate use. Thus, the dimensions chosen and the particular representation or map that is constructed is not determinate in any immutable lawlike way.

## Steps for Identifying Theory-in-Use

In the discussion below we shall identify several steps involved in identifying theories-in-use. We shall then illustrate these steps in greater detail. The special role of researcher creativity is treated at the end of the chapter.

Step 1. Identify appropriate theory holders. A theory holder is a person or group of people who are effective practitioners in the context of concern.

Step 2. Specify the indicators of effective practice. The indicators may be verbal statements or various behaviors. The best indicators are those which may be observed unobtrusively. While in the example at the beginning of the chapter we relied on statements made by the office equipment salesman, it would be better still to observe him in interaction with customers in a way in which our observation did not influence his behavior or thesis.

Step 3. Develop principles that describe the observed behavior or practice. This involves a statement which appears to govern what is observed.

Step 4. Identify the concepts involved in each governing principle.

Step 5. Describe the linkage(s) between concepts in each principle in propositional terms.

Step 6. Identify and describe possible linkages between concepts in separate principles.

Step 7. Know the "mapping" of the theory holder.

Step 8. Know the "mapping" of the theory builder.

Step 9. Collect several cases and develop syntheses.

Step 10. Identify ineffective practitioners and perform Steps 3 through 9.

Step 11. Identify the propositions that are common to both successful or effective practitioners and those who are ineffective.

Step 12. Determine whether the impact of the common propositions are for the unsuccessful or ineffective practitioners simply overwhelmed by the force of emulated "wrong" propositions or principles or whether other variables are operating which haven't been specified yet.


## An Illustration at the Market Level

We shall illustrate these steps using new product design as a context.

Step 1. *Identify appropriate theory holders.* In this instance we have selected a highly successful consultant in industrial design. This particular person is much sought after by major firms to assist them in the design of products ranging from wine glasses to asbestos gloves. He had training in marketing but little engineering sophistication. He does have an exceptionally well-developed ability to determine what people like. Because of this person's success in designing products with substantial market acceptance, we were particularly intrigued by the reality of product design as he experiences it. It must be recognized that many factors unrelated to him and not under his control affect the success (and lack of success) of the products he designs. Also, many of what he considers his best designs from an aesthetic standpoint are not feasible from an engineering standpoint and thus never reach a stage of being test marketed. Maybe some of these would be dismal flops as far as consumers are concerned.

Step 2. *Specify indicators of effective practice.* One indicator of effective practice is that the designer is hired repeatedly by the same firms. They must feel he does something right. Another indicator of effective practice is that he has very diverse clients with diverse problems. The designer's ability to range across a wide variety of problems suggests a set of generic skills, that is, knowledge that can be applied in different circumstances. This provides a kind of convergent validity to his knowledge. As indicated above, not all the success or lack of success experienced by the products he designs can be attributed to him. The lack of a real need for a product may cause a technically well-designed product to fail, or a poor promotional campaign may lead to the same result. Also, the presence of a very strong demand may contribute to the success of even a poorly designed product if the product offers some help to buyers and there is no better alternative. Thus to establish effective practice one must be able to attribute with reasonable accuracy some responsiblity for a product's success to the product designer. Once this is done, the researcher may then ask the theory holder—in our case a product designer—to describe what he or she knows. For example, we asked the designer to tell us what rules of thumb he would prescribe if he were a guest speaker before a group of students in an introductory course in industrial design. Several statements were given to us, a few of which (slightly paraphrased) are presented below:

Statement 1. Learn what is liked by the product's ultimate user and then design, redesign, and redesign still more until *they* tell you that you've got it (the user's likes) captured in the shape or label.

Statement 2. Learn what *you* like and make sure that it is not what your redesign efforts are trying to improve upon.

Statement 3. Learn what the buyer wants more of and less of in using a package or label.

Statement 4. Not everyone has the same aesthetic preferences; more than one design is often necessary.

These four statements are selected for discussion from among a larger array of statements given us because they relate to certain established ideas the reader will be familiar with in the marketing literature. Other statements concerned interpersonal and intraorganizational issues (how to deal with engineers, how to overcome the bad aesthetic taste of an executive's wife who insists on viewing preliminary design sketches, and so on).

Step 3. *Develop principles that describe the observed behavior or practice.* The first statement above might be cast more formally as the following marketing principle: During the concept testing and test use stages of product design, it is important to identify potential attribute gaps as perceived by buyers and redesign the product to minimize these gaps. An attribute gap is the discrepancy between a buyer's actual perception of an attribute or characteristic of a product and how that buyer would prefer to perceive that attribute. The greater the sum of all attribute gaps, the less likely the buyer is to buy the product. Gaps may exist concerning a very large number of attributes. It is necessary to determine which attributes are most salient to buyers and whether significant discrepancies or gaps exist. This may be done by initially having representative buyers react to the basic concept of the product or to a prototype of the product or to a limited trial use of the product.

Again, the industrial designer gave us only Statement 1, which suggested to us that the above principle might be operating. The discussion in the preceding statement reflects the kind of thinking that is associated with the principle and that *presumably* the designer also has in mind. This also reflects sound marketing practice as reflected by others in the product development field. Let us proceed now to the principles underlying the other statements.

The second statement was: Learn what *you* like and make sure that it is not what your redesign efforts are trying to improve upon. The basic marketing principle involved appears to be the following: During the concept testing and test use stages of product design, it is important to identify potential product designer-caused attribute gaps (which may adversely affect acceptance of the product) and redesign the product to minimize these gaps. A designer attribute gap is the discrepancy between what is a desired state of a product's feature as perceived by the designer and the actual status of that feature. For example, the designer may feel the wine goblet has too little stem (that it is too thin or too short), given the size of the bowl, when in fact the present stem is the preferred size as far as buyers are concerned or is correct given engineering or breakage considerations. The earlier designer biases or attribute gaps are identified, the earlier they may be corrected and the more effective the research and development process may be.

The third statement was: Learn what the buyer wants more of *and* less of in using a package or label. For example, what is supposed to result from the use of a new package? Less slipping of a carton from a child's hand? An easier way to read the listing of ingredients? Fewer burns when mixing chemicals? The basic principle this statement suggests is to design products that have both incremental and preventive effects. Incremental effects are produced by product attributes that increase the amount of some desired effect. More attractively designed and more comfortably worn safety equipment is more likely to be used by employees, and hence employee safety is likely to be increased. Attributes having preventive effects keep an undesired event from occurring. A milk carton for institutional use with a spigot keeps milk from spoiling as quickly as it does with an open-pour mouth container. This spoilage prevention attribute also has an incremental effect: money is saved. Similarly, the increase in employee safety resulting from more attractively designed and comfortable equipment also lessens employee absenteeism due to accidents. The designer indicated that those features which can be described to product managers as having both incremental and preventive effects (although these terms weren't actually used by the designer) were more likely to be accepted than features that had or were perceived to have only one type of effect.

The fourth statement reflects the fact that buyers are not all the same in their preferences and that different preferences may require different product design responses. This, of course, concerns market segmentation and product differentiation. More specifically, the underlying principle is: If discernibly different buyer groups exist, consideration should be given to the need for correspondingly differentiated product designs. The more important the differentiating characteristics of the buyer groups, the more important it is to take these characteristics into account in designing products. The product designer indicated that he also uses this idea in his approach to managers who make final decisions on what designs will be selected.

Step 4.    *Identify the concepts involved in each governing principle.* We shall link the execution of this with Step 5.

Step 5.    *Describe the linkage(s) between concepts in each principle.* The first principle discussed in Step 3 (see Table 6.1) involves at least three concepts or ideas: innovation testing among consumers, identification of buyer-perceived attribute gaps, and design development process effectiveness. Thus the following proposition or relationship is also implied by the principle: The greater the level of product design testing among buyers, the greater the likelihood of identifying buyer's perceptions of attribute gaps. A second proposition implicit in the same

*Table 6.1*

| Statements | Principles | Propositions |
|---|---|---|
| 1. Learn what is liked by the product's ultimate user and then design, redesign, and redesign still more until *they* tell you that you've got it (the user's likes) captured in the shape or label. | During the concept testing and test use stages of product design, it is important to identify potential attribute gaps as perceived by buyers and redesign the product to minimize these gaps. | The greater the level of product design testing among buyers, the greater the likelihood of identifying buyer's perceptions of attribute gaps. The more attribute gaps identified, the more effective the product design development process. |
| 2. Learn what *you* like and make sure that it is not what your redesign efforts are trying to improve upon. | During the concept testing and test use stages of product design, it is important to identify potential product designer-caused attribute gaps (which may adversely affect acceptance of the product) and redesign the product to minimize these gaps. | The greater the level of design testing among buyers, the greater the likelihood of identifying designer-caused attribute gaps. The earlier designer-caused attribute gaps are identified, the more effective the overall design development process. |
| 3. Learn what the buyer wants more of and less of in using a package or label. | Design products that have both incremental and preventive effects. | The greater the level of design testing among buyers, the greater the likelihood of identifying opportunities for combination effect designs. |
| 4. Not everyone has the same aesthetic preferences; more than one design is necessary. | If discernibly different buyer groups exist, consideration should be given to the need for corresponding differentiated product designs. | The more readily buyers can be segmented on the basis of different clusters of attribute gaps, the more desirable design differentiation is. The greater the level of design testing among buyers, the greater the ability to determine the desirability of design differentiation. |

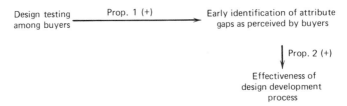

**Diagram 6.3**

principle is: The more attribute gaps identified, the more effective the product design development process. Concerning this last proposition, problems may be identified earlier in the development process through testing, thereby saving resources which might otherwise by expended on design features that would later have to be modified at greater expense. These two propositions are show in Diagram 6.3.

A basic idea or concept in the second principle is the early identification of designer attribute gaps. This involves the following propositions: The greater the level of design testing among buyers, the greater the likelihood of identifying designer-caused attribute gaps. Also, the earlier designer-caused attribute gaps are identified, the more effective the overall design development process. These two propositions (numbers 3 and 4) are shown in Diagram 6.4.

The third principle introduces the concept of having both incremental ("more of") and preventive ("less of") effects resulting from a particular design. We shall describe this as a combination effect. Thus the following proposition (number 5) is suggested: The greater the level of design testing among buyers, the greater the likelihood of identifying opportunities for combination effect designs. This is shown in Diagram 6.5.

The fourth basic principle introduces two additional ideas or concepts: the ease of segmenting buyers on the basis of attribute gaps, and the desirability of design differentiation. These concepts suggest two more propositions. One (number 6) is: The more readily buyers can be segmented on the basis of different clusters of attribute gaps, the more evident it is that design differentiation is desirable. The other proposition (number 7) is: The greater the level of design

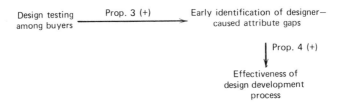

**Diagram 6.4**

**Diagram 6.5**

testing among buyers, the greater the ability to determine the desirability of design differentiation. These two propositions are presented in Diagram 6.6.

Step 6.   *Identify and describe possible linkages between concepts in separate principles.* The concepts in the various principles have been linked and described in the form of propositions. The diagrams indicate that some propositions involve a common concept and thus are linked with one another. This is evidenced more clearly by the solid lines in Diagram 6.7, which is a display of several related concepts that may explain, in part, the thinking and behavior of the industrial designer. There may be additional relationships as suggested by the dotted line. For example, the early identification of buyer-perceived attribute gaps may lead to an identification of designer-caused attribute gaps (and vice versa). Also, the more evident it is that design differentiation is desirable, the more effective the design development process will be (since differentiation can be undertaken early in the process).

Step 7.   *Know the "mapping" of the theory holder.* It is important to gain an understanding of the various psychological and sociological factors which could influence how the theory holder makes sense out of his or her experienced reality. For example, an industrial designer with a strong background in engineering but no background in marketing might display a rather different set of behaviors or give us a different set of statements than those given by the person in our example, who had an M.B.A. in marketing but no engineering experience. The person with formal engineering training would be more aware of the emphasis placed on those factors and less aware of the emphasis given to marketing factors. Thus the person would tend unwittingly to underreport the actual reliance on marketing factors just as our informant tended to say little about engineering factors until we presented Diagram 6.7 to him. When shown Diagram 6.7, he indicated that it was a reasonable expression of the four statements, but when elaborating, he proceeded to provide additional statements not given us earlier. Many of these additional statements included technical engineering issues.

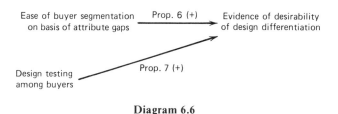

**Diagram 6.6**

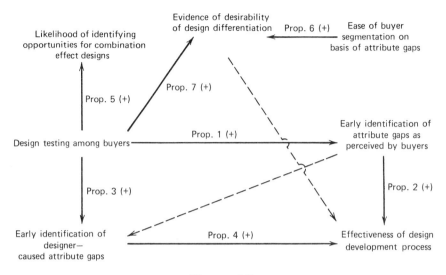

**Diagram 6.7**

*Step 8.   Know the "mapping" of the theory builder.* Theory holders may be unaware of the importance of certain factors. These factors may or may not actually be used by the theory holder, as suggested in Step 7. In our own mapping of the designer's theory, we undoubtedly "tuned in" and "tuned out" principles and concepts another listener would have filtered differently. Many of the issues discussed in Chapter 7 are appropriate considerations at this step.

*Step 9.   Collect several cases and develop syntheses.* It is, of course, desirable to collect maps of experienced reality from multiple theory holders. This increases the likelihood of identifying new concepts. Also, overlap among theory holders in the concepts they use and the way these concepts are interrelated may suggest a core theory. Also, focusing on differences among theory holders and asking why the differences may exist may suggest new ideas which explain why these differences exist. These ideas may become an important part of the theory.

*Step 10.   Identify ineffective practitioners and perform Steps 3 through 9.* Knowing what principles do not work effectively suggests propositions that are incorrect and hence are to be ruled out. It is true that successful practitioners may be a source of principles and hence propositions that do not work; however, a richer source would be ineffective practitioners. Let us consider first why it is important to identify wrong propositions. In all likelihood, effective practitioners will not be using all principles (propositions) that could be useful. In effect, their theories-in-use may not be fully complete; that is, they may not yet have identified all relevant variables. Those principles they do not use may contain relevant and appropriate propositions which, in turn, contain relevant concepts. The set of unused principles is potentially very large. We need to at least reduce the size of this set. One way of doing this is to determine which principles in the set of principles unused by effective practitioners are used by ineffective practitioners. We cannot automatically conclude that these principles and their implied propositions are wrong. However, we would want to allocate our time to discovering other principles in this set whose *a priori* likelihood of being correct is now higher.

Once we have identified an ineffective practitioner, we would perform Steps 3 through 9. Developing syntheses (Step 9) may be more difficult in that the number of wrong principles is probably greater than the number of correct principles. Thus, there may be less overlap in the principles used by ineffective practitioners. However, it is only where there is *convergent invalidity* that we would feel comfortable in rejecting particular propositions.

Step 11. *Identify the propositions that are common to effective and ineffective practitioners.* In this step, we isolate the propositions in use that are common to both effective and ineffective practitioners. It is also important to note what other unshared propositions may impact those which are shared.

Step 12. *Determine reasons why shared propositions have differential impact.* Let use assume that we have identified Proposition A as one which is practiced by several successful salespeople *and* several unsuccessful salespeople. Several possibilities exist concerning the validity of Proposition A, including the following.

1. Proposition A is actually valid but the unsuccessful salespeople are doing so many other things wrong that the beneficial consequences of using Proposition A cannot overcome the total negative effect of these wrong practices.

2. Proposition A is actually invalid but the successful salespeople are doing so many other things correctly that the negative consequences of using Proposition A cannot overcome the total positive effect of the correct practices.

3. The validity of Proposition A is mediated by other unspecified variables. This was illustrated earlier when we suggested that enacting consultant-like behaviors could lead to greater customer acceptance of advice *if* the salesperson was perceived to have the requisite experience to give sound advice. If the salesperson is not perceived to have this experience, then the more he or she tries to behave like a consultant the more suspicious or less trusting the customer will be and the less likely the professed advice is to be accepted. To explore this type of possibility, we have to hold constant the effect of other unrelated propositions which could affect the sales outcome. Basically, we ask the following question: If this were the only proposition operating, what other variable we hadn't considered before could account for its having a beneficial impact in one set of cases and a negative impact in another set of cases?

Consider an industrial design example. Assume we have explored the theories-in-use of several successful as well as unsuccessful industrial designers. Let us also make two other simplifying assumptions: (1) that most designers in both categories practice principle 4 in Table 6.1 from which we derived proposition 6 (see Diagram 6.6), and (2) that we can hold constant the effects all other variables in Diagram 6.7 and in the comparable diagram we might have developed for the unsuccessful designers. Alternately we could assume that proposition 6 is the

### Exhibit 6.2

A Primer for Yacht Salesmen: Stress Romance—But Don't Go Overboard

Norwalk, Conn. — Anyone can sell brushes door-to-door, but moving $500,000 yachts is trickier. Here are three rules of the game, gleaned from salesmen at the huge In-the-Water Boat Show here.

1.  "Don't call them boats. Call them yachts. Boats float. Yachts create."

Most people don't need a $280,000, 46-foot cabin cruiser. To sell them one, it helps to ignore depressing topics like seasickness and the cost of moorage and fuel, while emphasizing the romance of nautical life that feeds every boat lover's inner fires.

Harry Bernstein, a salesman at Schatz Bros. Marine Center in Brooklyn, is doing just that on Pier A. His male-model good looks—flashing teeth, a deep tan, blue linen blazer, and khaki slacks—blend seductively with dozens of gleaming white hulls, baking in the autumn sun. Mr. Bernstein's patter evokes the atmosphere of cocktail hour at a quiet anchorage. No storm warnings here.

2.  "Never try to close a sale. Lay back and let the customer decide what he wants to buy and how it should be equipped."

Existing boat owners, not yachting newcomers, are the best sales prospects, says Mr. Bernstein. That's because most people with boats are afflicted with the urge to buy something bigger, faster, or just more expensive.

"I'd like to get a little more boat speed," says an elderly gentleman in an ascot. "You know, so I could get out to the Grand Banks for a little fishing and get back the same night." The salesman nods sympathetically.

3.  The cut of a customer's clothes is a quick way to sort out potential big spenders from sightseers, but the rule isn't infallible.

Viking 43-foot Diesel, S187, 170.

Larry White of Rex Marine Center Inc. in South Norwalk has just salvaged a $430,000 contract on a 50-foot Hatteras luxury cruiser. The sale nearly got away. "This guy was here last year but he dressed in old work clothes and everybody ignored him."

Adds Mr. White: "Just try to remember that sometimes that dirt under their fingernails is from burying money in the back yard."

*Source.* Tom Metz, *Wall Street Journal,* October 8, 1980, p. 37.

only proposition to have any real impact on the effectiveness of the design development process.

The question we must ask is, why are some people more effective than others in the design development process when both groups can equally readily segment buyers on the basis of attribute gaps and thus determine how desirable it is to differentiate design? To answer this question, we must look for a phenomenon we have previously overlooked. This may require going back to our informants or reprocessing the information they have already given us. In either case we may obtain a new insight. For example, we might notice or be told that the availability of financial and nonfinancial resources affects the ability of designers to experiment with differentiated designs once it is evident that such differentiation is desirable. The more successful designers may have more assistants available to help develop alternative designs than do the less successful designers. Thus successful designers may tend to generate more ideas (since they can receive help in developing these ideas) and hence have a greater pool of designs to select from, a situation that in turn enhances the effectiveness of the design development process. Thus we would add a new variable to our theory: the ability to respond to evidence of the desirability of design differentiation. Under the simplifying assumptions we have made, this new variable would account for the differences in the success of the two groups of designers.

## The Reader's Turn

An article in the *Wall Street Journal* contained an offering of rules for selling yachts (Exhibit 6.2). These rules reflect the experience of apparently successful sales personnel. Read Exhibit 6.2 carefully and spend a few minutes thinking about the rules. Refer back to the steps for constructing theories-in-use. Can you develop a theory for selling yachts?

## Concluding Observations Concerning Theories-in-Use

### The Role of Researcher Creativity

The discussion thus far may suggest that the researcher has little opportunity for creative value added in developing theories-in-use. If the researcher merely provides a descriptive map of the theories held by, say, purchasing agents concerning supplier behavior, this might be correct. In this case it is the purchasing agents who are acting as the major creative agents in uncovering a theory of supplier behavior. It would be unfortunate if the researcher did not go beyond simple journalistic reporting or only assumed the role of translator. The researcher, when examining the theories-in-use of multiple purchasing agents among whom there is variation on significant dimensions, has an opportunity for discovering the importance of these dimensions and developing an explanation of how they work. Creativity is also involved in determining what dimensions are potentially important, in monitoring these dimensions, and especially in explaining how or why they are important. Since individual purchasing agents are generally not in a position to observe variations on different dimensions in the theories of other purchasing agents, they are less able to offer insights on these issues.

Additionally, the researcher who is developing a general, more formal theory on the basis of several individual theories-in-use has an opportunity to (1) discover existing relationships among concepts that were not evident to the purchasing agents, and (2) propose new relationships which could enhance purchasing agents' understanding of supplier behavior.

It was said earlier that the theory-in-use approach is just one approach and should not be used to the exclusion of others. There is opportunity to be creative in the blending of insights from different approaches. For example, there may be a real or apparent contradiction between what a theory-in-use approach suggests is important and what other approaches have suggested. Very substantial creativity may be required by the researcher to reconcile this contradiction.

**Micro-Macro Application**

The examples used in this chapter reflect rather micro-level applications of the theory-in-use approach. In all instances individuals were the unit of analysis. However, the approach is equally appropriate when focusing on other more macro units of analysis such as formal organizations or subgroups, a market segment, an industry, or other groups. In such cases the verbal statements or guidelines of individual members of these large units of analysis are important. However, nonverbal statements in the form of action assume more importance as indicators of guidelines from which propositions would be derived. This is also the case when one is mapping theories concerning social processes such as social change.

## *Summary*

This chapter has suggested that researchers and practitioners are both theory holders and theory builders. Often researchers are more concerned with formal theory, which might be expressed as a causal model consisting of concepts with explicit empirical referents connected to form testable hypotheses under carefully controlled experimental conditions. Practitioners, on the other hand, are generally more concerned with informal theory based on everyday observations (versus controlled experiments), having less than precise concepts (versus explicit empirical referents), and being related to one another intuitively (versus in rigorous testable relationships). The informal theories built and maintained by practitioners in their everyday activities represent an important source of insight for the researcher concerned with formal theory. By mapping these informal theories and applying their own creativity, researchers may gain insights into marketing phenomena which might not otherwise be obtained.

A methodology for eliciting theories-in-use by practitioners was developed. Certain problems in selecting appropriate theory holders among practitioners were mentioned, as was the unresolved issue of sample size. Although no example was presented to illustrate the point, it is important to repeat here that a theory-in-use approach is equally useful in uncovering theories held by formal organizations and other multimember units of analysis such as markets, industries, and social groups.

In many ways a theory-in-use approach is an exercise in reconstructed logic, although the reconstruction is performed by another party. It is one person's reconstruction of another person's or group's logic. This very act of reconstruction may introduce or exclude subtle yet important ideas. Thus there is a good deal of putativeness in developing theory-in-use.

# SEVEN

# HOW DO WE KNOW WE
# KNOW: REALITY TESTS

*This chapter introduces a number of tests people employ when deciding whether, or to what extent, they believe something. These tests may be used jointly. Thus it is not always easy to know in a given instance when a particular test is especially important. These so-called reality tests interact with our frames of reference, which are our general set of assumptions, decision rules, and expectations. The purpose of this chapter is to sensitize the reader to the relevance of frames of reference and reality tests. This is important partly because they pervade our thinking, especially about new ideas, and partly because generally we do not give them explicit consideration while they are in use.*

140

It's not what we don't know that gives us trouble. It's what we know that ain't so.

**Will Rogers**

Men occasionally stumble over the truth, but most of them pick themselves up and hurry on as if nothing happened.

**Winston Churchill**

Awareness is a key factor in understanding any phenomenon. The creation of knowledge is no exception to this principle. Researchers who are aware of the approaches they typically take in exploring ideas and solving problems are more likely to develop consistently better information than those who are less conscious of their approaches. This awareness includes identifying the assumptions and concepts used, determining how assumptions and concepts are combined to develop propositions and theories, and knowing what it means to say something "causes" something else.

The construction and contemplation of ideas and problems ultimately leads to an evaluation of their truth and utility. The tests used to determine truth and utility are derived from the frame of reference brought into a situation. This frame of reference can focus on formal, scientific criteria as well as more informal, experiential ones. What we present here are some simple points of view about the frames of reference and *tests* we use to determine whether an item of information or observation is true and/or useful.

## Frames of Reference

As researchers, managers, or consumers, we are constantly making observations about our environment, which are organized to form the "map" of our experiences referred to in earlier chapters. This map represents our point of view or frame of reference in approaching a particular problem, developing a theory, or collecting and interpreting observations. It reflects our perception of the world—our "reality."

This frame of reference is characterized by our standard assumptions concerning how the world works, by our preferences for particular symbol systems (mathematical, logical, and so on), by our preferences for certain analytical devices to be used in an inquiry, and by our particular role (consumer, manager, researcher) or purpose in attacking the problem in the first place. As Charlie Brown suggests in Figure 7.1, our perceptions of reality may change abruptly and dramatically with very little effort.

However, most people are not always aware of their own frame of reference nor of that used by others. The following scenario, which the reader may have encountered elsewhere, illustrates how costly this lack of awareness can be.

141

**Figure 7.1**

*Source.* Charles Schultz, Peanuts Cartoon, *The Pittsburgh Press*, August 24, 1979. Copyright © 1979 United Feature Syndicate.

The manager of a large hotel in Chicago had been receiving an ever-increasing number of complaints concerning the long waiting time for the elevators. Recent drops in occupancy rates encouraged the manager to act quickly on this problem. He consulted a local engineering company, which performed extensive cost/benefit analyses and determined that the manager had two feasible alternatives. First, an extra elevator could be added at a cost of $250,000. This would take six months. Second, the existing elevators could be fitted with high-speed motors at a cost of $350,000. This would take one month.

The manager was somewhat dissatisfied with these alternatives. He discussed the current alternatives with a friend who was a psychologist. His friend pointed out another alternative that would cost $5,000 and could be implemented within a week. He suggested that the complaints were due to people's *perception* of time. Accordingly, if this perception of the time spent waiting for elevators could be altered, there would be no need for costly structural changes in the hotel. The psychologist recommended placing large mirrors as well as a variety of displays or information counters in the lobby. These devices would distract people's attention from the slow arriving elevators. The manager implemented this alternative and noticed a significant decline in the number of complaints.

The traditional modes of thinking did not incorporate the psychological alternative in approaching this problem. Other approaches—for example, social, cultural, or ecological explanations—could also be developed to aid the decision maker. The importance of explicitly identifying the frame of reference cannot be overstated. Frames of reference serve several major functions: they provide orientation, they determine conceptualization of problems, and they determine possible solutions. Each of these functions is discussed below.

### Frames of Reference Provide Orientation

We focus on some objects but not others because of our frame of reference. In our example, the engineers focused on the elevators while the psychologist focused on people and their physical surroundings. In determining the "health" of a company, an accountant focuses on the financial statements, the economist on competition and market structure data, the marketing manager on the consumer as well as current and future product lines, the psychologist on the people running the company, and the sociologist on the structure of the organization and the interaction among its members. Each professional can be oriented toward different objects and people. More important, each can see the *same* object or person in quite a different way. Though they all may speak English, they are not sharing the same meanings.

### Frames of Reference Determine Conceptualizations of Problems

The second function of frames of reference brings up the distinction between asking what *is* a problem versus representing a situation *as* a problem. The use of the word "is" in exploring problems and theories conveys a sense of trying to find something. It is echoed by the sentiment that somewhere in a situation, if we search long enough and hard enough, we will find the right answer. However, this assumes that we know what we are looking for and that there actually exists a correct answer. Anyone familiar with political discussions, business meetings, or simple family decisions knows that substantial time may be spent just determining if something *is* a problem or not.

A *Journal of Marketing* article by Farris and Albion illustrates this point when discussing the impact of advertising on the price of consumer products.[1] Table 7.1 indicates the two schools of thought regarding this issue. Notice that they are based on two different sets of assumptions concerning how consumers behave. These assumptions have been derived from two quite different frames of reference and result in dramatically different conceptualizations of how advertising affects prices. This example illustrates how different people map the workings of the marketplace. This mapping results in unique conceptualizations, theories, and tests for these theories concerning marketing phenomena. The interesting aspect of both conceptualizations presented in Table 7.1 is that empirical support can be found to support each one.

This can occur because particular frames of reference lead to a tendency to find things as they are expected to be found. Francis Bacon noted this years ago:[2]

The human understanding, from its peculiar nature, easily supposes a greater degree of order and equality in things than it really finds. When any proposition has been laid down, the human understanding forces everything else to add fresh support and confirmation. It is the peculiar and perceptual error of the human understanding to be more moved and excited by affirmative than negative.

---

[1] P. W. Farris and M. S. Albion, "The Impact of Advertising on the Price of Consumer Products," *Journal of Marketing*, Summer 1980, pp. 17–35.
[2] Francis Bacon, 1853.

*Table 7.1*
**Two Schools of Thought on Advertising's Role in the Economy**

| Advertising = Market Power | | Advertising = Information |
|---|---|---|
| Advertising affects consumer preferences and tastes, changes product attributes, and differentiates the product from competitive offerings. | Advertising | Advertising informs consumers about product attributes and does not change the way they value those attributes. |
| Consumers become brand loyal and less price sensitive, and they perceive fewer substitutes for advertised brands. | Consumer Buying Behavior | Consumers become more price sensitive and buy best "value." Only the relationship between price and quality affects elasticity for a given product. |
| Potential entrants must overcome established brand loyalty and spend relatively more on advertising. | Barriers to Entry | Advertising makes entry possible for new brands because it can communicate product attributes to consumers. |
| Firms are insulated from market competition and potential rivals; concentration increases leaving firms with more discretionary power. | Industry Structure and Market Power | Consumers can compare competitive offerings easily and competitive rivalry is increased. Efficient firms remain, and as the inefficient leave, new entrants appear; the effect on concentration is ambiguous. |
| Firms can charge higher prices and are not likely to compete on quality or price dimensions. Innovation may be reduced. | Market Conduct | More informed consumers put pressures on firms to lower prices and improve quality. Innovation is facilitated via new entrants. |
| High prices and excessive profits accrue to advertisers and give them even more incentive to advertise their products. Output is restricted compared to conditions of perfect competition. | Market Performance | Industry prices are decreased. The effect on profits due to increased competition and increased efficiency is ambiguous. |

*Source.* P. W. Farris and M. S. Albion, "The Impact of Advertising on the Price of Consumer Products," *Journal of Marketing*, Summer 1980, p. 18. Reprinted with permission. Published by the American Marketing Association.

The intriguing aspect of Bacon's observation is that different theorists are able to see support for their theories in the same body of data. Not only are observations laden with theory, but more important, because they are socially construed, they are laden with multiple theories.[3] Frames of reference can be used very creatively to organize any particular sets of facts.

Accordingly, we must scrutinize our own preferences for particular concepts and the assumptions that we bring to a situation. Failure to recognize and surface these assumptions ultimately leads to the "convenient light syndrome," which is reflected by the following situation:

Late one evening a policeman comes upon a young man who is down on his knees feverishly searching under a light post. The policeman asks what he is looking for. He replies that he has lost his wallet. The policeman inquires where he last had it. The young man replies that he purchased some flowers from a vendor about a half a block away. "Why not look there?" the policeman responds. Questioningly, the young man looks up and states, "The light is better here."

If the nature of facts bears the imprint of the observer, why is it that we still feel comfortable when reporting facts? One answer seems to be that "observations are impregnated" with several different theories. The following quote is especially relevant as it is drawn from a discussion of the misuse of research evaluating programs of applied change. Although the programs are not explicitly marketing programs, the discussion might well have been addressing the evaluation of marketing programs.

*The epistemological problem.* The postpositivist thinking that currently predominates in the philosophy of science literature denies the existence of theory-neutral observations. It posits instead that all observations are impregnated with the theory or theories of observers. If this is so, and we believe it is, one implication is of great moment: This is that no single test of a proposition about the effects of a program will involve confronting expectations about the data with theory-neutral observations that provide unambiguous tests of the program. Instead, the effects of the program and the theories (expectations) of the observers are inevitably confounded.

To deny theory-neutral observations does not necessarily imply that scientific observations are impregnated only with the observer's theory. Stegmuller (1976) believes that observations are influenced by multiple theories and Kuhn (1975) now appears to accept this. The possibility that observations are impregnated by many theories may explain the skepticism of some practicing scientists about the denial of theory-neutral observations, for these scientists have seen some stubborn "facts" survive many theories that attempted to explain them. The theories have come and gone, but the "facts" have survived the many different paradigms buttressing the way the observations were made. The point is not that theory-free facts are possible; rather

[3]Thomas D. Cook and Donald T. Campbell, *Quasi-Experimentation: Design and Analysis Issues for Field Settings* (Chicago: Rand McNally, 1979).

it is that some observations have been repeated across observers whose operating theories were extremely diverse.[4]

### Frames of Reference Determine Possible Solutions

Closely associated with determining the concepts used in a theory, a particular frame of reference also determines the acceptable types of solutions as well as the means to generate them (that is, analytical devices used).

Considerable effort is expended in business and research trying to find the correct answer for a particular problem. The pleasure we derive from being correct can range from a good feeling that the uncertainty is over to the acclamation of respected peers or some form of monetary reward. The particular frame of reference used determines which answer or theory is judged correct, or more precisely, which answer or theory might be *more* correct than the other.

In marketing research, there are standard sets of procedures that determine the quality of a particular research study. These include various tests for validity and reliability of the research results.

Computer models have been developed in marketing to determine "optimal" solutions for various advertising decisions. One model in particular is DEMON, or Decision-Mapping Via Optimum GO-NO Networks.[5] The focus of the model is finding a profit-maximizing advertising budget for new products. The particular frame of reference used includes a mathematical program that links advertising, sales promotion, and distribution to consumer demand. For different mixes of the three marketing variables, costs are compared with the revenue generated to produce an estimate of expected profits. Note that specific assumptions must be made in this model that determine the link between advertising and demand. These assumptions ultimately determine what the "correct" solution will be. If the assumptions or the way the variables are measured change, the "correct" solution will also change.

## Reality Tests

The concern for arriving at the correct or better answer is further exhibited in particular disciplines or professions. For example, the field of mathematics has spent a great deal of time and effort developing complicated *proofs* for mathematical theorems. The field of statistics reveals methods to determine the

---

[4]Thomas D. Cook, Judith Levinson-Rose, and William E. Pollard, "The Misutilization of Evaluation Research: Some Pitfalls of Definition," *Knowledge: Creation, Diffusion, Utilization*, 1, no. 4 (June 1980), 477–499.

[5]D. B. Lerner, "Profit Maximization Through New Product Marketing Planning and Control," in Frank Bass, C. King, and E. Pessimier (Eds.), *Applications of the Sciences to Marketing Management* (New York: Wiley, 1968), pp. 151–167.

likelihood of an observation's being true or false (Type I and Type II errors). The decision sciences emphasize methods for finding the optimal solution to problems given certain objectives and constraints (linear programming). On a different level, the court system seeks to determine innocence or guilt depending on certain procedures or tests and as judged by the defendant's peers. A doctor determines whether a patient is sick or healthy, and one particular treatment is recommended rather than others. An accountant calculates specific statements and ratios to determine if a company is "sick" or "healthy." Environmentalists, sociologists, and social planners develop quality of life indicators to ascertain whether we live in a "sick" or "healthy" society. Each group has a preferred "reality" which reflects its own map of the world and how it works. These maps reflect the reality tests each use. The tests "are relatively structured occasions in which some symbolic representation claiming the status of fact is subjected to scrutiny in terms of criteria of truth. They are essentially procedures for *validating* an experience or observation . . . , and involve the testing of a cognition, a decision, or a performance based on a decision."[6] The different types of reality tests used will be discussed in the next section.

It is important to understand that reality tests derive from the particular frame of reference we bring with us to a situation. As was mentioned earlier, a frame of reference is characterized by the following:

- Standard assumptions concerning how the world works (anchor points).
- Preferences for particular symbol systems (mathematical, logical, verbal, and so on).
- Analytical devices used in an inquiry (rational and symbolic in nature).
- A specified purpose and a specified role or social context.

Reality tests are the procedures used for validating a particular experience or observation; they are tests of the adequacy of the data. They reflect the types of information that will be collected as well as the types of explanations that will be accepted in determining whether a theory or solution is true or useful. In a legal setting these are the procedures used to determine the innocence or guilt of a person. Sworn testimony is the information accepted. Jurors or the judge must use the assumptions of guilt beyond reasonable doubt, and it is better to let a guilty person go than to convict an innocent person. In medicine other procedures and tests are developed to determine the healthiness of a patient. This determination is made on the basis of the patient's own account of his or her conditions plus various biological indicators as filtered through the physician's accumulated experience, consultation with other doctors, codified knowledge in the area (textbooks, cases, and the like), and various technical instruments (such as blood pressure machines, EKG, and X-ray machines).

[6]B. Holzner and J. Marx, *Knowledge Application: The Knowledge System in Society* (Boston: Allyn & Bacon, 1979).

The key components of any reality test are as follows:

*Subjective experience.* As was stressed earlier, testing a theory or solution involves validating individual experiences. This entails comparing a particular experience with the "map" that has been developed. Does it fit on the map? If so, where, and what does this mean? For example, if you ask salespeople about "what sells a product," you may receive as many different reasons as persons you interview. Each reason reflects the person's interpretation of numerous selling experiences and what caused success or failure.

*A method of observation.* In testing the truth or utility of an observation, we must have some method for collecting the observations.

*Interpersonal confirmation.* In any area the tests that become widely accepted usually reflect the consensus of a large number of people. In reviewing the abilities of potential M.B.A. students, most schools use the GMAT as a key indicator. This high degree of acceptance is due in part to interpersonal confirmation. That is, a variety of people in a variety of situations have independently found the test results to be reasonably accurate predictors of a student's performance in the M.B.A. program. It should be noted that in the early stages (before interpersonal confirmation has had a chance to take hold) people are likely to rely on the *source* of the test. Is the developer credible, trustworthy, authoritative? These factors again can be evaluated on the basis of interpersonal confirmation, that is, whether many other people use other products or services from this source.

*Consistency.* The tests that are used to validate theories or solutions can be based on a determination of their logical or symbolic consistency. From a *logical* standpoint: are there any inconsistencies in the argument? If a person says advertising creates interest in a product, and interest leads to purchase, then the logical conclusion would be that advertising leads to purchase. This argument is made independently of whether it is empirically tested or not. For the person making the argument, it is logically true.

From a *symbolic* standpoint, do we share the same meaning for various objects, ideas, words, or people? On one level this can be represented by a commonality of language used in developing and testing theories and solutions. For example, statisticians use such terms as normal distribution, t-test, regression, and correlation. Businesspeople use terms like gross margin, market share, rate of return, and profit. Clearly, there must be a sharing of terms and what these terms mean if particular tests of theory are to be communicated effectively.

Another level of symbolic consistency revolves not around commonality in language but around how any particular concept or theory is linked back to our experiences in a consistent manner. Scientists refer to these as *operational definitions.* In more common sense terms, this refers to the types of things you have to experience to indicate that something does or does not exist. This issue is developed more fully by raising the following questions when solving a business problem or doing research. These questions are raised after a problem is given a particular definition.

1. Given your current goals and knowledge, which indicators and how many indicators of this problem or concept must you attend to before you actually count a problem or concept as being observed?

2. Is it possible that you could view some subset of the indicators/ observations in item 1 and *not* recognize the problem or concept or, more importantly, label it as another problem or concept altogether?

3. Do the indicators used allow you to recognize the problem or concept when they are hidden or masked in some way (for example, where there's smoke, there's fire)?

4. If you view these indicators as truly representing the problem or concept, how much distortion (bias, magnification, reduction) can you ascertain?

5. Are the indicators you use of a primarily similar or dissimilar nature; that is, are you digging in one hole all the time, or are you consistently exploring and digging new holes?

6. Are the indicators used likely to be understood and shared by others who are interested in solving the problem or researching the concept?

## Types of Reality Tests

The previous discussion and guidelines should help sensitize the reader to the possible dimensions of reality tests. This section will make these dimensions more explicit. Seven types of reality tests are discussed. These are shown in Table 7.2.

The key dimensions of the typology are as follows:

- In evaluating an experience or observation, are you focusing on the source (who says so?) or the consequences (what will or did happen?)?

*Table 7.2*
*Typology of Reality Tests*

|  | Source | Consequences |
|---|---|---|
| Application | Traditional<br>Authoritative | Magical<br>Consensual |
| Learning | Rational | Empirical<br>Pragmatic |

- What is your prime reason for testing a theory or carrying out a particular research study? Are you interested in learning why something occurs (to create *new* skills, knowledge, or understanding of a phenomenon or problem) or applying what is already known (application)?

It is important to make explicit which particular tests you or others are using to validate an experience or observation. As you read the explanation of each type of reality test, ask yourself the following questions.

- Who is most likely to use these tests?
- In what context or situation would they be most useful?

## Traditional Reality Tests

Traditional reality tests draw heavily on past experience and beliefs to determine the validity of a current observation or experience. These tests reflect information, beliefs, and customs that were developed and handed down from one generation to another.[7] This ensures a continuity in practices and beliefs over time where standard benchmarks are developed and maintained.

In reviewing the concepts and results of a particular marketing research study, an individual using traditional reality tests would ask the following questions.

1. Are the concepts and results consistent with a body of previous knowledge?
2. Are the results compatible with existing assumptions and institutional arrangements in the company?
3. Do the results imply a major change in philosophy, organization, or marketing programs?
4. Do the results agree with the marketing manager's particular sense of the situation?
5. Is the source of the marketing research results someone who knows and agrees with the prevailing ideas and values of the company's marketing management?

The use of traditional reality tests represents an effort to imitate what has gone before and tries not to "rock the boat." It should be stressed that this does *not* mean that new ideas are not accepted. Rather, new ideas are accepted so long as they are compatible with existing ideas and values. In fact, traditional reality tests can be applied in extremely creative ways to show that a particular observation or experience is in fact compatible with prior ideas and values. This occurs regularly in the fields of science, politics, business, and particularly religion. This creativity is represented by the following story:

---

[7]A generation can refer to any group of individuals who hold the same status over a similar but limited period of time—for example, a class of students.

A psychoanalyst has been treating a man who firmly believes he is dead. He has believed this for years and has thwarted the efforts of many people to dissuade him. However, the psychoanalyst presents the man with the following argument:

"John, do you believe that you can bleed if you are dead?"

"Certainly not," replies the man.

The psychoanalyst grabs the man's hand and cuts it lightly with a knife. Blood flows from the cut.

"Well, John, what do you say now?"

Astonished, the man replies, "Well I'll be darned, dead men *do* bleed!"

## Authoritative Reality Tests

Authoritative reality tests determine the validity of a particular experience or observation based on an evaluation of the source(s) presenting or backing it. The experience or observation is accepted as "real" only because the source is highly credible and certified as legitimate.

If the authoritative reality test setting were used in reviewing a particular research study, the validity of the results would be determined on the following grounds.

1. Who is the source (person or institution) of the results?
2. What is his or her background and reputation?
3. What degree of trust or confidence do I have in this person or institution?
4. What are the sanctions for not complying with the implications or recommendations put forth by this source?

Examples of authoritative reality tests include the following: choosing between two research companies based on their name or reputation (e.g., Nielsen, Harris, Market Facts); believing the results of a study because they have been presented and endorsed by a senior official in the company; using certain concepts and methods to study a problem because the person who most acted on the problem favors those concepts.

Authoritative reality tests take on particular importance in certain types of advertising involving testimonials by credible sources. Diamond Shamrock, for example, used midwestern farmers to promote their agricultural chemicals in the print media. Respected farmers, identified as opinion leaders within their communities, were featured in ads which contained their pictures, names, and addresses and were accompanied by a direct quote in support of the Diamond Shamrock product. This approach proved to be far superior to any other tried by the company, since it provided the degree of assurance needed in the context of a social structure that recognized the legitimacy of the successful practitioner.

## Consensual Reality Tests

Consensual reality tests rely on group opinion to determine what is true or not. They reflect tests in which what most people agree is real is taken as the final judgment.

Probably one of the most vivid and classic examples of this type of test occurred in a study conducted by Solomon Asch. Asch developed an experiment in which groups of seven students were gathered in a classroom and told they were going to take a perceptual test. The experimenter placed in front of them two white cardboards which had vertical black lines pasted on them. On one card was a single line which was used as a standard. On the other card were three lines differing greatly in length, one of them being equal in length to the *standard* line. People were individually asked to choose which of the three lines was equal in length to the standard line. Twelve different comparisons were made. After the third trial, six of the seven students (confederates of the experimenter) chose the line that was not the correct match. This pattern varied somewhat but continued through the rest of the experiment. The seventh person, the naive subject, responded after most of the other members of the group had made their choice. Although many of the naive subjects stood fast and chose the correct line, over 50 percent of them agreed with the group's choice when it was wrong (when it was picked as correct two or more times in their choice over the twelve trials). This became even more pronouned as they progressed through the twelve tests and group pressure mounted. Although the measured differences were significant, the prime reality test used by many subjects was the consensus of other members.

Although the Asch study reflects consensual validation through group pressure, there are other instances in which consensual reality tests are used: political elections (who is the "best" candidate) and beauty contests (who is the "most beautiful" woman).

Consensual reality tests are also used in advertising: "Nine out of ten doctors recommend Bayer aspirin to their patients who use aspirin." California Cellars combines authoritative with consensual reality tests in their comparative advertising campaign in which a group of recognized wine "experts" *agree* that California Cellars is superior to a well-known competitor. In a series of ads, the wine always emerges as that "chosen" over an array of similarly perceived brands.

Since consensual reality tests do not draw heavily from empirical or rational grounds, they tend to be very difficult for any *one* individual to challenge, especially if these tests have become institutionalized on a broad scale. A new majority rule or an exceptional individual performance is usually needed to change a particular type of consensual reality test.

## Magical Reality Tests

Whereas consensual reality tests focus on what people have in common, magical reality tests rely on the uncommon. They reflect situations where only a very limited number of people are able to produce a certain outcome. The manner in which this outcome is produced remains a mystery to the common person. In fact, many times this outcome is seen as the result of a power or influence that derives from a supernatural force.

However, magical reality tests rely on consensus to a degree. This reliance focuses on shared agreement that the final outcome has actually occurred. We do not understand how Houdini performed his feats, but we can experience and agree on the outcome—he escaped in good condition. Similarly, the athlete who far outclasses his field is labeled as "gifted"; or the advertising manager who is always able to come up with the right strategy is labeled a "wizard."

Magical reality tests are similar to pragmatic reality tests in that they focus on the consequences of a particular performance: they are different in that magical reality tests do not promote an understanding of *how* the outcome occurred whereas pragmatic reality tests do. If you have been in business or spent some time interpreting research results, you have probably heard the expression "I don't know why it works, I just know it works." The person using magical reality tests would attribute it to "luck" or "fate," while a person using pragmatic reality tests would attribute it to "skill" or "dexterity."

Magical reality tests are best exemplified in advertising campaigns for products such as perfume and cosmetics. Most consumers don't understand or care how perfume or cosmetics work; their main interest is in the result. Thus, we are told only that "Second Debut's" secret ingredients magically remove wrinkles and transform you from a middle-aged into a young woman. Magical reality tests are also used by many consumers in the evaluation of truly innovative products and services (such as television, photocopying machines, and microwave ovens). We do not understand how they work nor could we produce the same result, but we accept them because they allow us to do something we value but could not do before. Companies developing some products are frequently viewed with awe and develop a brand loyalty akin to that of a magician or wizard. Accordingly, their name becomes synonymous with the product—for example, Xerox in photocopying.

## Rational Reality Tests

These tests typically assess the formal structure of a theory or problem in terms of its logical consistency. This is similar to the example used earlier of advertising → interest, interest → purchase, therefore, advertising leads to purchase. The key point is that the people who use rational reality tests believe that reason and logic *alone* are sources of knowledge superior to and independent of actual empirical observations. If you were to present a marketing research report to someone who stressed rational reality tests, he or she would focus on the internal consistency of the arguments made in the reports. Do the conclusions logically follow from the initial theories and assumptions? Are the concepts included comprehensive? Are they related in a consistent manner? The actual results of the report are of lesser interest when using rational reality tests.

Rational reality tests are used in some types of personal selling techniques. The object is to present a potential buyer a very tight rational argument for buying. One of these techniques is the "balance sheet" approach. In this approach the salesperson suggests to the buyer that the only rational way to decide on a particular purchase is to develop a balance sheet with the "pros" on one side and the "cons" on the other. They then generate items under each heading. After doing this, they count up the number of "pro" reasons and then the "con" reasons. If the number of "pros" is greater than the number of "cons," then it should be "obvious" that the buyer should purchase the product. The use of this approach focuses on getting the buyer to employ a frame of reference that the salesperson can control, where irrational objections don't count because only rational ones are supposed to be used. Since the number and strength of reasons are the key determining factors, to be logically consistent the buyer must choose that course of action which has the largest number of strong reasons. The salesperson tries to control this by helping the buyer generate "pro" reasons but leaving the buyer on his own when developing "con" reasons.

## Empirical Reality Tests

Empirical reality tests rely directly on experience or observation to determine if something is true or not. Many times these tests are used without regard to identifying the particular theory, concept, or assumption that may have "caused" particular observations or experiences.

Examples of empirical reality tests are found among the standardized set of methodological procedures used by a scientific community, such as various tests of internal and external validity, procedures for random assignment, and establishing control groups. There is great concern for controlling any possible biases in the manner in which an observation is collected, analyzed, or interpreted. Debate usually centers on the correct use of a method or if in fact a particular method was the correct one to use in the first place.[8] There is also greater reliance on quantitative rather than qualitative data.

In discussions of what to include in a particular marketing research study investigating the impact of advertising on sales or evaluating an advertising allocation model (DEMON, mentioned earlier), someone would ask the following questions.

- How do we define advertising and sales?
- Can we accurately measure advertising and sales? What methods are most appropriate?
- What other factors do we have to control so that we can say, in fact, that advertising causes sales to increase? Can these factors be readily measured and controlled?
- How many observations do we need to collect and where will they come from?
- How many times do we have to collect observations? That is, how many

---

[8]Cook and Campbell, *op. cit.*

different times do we have to observe that advertising results in sales before we believe it?

- How generalizable will the results be? Can we use these same results in situations slightly different than the one for which we orginally tested (if advertising → sales for facial soap, will that also be true for laundry detergents)?

Criticisms of the results of a study are likely to focus on deficiencies in method rather than on deficiencies in logic.

## Pragmatic Reality Tests

Pragmatic reality tests have as their foundation the belief that the meaning of concepts is to be sought in their bearings on actual practice. Their chief function is to guide action. Their validity is tested by their practical consequences or implications.

Internal logic and the application of the scientific method stand secondary in importance to the action implications of using a particular concept or solution in everyday practice. For example, if the results of a research study were presented to someone employing pragmatic reality tests, the following questions would serve as the key criteria in assessing their truth and usefulness.[9]

1. Does the study analyze the effects of factors that decision makers can do something about?
2. Is the study targeted; that is, does it focus on a narrow set of factors?
3. Does the study contain explicit recommendations?
4. Do these recommendations have direct implications for a course of action?
5. Do the results add to practical knowledge of the operation of current or future policies and programs?

These questions are representative of what many would call the prevailing philosophy of businesspeople. This philosophy is commonly used to discredit much academic research as being too "ivory towerish." "You don't know what's going on out there—that won't work in the *real* world." "Real" to the user of pragmatic reality tests focuses on the feasibility of implementing results or recommendations in day-to-day affairs—predominantly in the short run. These daily realities can be represented by the economic, legal, political, or social constraints that might restrict the believability or usefulness of the results. There is thus sometimes a poor fit between how map makers and map users evaluate information. For example, assume you are located in a large jungle and face the task of finding your way out. Apart from an assurance that you won't come to physical harm, you would probably want some navigation aid such as a map of

[9]Carol H. Weiss and Michael J. Bucuvalas, "Truth Tests and Utility Tests: Decision-Makers' Frames of Reference for Social Science Research," *American Sociological Review*, 45 (April 1980), 302–313.

the jungle. As luck would have it, you stumble upon a document labeled "Map of the Jungle." How would you feel upon the initial discovery of this document? How would you feel afterwards when, upon opening the map, you discover that it displays only features of the jungle that are rather unimportant for finding your way out? The situation is not unlike many areas of research in marketing. Often it is only rather inconsequential matters which get mapped. The mapping of inconsequential matters may be done so well in terms of other reality tests (citation of other research, justification of methodology) that the results appear more consequential than they are. Exhibit 7.1, "Do Chickens Have Lips?" is a tongue-in-cheek illustration of this point.

A theory or piece of research that is "interesting," as discussed in Chapter 2, is likely to be consequential. This is especially so if the ideas (theory, research findings) might result in many people altering much of their thinking. One way of deciding what important features of a problem or issue area should be investigated, that is, what the salient features of the jungle are which should go into the map, is by making observations in a natural setting. Robert B. Cialdini uses the metaphors of trapping and scouting to illustrate this point.[10] The construction of a trap (for example, an appropriate field or laboratory experiment) to ensnare the effect of a promotional theme or a product attribute or a sales training program is extremely important. It also requires substantial skill. But how does one know that what has been trapped is worth going trapping for? Advance scouting will help identify the big game. The scouting should not be done in the trap but rather in the natural environment where the game live. Cialdini provides a number of examples of important social psychological principles which were first observed in their natural settings. This is the start of "full-cycle" social psychology.

Wherein initial natural observation gives direction to subsequent controlled experimentation, the outcomes of which can then be given external validation through further natural observation that may stimulate still further experimentation. Systematic recourse to the evidence of the real world both before and after performance of the experimental work may thereby reduce the extent to which current social psychological research can be criticized as artificial and epiphenomenal.[11]

This approach, if pursued more rigorously in marketing, would probably yield more academic research which could pass the pragmatic validity tests for practitioners.

The reality tests discussed above are far from exhaustive and are not mutually exclusive. They may be used in various combinations, and the same individual may employ different ones in a situation to draw out preferred modes of

---

[10]Robert B. Cialdini, "Full Cycle Social Psychology," in L. Bickman (Ed.), *Applied Social Psychology Annual*, Vol. 1 (Beverly Hills, CA: Sage, 1980), pp. 21–47.
[11]*Ibid.*, p. 44.

### Exhibit 7.1
On Fowl Oral Apertures: Do Chickens Have Lips?

*Lawrence H. Frank*
3222 Cottonwood Avenue
Bellingham, Wash. 98225

*James C. Gange and Robert K. Klepac*
Department of Psychology
Fargo, North Dakota 58102


Chicken Little
Department of Farmology
North Dakota State University
Fargo, North Dakota 58102


Although the piercing question has plagued serious thinkers since the time of Aristotle, Bloodlip (1923) was the first to apply the methods of science to the question: do chickens have lips? Bloodlip kissed 38 chickens, recording his impressions carefully after each kiss, and concluded that chickens have sharply pointed beaks, but not lips. Bloodlip's procedures, however, call this conclusion to question: in addition to his small $N$ and the lack of adequate controls, Bloodlip by his own report did not know the chickens very well (1923, p. 42) and may have been perceived as a masher, therefore inhibiting the animals' lip-pucker response. This suspicion is supported by Bloodlip's discussion, in which he notes that the experimenter required 33 stitches in and around his lips during data collection (p. 246).

Other studies present indirect evidence for the existence of lips in chickens. Henlover and Strange (1969), for example, offered chickens a choice between identical gold-colored tubes, one of which was filled with Mealworms[1] the other with lipstick (Avon, Passion Apple Red). All subjects showed a marked preference for the lipstick. Similar results were obtained in replications using Come-To-Me Pink and Tempting Tangerine (Henlover and Strange, 1969, p. 4). The hypothesis that these results may be a simple result of the lipstick's greater nutritional value may be ruled out by the authors' incidental observation that the chicks did not engage in consummatory behavior, but rather smeared the substance around their oral orifices by rotating their heads in a manner reminiscent of the oscillating behavior so long noted among graylag geese.

These findings were extended by Feather and Comb (1971), who found an interaction between chicken strain and lipstick preference. When offered a choice, White Leghorn hens preferred Primrose Pink to Candy-Apple Red, while Rhode Island Reds preferred the darker shade. The authors' prediction that, like females of other species in whom the presence of lips has long been demonstrated, chicks would select colors more flattering to their complexions, and avoid choosing a shade which might render lips conspicuous.

While the studies of Henlover and Strange (1969) are compelling, they suffer from two weaknesses. Their heavy reliance upon lipstick preference as the sole dependent variable requires a greater degree of inference than Bloodlip's more direct approach. Secondly, the studies used subjects who were housed in barnyard chicken coops, leaving open the possibility that lipstick application is the result of drab sociocultural backgrounds rather than a natural consequence of one's having lips. The present study represents an attempt to rule out these factors in a further exploration of the lip-beak controversy.

## Method

*Subjects: Source and Maintenance.* Subjects were 60½ adult Female Bantam roosters obtained from Honest Harry's Restaurant and Experimental Station, Fargo, North Dakota. Prior to data collection, subjects were housed for three months in individual parlors, equipped with mirrors, showers, and self-grooming aids. *S*s were maintained on a 10-hr. photo-period, which began each day at 5 A.M. when *S*s were awakened by an alarm clock (Baby Ben #4348).

*Experimental Design and Procedure.* Two tests of lip-presence were employed. In the first, chickens were grasped by the neck and pressure was increased until visual apparati protruded at least .4 millimeters from their sockets. (It had been found in pilot studies that at this point, all chickens open their mouths in protest.) A smooth square of malleable material (Play-Doh Corp. #14586—green) was inserted into the mouth, and neck pressure immediately released. Pressure was then reapplied, and the material removed. Imprints of each subjects oral aperture were thus obtained.

The second test was a variation of Bloodlip's (1923) earlier technique. Sixty male college sophomores served as chicken-kissers,[2] and each was randomly paired with a chicken.[3] Pairs were given an opportunity to get to know each other, during which time the chicken kissers spoke pleasantly to the hens, occasionally offering a bit of grain, and engaging in any additional pleasantries which they saw fit. When the chicken kisser felt that adequate rapport had been established (in no case less than two hours nor greater than three hours), each male placed his right hand behind the hen's comb, looked wooingly into her eyes, and gave her a 7-sec peck upon the oral aperture. Kissers then rated their impressions of the experience on a seven-point bipolar scale, bracketed by the words "lips" (1) and "beak" (7).

## Results and Discussion

Microscopic examinations of the mouth imprints by 14 lip experts (all professional politicians) showed conclusive agreement that chickens do have lips. A typical fly-by-night analysis of variance (Frank, 1973) was run on the chicken-kissing data. The analysis yielded a significant difference between the number of students reporting that chickens do have lips and those reporting that the opposite was true. Subsequent analysis revealed results which were contrary to the experimenter's hypothesis, hence the data were unfortunately lost in a fire and cannot be reported here.

The present findings are in direct contradiction to those reported by Bloodlip's (1923), suggesting that his study was grossly affected by experimenter bias. Rather, the findings presented here support the contents of Feather and Comb (1971) and Henlover and Strange (1969), that chickens do in fact have lips. In post-experiment interviews, however, all participants claimed extensive knowledge about lips, and claimed to be experienced in kissing.

In a subsequent study, college students were blindfolded and presented either with a chicken or a volunteer housewife, which they kissed. In every case (n = 243) students reported having kissed lips, regardless of the species with which they had been presented. In addition to removing any doubt about the existence of chicken lips, these data have interesting implications for the study of henpecking in marital constellations.

It having been demonstrated conclusively that chickens have lips, further research is needed to determine the biological significance of the beaktype like appearance of those lips. Informal observation by the present authors suggest that hens find human kisses noxious, suggesting that evolutionary pressure might account for the phenomenon. This notion requires validation but is consistent with Bloodlip's (1923) observations, and with the widely accepted fact that humans seldom kiss chickens except for the sake of science.

## Footnotes

[1] Frieda Falic (1953) demonstrated that chickens prefer mealworms to snakes ($p$. 0001).
[2] The other ½ subject was dropped from the study because the $E$s were unable to locate ½ of a male college sophomore.
[3] Ethical considerations dictated against allowing $S$s and kissers free choice of partners, since undue extra-experimental involvement might then ensue.

## References

Bloodlip, R. H. Behaviors of the Drunk: The Chicken Kissing Syndrome. *Journal of Special Relations*, 1923, 21–24F.
Feather, F. F., and Comb, C. F., Lipstick Preference in Two Strains of Chickens. Reported at a meeting of the Uptown P.T.A., 1971, 1–10.
Frank, L. H., Figures Don't Lie, But Liars Do Figure. Analyses useful with questional data. *The Weekly Wheatgrower*, 1973, 45, 14–14.5.
Henlover, H. H., and Strange, V. V., The Avon Lady and the Chicken. *Journal of Believe It or Not*, 1969, 1–4.

---

ascertaining truth or utility. It is particularly important, however, to determine how these reality tests are distributed among various participants with regard to a particular marketing problem.

It should also be kept in mind that reality tests can be described in different ways. For example, William Dunn offers an interesting perspective.[12] He suggests that three standards are used to assess the usefulness of knowledge. One standard relates to *relevancy*: Is the information appropriate to a given problem? Was it on time? A second standard concerns *adequacy*: Does it satisfy a manager's criteria for truth? Were appropriate statistical tests used or research designs employed? A third standard concerns *cogency*: How persuasive is the finding? What are the statistical confidence limits used?

Elsewhere Dunn has suggested alternative models which may account for the use and nonuse of knowledge by public policy makers:[13]

1. *Product-contingent model*. The characteristics of products of social science research (form, content, language, length, reliability, validity, timeliness) determine the scope of knowledge use by policy makers.

[12] William N. Dunn, "Reforms as Arguments," in Burkhart Holzner, *et al.* (Eds.), *The Political Realization of Knowledge: Toward New Scenarios* (West Germany: Physica-Verlag, 1982).
[13] William N. Dunn, "The Two-Communities Metaphor and Models of Knowledge Use," *Knowledge: Creation, Diffusion, Utilization*, vol. 1, no. 4, June 1980.

2. *Inquiry-contingent model*. Differences in modes of inquiry used to acquire, process, and interpret information (research design, analytic techniques, observational methods, sampling) determine the scope of knowledge use by policy makers.

3. *Problem-contingent model*. The characteristics of policy problems (levels of conflict, uncertainty, and risk associated with attempts to satisfy needs or realize opportunities) determine the scope of knowledge use by policy makers.

4. *Structure-contingent model*. Variations in the structure of organizations (authority responsibility, power, and incentive systems) determine the scope of knowledge use by policy makers.

5. *Process-contingent model*. The nature of interaction (authoritarian, delegative, collaborative) among producers and potential users and beneficiaries of knowledge determines the scope of knowledge use by policy makers.

Another study strongly suggests that these models are highly appropriate (although differentially so) to marketing managers.[14]

## *Summary*

Reality tests have the following functions.

1. *Reality tests determine acceptable solutions to a problem*. Becoming aware of the different reality tests increases our chances of "seeing" different solutions to a problem and decreases our chances of solving the "wrong" problem (that is, developing solutions that don't change the things we want or developing solutions that are *worse* than the original problem).

2. *Reality tests determine resistance to new ideas*. Habit is a strong motivator for all individuals—most people will do as they have done before rather than try something new. To understand people's resistance to new ideas or their rejection of the results of a particular research study, you must tap into the particular reality tests they are using. As was pointed out earlier, people can be very creative in retaining a particular mode of thinking even when faced with what others consider the "empirical facts."

3. *Sensitivity to different reality tests reduces translation problems*. Frequently we reject an idea or observation because we don't understand the jargon used to present it. More seriously, we may reject it because we don't understand or agree with the underlying assumptions or analytical

---

[14] Gerald Zaltman and Rohit Deshpande, "The Use of Market Research: An Exploratory Study of Manager and Researcher Perspectives," A Report to the Marketing Science Institute, 1981.

devices used to generate the idea or observation. Identifying reality tests explicitly aids in the translation process that is needed if people are to communicate effectively. This becomes all the more important given that a substantial number of business and academic research projects are group projects.

Two other observations will conclude this discussion of reality tests.
First, *reality tests are interdependent not independent*. The presentation of reality tests in this chapter may give the impression that they can be applied *independently*. In some situations this may be the case, however, most problems or concepts we deal with are sufficiently complex that *multiple* reality tests are used to determine their validity. Earlier the case of GMAT's was presented. However, when the eligibility of a student is being determined, other reality tests will play a role (examples: are the parents alumni (traditional); have we admitted enough minority students to meet current government policies (authoritative); will the student do well in the business world (pragmatic). A researcher uses *both* rational and empirical tests to evaluate a theory. Consensual plus pragmatic tests make up what we call "common sense." It is the *interdependence* of reality tests that must be understood if modern-day problems and concepts are to be solved and tested in an interesting and creative manner.

Second, *reality tests are contextual in nature*. The interdependencies of reality tests are reflected in the wide variety of roles that *we* play (consumer, manager, researcher, or whatever) or that are played *by others* in a particular situation. One of the goals of this chapter has been to sensitive the reader to the situations in which different types of reality tests might be used. Determination of the contexts in which particular reality tests might be used and are most useful remains an important yet unresolved issue. However, the degree of resolution will increase as awareness of the different types of reality tests used and their role in determining your particular "map of the world" is explored through everyday experience.

# EIGHT

## EVALUATING THEORY

*Chapter 7 was concerned with the question, "How do we know?" Different* summary *tests used to answer this question were discussed. In this chapter we review a number of* specific *characteristics of a theory that are assessed when we judge its quality, worth, and significance and the need to alter it. The relative strength of these characteristics is the criterion for evaluating the theory. These specific criteria are used in the summary reality tests discussed in the last chapter. The criteria in this chapter should be used as design guidelines in developing or forming a theory. If they are attended to in the development of a theory, the chances of having an interesting theory that meets most reality tests are fairly high.*

Since all models are wrong the scientist must be alert to what is importantly wrong. It is inappropriate to be concerned about mice when there are tigers abroad.

George E. P. Box[1]

Theories are evaluated in order to determine their potential contribution to marketing. The theory builder has several opportunities to receive feedback during all phases of theory construction. Interactions with colleagues, customers or clients, and students are important in the initial stage. Seminars, response to working papers, and professional conferences are other means of receiving evaluations. Research submitted for publication is subjected to the evaluation of reviewers who are respected experts in the field.

A theory may go through numerous revisions before publication. Subsequently, the scientific community, both academicians and practitioners, may challenge parts of the framework and extend the work by examining specific parts of the model. Thus, an exchange of ideas takes place within the marketing community.

A variety of evaluative criteria have evolved from the philosophy of science and other areas which are useful in evaluating theories in marketing. The choice of a particular set of criteria, however, is somewhat idiosyncratic to the person doing the evaluation. It may also depend upon the nature and purpose of the theory itself. In this chapter we will present two sets of criteria that can be used to evaluate marketing theory *especially* in the formative or developmental stages. We will begin with some well-established general criteria adapted from the philosophy of science literature, and continue with nontraditional criteria for theory evaluation.[2]

# Philosophy of Science Criteria

What are the properties of a good theory? Table 8.1 lists some important properties. Note the similarity of some of these to the reality tests discussed in the previous chapter.

A theory is *internally consistent* if it follows the basic rules of logic; thus $A > B, B > C, C > A$, would fail the test imposed by this criterion. If a theory of consumer complaint behavior draws upon other bodies of knowledge, such as social learning theory, role theory, and attribution theory, it displays a high degree of *strength*. If the mechanisms involved in the theory are basic ones, it is

---

[1] George E. P. Box, "Science and Statistics," *Journal of American Statistical Association*, vol. 71, no. 356, December 1976.

[2] For an excellent treatment of cognitive aesthetics as nontraditional criteria, the reader is urged to consult Richard H. Brown, *A Poetic for Sociology* (New York: Cambridge University Press), 1977.

*Table 8.1*
*Properties of a Good Theory*

| *Property* | *Meaning* |
| --- | --- |
| Internal consistency | Has no logical contradictions |
| Strength | Entails other theories |
| Representativeness | Deals with deep mechanisms |
| Empirical interpretability | Is operationalizable |
| Falsifiability | Falsifiable when confronted with reality |
| Confirmation | Coheres with facts |
| Originality | Increases knowledge by deriving new propositions |
| Unifying power | Connects previously unconnected items |
| Heuristic power | Suggests new directions for research |

*Source.* G. Zaltman, C. Pinson, and R. Angelmar, *Metatheory in Consumer Research* (New York: Holt, Rinehart & Winston, 1973), p. 44.

considered to have *representativeness*. Theory should be capable of being tested empirically; out of social learning theory came the concept of interpersonal trust and a scale developed by Rotter[3] to measure it. Such a theory therefore has a high degree of *empirical interpretability*, at least in this instance. When possible hypotheses should be stated in a way that they can be proven wrong, meaning that the theory is *falsifiable*. A theory should cohere with facts (*confirmation*). The interesting theorist will pay particular attention to the criterion of *original-ity*, expanding the boundaries of knowledge beyond the taken-for-granted world. Thus a theory might be evaluated in terms of how interesting it is (see Chapter 2). *Unifying power* also carries a high interest quotient, with the creative process being invoked in seeing relationships where others have seen only separateness. Finally, a theory high in *heuristic power* raises interesting questions that stimulate further inquiry. As in the famous story of the Lady and the Tiger, a good theorist raises more questions than can be answered immediately and leaves the reader to his or her own devices in finding the answers—in extending the chain of inquiry.

## Applying the Criteria: An Example

Several of the better known theories of consumer behavior, including ones by Howard-Sheth; by Engel, Kollat, and Blackwell; and by Kerby, have been evaluated elsewhere.[4] We will apply these criteria to a basic theory of buyer

[3]Julian B. Rotter, "Generalized Expectancies for Interpersonal Trust," *American Psychologist*, 26 (1971), 443–452.

[4]Gerald Zaltman and Melanie Wallendorf, *Consumer Behavior: Basic Findings and Management Implications* (New York: Wiley, 1979); and G. Zaltman, C. Pinson, and R. Angelmar, *Metatheory in Consumer Research* (New York: Holt, Rinehart & Winston, 1973).

behavior in housing markets, developed by Hempel and Ayal.[5] This particular theory (or theoretical attempt) is chosen somewhat arbitrarily, not because it necessarily represents either a "good" or "bad" example. Most theories score high on some criteria and low on others, and this one does so as well. Figure 8.1 shows the basic processes involved in the theory.

Briefly, the theory can be illustrated using a graduate business student who has accepted his or her first position with a marketing research firm in another city. An abrupt shift occurs in the life space, from dynamic equilibrium, in which

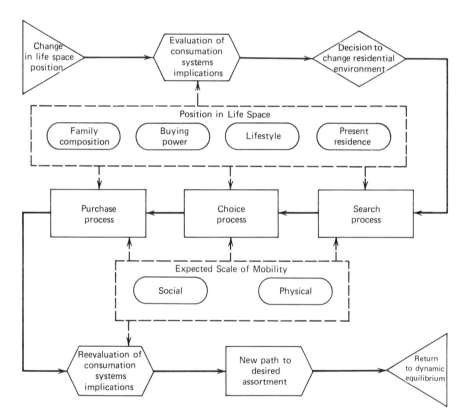

**Figure 8.1.** A simple model of transition period influences on the home-buying process and related consumption systems.

*Source.* Donald J. Hempel and Iqal Ayal, "Transition Rates and Consumption Systems: A Conceptual Framework for Analyzing Buyer Behavior in Housing Markets," in A. G. Woodside, J. N. Sheth, and P. D. Bennett (Eds.), *Consumer and Industrial Buying Behavior* (New York: Elsevier North-Holland, 1977, p. 207).

[5]Donald J. Hempel and Iqal Ayal, "Transition Rates and Consumption Systems: A Conceptual Framework for Analyzing Buyer Behavior in Housing Markets," in A. G. Woodside, J. N. Sheth, and P. D. Bennett (Eds.), *Consumer and Industrial Buying Behavior* (New York: Elsevier North-Holland, 1977), pp. 201–218.

gradual acquisitions were made (cross-country skis, stereo system speakers, bookcases), to a state in which the rate of change accelerates. This transition period involves changes in cognitive processes, intense deliberation over purchase decisions, and the emergence of new criteria for decision making. The home ownership versus rental decision, for example, may emerge for the first time. The household is the unit of analysis in the model; for the married student, joint decision making would be expected in the two consumption systems: (1) the primary system consisting of housing and related services, such as realtors, and (2) the secondary system, including durables to equip and operate the home.

The change in life space position will probably involve changes in one or more of the following variables: family composition; buying power (increase); lifestyle (activity patterns); and attitudes toward the current residence.

The couple may spend a long weekend in the new city, searching for a suitable home. Of the several possible residences shown them by the realtor, they decide upon a two-bedroom condominium since it satisfies their most salient criteria of privacy, proximity to work, recreational facilities, and acceptable price range. The student may expect to be transferred in a couple of years, so resale value is important, and the adjoining condos are occupied by other young professional couples (expected state of mobility). They sign the purchase agreement and arrange the bank loan (on the basis of the increased buying power). A reevaluation of their current consumption system then takes place, as they consider their preferences for furniture and appliances, set priorities, and design a sequence of planned purchases of these items. The move is completed and the household returns to dynamic equilibrium.

Hempel and Ayal derive the following six propositions from the theory:[6]

1. Where major durables are concerned, the purchasing behavior of households during periods of dynamic equilibrium will represent a gradual adjustment of existing stocks to a desired assortment. The process of gradual adjustment will be reflected by purchases of durables item by item, at relatively long time intervals.

2. The period immediately preceding and following an abrupt shift in the household's position in life space will be marked by a distinct disruption in the regular purchase behavior of the household. This disruption will appear as a "compression" effect in the household's pattern of major durables purchased. In effect, the transition period precipitates a concentrated planning process for durable goods acquisitions. For these plans to materialize, however, enabling conditions must permit purchase.

3. Purchases of durable goods during transition periods will reflect a household's reevaluation of the total existing and desired stock. Compared to stable time periods of equal length, these purchases will be more interrelated into a recognizable pattern, reflecting a reorganization of the total consumption system.

4. Buyer behavior for durable goods, and particularly buyer behavior and post-purchase satisfaction in housing, can be explained and predicted on the basis of position in the life space (and changes in it), search behavior, and availability of alternatives. These elements can serve as useful bases for market segmentation.

[6]*Ibid.*

5. A "consumption system" entrepreneurial approach to marketing and financing housing the major durables can benefit both the suppliers and the consumers.

6. The house buyer's immediate satisfaction with his new home and with the commercial organization involved in its sale (e.g., brokers and builders) will be lower for households in transition periods than for those in dynamic equilibrium.

How does the Hempel and Ayal theory hold up under the criteria listed in Table 8.1? Keeping in mind that these criteria are only a subset of the range available to the evaluator, we can illustrate how each applies to the theory.

A weakness of the theory is the imprecision in the stating of propositions, a problem of internal consistency. For example, Proposition 5 states that the consumption system approach *can* benefit both the buyer and seller, a statement that cannot be readily contradicted. In the interest of improving explanation, the Lewinian concept of balance[7] (whether the situation is perceived positively or negatively by the household) could be added to Proposition 6. Some households may adjust to rates of change in a positive way, partially because of their experience. If balance is not added, empirical findings that some households were more satisfied when in transition would appear contradictory.

The Hempel-Ayal theory is high in strength. Some aspects of the theory are general—that is, collective, household decision making—rather than individual— the accommodation of several transitions precipitating the move, and the inclusion of both social and geographical dimensions of mobility.

Underlying the Hempel-Ayal theory is the process of social change, which Rogers and Shoemaker[8] define as an alteration of the social structure (status) and the functioning elements (roles). Role is a deep (basic) mechanism, and role transitions are an important element in the movement from one steady state to another. The impact of role transitions upon the consuming household—the individual and his or her role partner—varies according to many criteria, including whether they are anticipated or unanticipated, and whether they are structurally incremental (a gain in status when the graduate student moves into a managerial or researcher role) or decremental. If we regard consumption as a role-prescribed behavior,[9] then it is useful to study role transitions and the behavioral traces apparent in markets such as housing. Persons moving from one steady state to another provide an excellent sample for a natural experiment in which several interesting propositions could be tested. For example, the stages of socialization that the person goes through in acquiring a new role set could be examined. In the initial stage of socialization, the consumer would be expected to conform to the formal aspects or stereotypes of the role. Later, after having acquired some experience with the role, the individual (household) would be

---

[7] Kurt Lewin, *Field Theory in Social Science: Selected Theoretical Papers* (New York: Harper, 1951).
[8] Everett M. Rogers and F. Floyd Shoemaker, *Communication of Innovations: A Cross-Cultural Approach* (New York: The Free Press, 1971).
[9] Melanie Wallendorf, "Social Roles in Marketing Contexts," Working paper No. 258, Graduate School of Business, University of Pittsburgh, 1978.

expected to shape the role according to his or her identity. In this way, improvements to the theory can be made—explanatory power is enhanced.

Some parts of the theory lend themselves more readily to empirical interpretability than do others. Buying power, for example, is operationalized through twenty separate measures, including total amount and source of income and duration of employment. More problematic is the measurement of concepts lacking in linguistic exactness, such as "compression effect" in Proposition 2 and "recognizable pattern" in Proposition 3.

Regarding falsifiability, Propositions 1 and 2 could be tested together. Proposition 3 would be difficult to falsify based upon the previous objection to the lack of clarity in the use of the term "recognizable pattern." Proposition 5 is a managerial statement, not a proposition.

In terms of confirmation, Propositions 2, 4, and 6 were subjected to empirical test in three housing markets. Life space measures were highly consistent across markets. Those households in transition engaged in less search behavior and expressed lower satisfaction than households in dynamic equilibrium, and they had higher expenditures. However, cases with low rates of change were not included in the analysis.

The theory is original in relating transitions to consumption behavior, and this is a strong point. Hempel and Ayal consider the disposition process as well in their discussion of the implications of the theory: "Consumer satisfaction and the quality of life can be improved by marketing systems that recognize significant states of change. These systems should be capable of suggesting and providing appropriate revisions in the total assortment as well as easing the transition by providing effective disposal for replaced assortment items."[10] Jacoby et al. have noted that virtually no theory development or empirically oriented research has addressed the issue of disposition by consumers.[11] The Hempel-Ayal theory lacks originality, however, in some of its concepts. The family life cycle, for example, needs to be updated, given changes in social trends. Some attempts have been made in this direction: Jain proposes three life cycles (divorced/widowed, single, married), while Wortzel recommends attention to trends such as cohabitation.[12,13]

The theory has a high degree of unifying power, relating transition periods to at least two consumption situations. Clear specification of potential connections, such as social mobility and lifestyle, would add to this unification.

---

[10] Hempel and Ayal, op cit., p. 218.

[11] Jacob Jacoby, Carol K. Berning, and Thomas F. Dietvorst, "What About Disposition?" Journal of Marketing, 41, no. 2 (April 1977), 22–28.

[12] Subhash C. Jain, "Life Cycle Revisited: Applications in Consumer Research," in Mary Jane Schlinger (Ed.) Advances in Consumer Research, Vol. 2 (Chicago: Association for Consumer Research, 1975), pp. 39–49.

[13] Lawrence H. Wortzel, "Young Adults: Single People and Single Person Households," in William D. Perrault, Jr. (Ed.), Advances in Consumer Research, Vol. 4 (Atlanta: Association for Consumer Research, 1977), pp. 324–329.

By far the strongest point to be made in favor of the theory is that it is high in heuristic power. As mentioned above, the disposition process can be investigated by examining, for example, the relationship between social mobility and the decision to replace versus to retain possessions upon changing residences. A theory that raises interesting research questions contributes to science. Through the continual process of evaluation, constructive criticism, implementation of suggested improvements, and empirical testing is gradually woven the fabric of a mature discipline.

## Nontraditional Criteria

### Di-Stance

The reader may recall, perhaps all to easily, having had the following kind of experience. You have entered a lecture hall, assumed a customary seat, opened a notebook, and begun attending to the speaker's introductory comments. Perhaps a few notes are made as you attempt to reproduce what the speaker is putting on the blackboard. Twenty minutes pass on the clock and you are rather involved in the content of the lecture. Another twenty minutes pass and you are reminded by a numbness in a certain area that seats in the hall are wooden and uncushioned. Fifteen minutes later (by the clock) you inhale deeply, attempt an unobtrusive stretch of your upper and lower torso, glance up at the clock, and groan inwardly, almost unconsciously, noting that another thirty-five minutes remain of the lecture. You begin to look around the hall: (a) spotting a previously unnoticed ventilation shaft with colored yarns hanging limply from it, (b) noticing a section of overhead lights which do not work and which cause you to wonder whether it has been like that since the course began five weeks ago, (c) realizing that the same students are always in the front and then realizing further that nearly everyone in the room including yourself is in the same seat that he or she always assumes for this class, although that is hardly mandatory. You become more conscious of the physical movement of the instructor while trying a bit harder to identify the geographical origin of his or her accent. While these musings are going on you have not totally disengaged from the content of the lecture and something said brings you back, perhaps briefly, to the instructor and you make a few more written notes.

The experience described above reflects a special kind of distance, a psychological *di-stance*, a divisional posture in which one is able both to be *a* part of the phenomenon (here, a class lecture) and yet to be apart from the phenomenon much like a fly on the wall. If we are to explain fully a particular marketing phenomenon such as conflict between different participants in a distribution channel, the insights should reflect both the "detached" and "attached," or "objective" and "subjective," points of view. For example, an explanation of classroom activity should reflect the insights of the student in the example above who would be able to give an account of the lecture in terms of (1) the verbal content delivered by the instructor and (2) the general ambiance of the setting as he or she experienced it. Great novels and memoirs display the quality of di-stance; they offer the point of view of the detached observer as well as the experiences of the participants. A good theory requires no less a quality.

## Metaphor

A metaphor is a "thing" to be used for viewing another "thing." A theory is a metaphor used for viewing a phenomenon. No one would confuse the actual phenomenon with the theory. They are different entities even though we hope they are related. In fact, metaphor is itself a logic of discovery.[14] Interestingly, the positivist tradition in philosophy considers methaphor to be of minor relevance in understanding reality.

There are probably few areas of inquiry in the social sciences that rely on metaphor to the degree marketing does. Whenever we "borrow" a theory or concept from psychology, sociology, operations research, or another discipline for the purpose of viewing a marketing phenomenon, we are using a metaphor. Similarly, we actively "lend" marketing metaphors such as "market segmentation" or "product life cycle" to people or agencies in the so-called nonprofit sector for use in viewing their activities and problems. We often examine research literature in other sciences such as educational psychology, rural sociology, or organizational behavior even though we are not particularly interested in the learning of nonsense syllables among fourth graders, the type of farmer who is most likely to try a new breeding technique for his commercial livestock, or which hospitals are most apt to adopt the latest tool in management science. We survey other literatures looking for a pleasant insight or surprise which might be transferred to contexts that are of greater concern to us. Both the data and the concepts or theory in a research study outside marketing may serve as metaphor. For example, there may emerge from the data an idea that the researchers did not originally specify. The well-known two-step flow of communication metaphor arose this way, as have many major advances in science.

The very notion of a controlled experiment is an example of the use of a metaphor. For example, we use the control group as a perspective from which to view the experimental group. The two groups are intended to be alike in certain important ways. In fact, this alikeness is absolutely essential in order for us to spot the effects of a particular phenomenon (treatments) in the experimental group. The reader may now recognize that he or she has probably received very substantial training in the construction and use of metaphors in various research

---

[14] A fascinating discussion of metaphors can be found in George Lakoff and Mark Johnson, *Metaphors We Live By* (Chicago: University of Chicago Press, 1980).

methods courses. Thus the very logic of inquiry involves metaphor, as does the results it produces.

Metaphor involves a transfer of a symbol from one setting to another. The symbols of mathematics and operations research may be used to describe buyer behavior, as may the cognitive symbols of the anthropologist and archeologist. If we invited an anthropologist and an operations researcher to view consumers in a supermarket and provide us with an account of their observations using their professional points of view, we would receive very different looking reports. And neither might resemble what the store manager would tell us. In fact, the symbols used by each party may affect our insights in unintentional ways because the symbols may carry certain "baggage" or connotations that broaden or delimit our perspectives. It is thus important to ask of a theory whether the metaphors used help broaden thinking or limit it in special ways. Does the term "exponential" and its algebraic expression add to our thinking about consumers' behavior as they wait in line at the checkout counter in a way which the term "rising impatience" or "increased nervous actions" does not? And vice versa? The metaphor of social marketing or nonprofit marketing is enriching because it widens the domain of contexts in which marketing tools and concepts (marketing itself is a metaphor for these contexts) may be applied. These metaphors may be restrictive in the sense that they may imply too great a distinction between the profit and nonprofit marketing or may suggest that these other areas have not themselves independently developed so-called marketing tools and concepts.

Many theories in marketing rely heavily on spacial metaphors to organize ideas and concepts. For example, we speak of attitude and market *structure, rank order* of preferences, preference *surfaces*, attribute *ideal points, hierarchy* of effects, *middlemen*, and *asymmetrical* power structures in the marketing *channel*. Notions of movement (brand switching, stock turnover) and *up* and *down* are especially important, with "up" generally being better than "down." Certain insights are gained and others lost when one particular orientational metaphor is used. What is helpful—and generally difficult—is to try to express the same idea using different metaphors. Metaphors from chemistry, biology, economic development, cultural change and marriage, family and divorce are as appropriate as metaphors from physics for conveying ideas about attitudes, choice, interorganizational relationships, and so forth. The reader who is inclined to dismiss this idea as "absurd" and thus "uninteresting" might try to explain why physical spacial metaphors are more appropriate than other metaphors. The reader who dismisses this idea because it is so "obvious" is invited to express ideas about attitudes, product attributes, manufacturers, wholesaler relations, and so forth, using nonconventional metaphors.

Even the way we speak of theory conveys certain biases in metaphors. Consider the title of this book "Theory *Construction* in Marketing" and our frequent use of the expression theory *building*. Apparently, theories and arguments or propositions are buildings.

Is that the *foundation* for your theory? The theory needs more *support*. The argument is *shaky*. We need some more facts or the argument will *fall apart*. We need to *construct* a *strong* argument for that. I haven't figured out yet what the *form* of the argument will be. Here are some more facts to *shore up* the theory. We need to *buttress* the theory with *solid* arguments. The theory will *stand* or *fall* on the *strength* of that argument. The argument *collapsed*. They *exploded* his latest theory. We will show that theory to be without *foundation*. So far we have put together only the *framework* of the theory.[15]

Thus, in evaluating the metaphor used in a theory, we should ask whether it is guilty of "cookbookery." This is a "tendency to force all problems into the molds of one or two routine techniques, insufficient thought being given to the real objectives of the investigation or to the relevance of the assumptions implied by the imposed methods."[16] Is the metaphor really appropriate? For example, the use of the "life cycle" metaphor in product planning assumes an end and thus tends to preclude notions of rejuvenation, especially when the term is applied to specific brands. Reliance on the metaphor may itself have hastened the discontinuance of some products.[17] The reader might evaluate the appropriateness of metaphors from music (the stages of a symphony), botany (seasonal changes of trees), and astronomy as alternatives for thinking about the same product phenomenon that life cycle refers to. What insights or ideas are gained and lost with such other metaphors?

### Generative Capacity and Irony

In Chapter 1 we introduced the notion of the generative capacity of theory. This refers to the ability of a theory to challenge commonly accepted assumptions and to suggest alternative ways of looking at phenomena. Thus an important criterion becomes: Does this theory challenge an important assumption *and* does it do so in a fashion which suggests an alternative way of viewing an event? It is not sufficient simply to challenge an assumption. Making counterassertions is relatively easy. What is most useful is the offering of a new viewpoint. A very good example of a carefully developed conceptual scheme which both challenges traditional perspectives and offers a new viewpoint may be found in an article by Stern and Reve analyzing distribution channels as political economies.[18] The metaphor of a political economy allows the authors to generate a number of provocative propositions, including propositions that challenge one another.

[15] *Ibid.*, p. 46.
[16] Box, *op. cit.*, p. 797.
[17] N. K. Dhalla and S. Yuspeh, "Forget the Product Life Cycle Concept," *Harvard Business Review*, January–February 1976, pp. 102–112.
[18] Louis W. Stern and Torger Reve, "Distribution Channels as Political Economies: A Framework for Comparative Analysis," *Journal of Marketing*, Summer 1980, pp. 52–64.

This creates the opportunity to generate additional notions which could accommodate apparently conflicting propositions or to provide corrective data.

Generative capacity is related to irony, which is a way of seeing an idea through viewing its opposite. When a surprise quiz in class greets us—unprepared—or we find that a deadline for which we are already in trouble has been moved up, we commonly respond with something like, "Great! Just what I need." Our tone of voice and facial gestures leave little room for doubt as to exactly what we do feel. In fact, our true and opposite feelings may sometimes best be expressed in this way. Irony may also serve as a logic of discovery.[19] By deliberately building irony into a theory, we may better understand the phenomenon we are trying to explore and explain. Thus, the presence of irony is a criterion of a potentially good theory.

Irony is somewhat akin to understanding the value of a cash register at a busy checkout line by removing it for a while. We might more readily appreciate or understand its importance by viewing the situation this way than by watching the cash register being used. We might not perceive as readily the value of the cash register in terms of customer and especially clerk or checker mental stress if we watched only the register in use. If a theory of the role and importance of cash registers at busy checkout counters possessed irony, it would enable us to see the effects of the absence of the register without having to actually remove one. (Note: building such a theory might be a good topic for a surprise quiz.)

A good illustration of the explicit use of irony in a theory of information system design can be found in Mitroff, Kilmann, and Barabba's discussion of management information and misinformation systems.[20] Their work reports a theory of design which underlies a market intelligence system developed for the marketing division of the Xerox Corporation. A major feature of this system is the presence of a dialectic technique which deliberately induces conflict under controlled circumstances. This technique challenges all facts and interpretations. An interpretation or explanation of certain market research results are viewed through what the opposite of what those interpretations would be and what the opposite of those results would be. For example, a theory describing the "Office of the Future" might be developed in the form of a scenario to examine the market potential of certain innovations in document processing. Current research about trends in the quality of training of office clerks and the basic competencies of people choosing such careers is an example of the type of data used to develop such a descriptive theory. The scenario expressing a theory of the office of the future should permit irony. That is, the feasibility of introducing a particular item of equipment when general competencies among clerical

---

[19] Brown, *op. cit.*, pp. 172–220.
[20] Ian I. Mitroff, Ralph H. Kilmann, and Vincent P. Barabba, "Management Information Versus Misinformation Systems," in G. Zaltman (Ed.), *Management Principles for Nonprofit Agencies and Organizations* (New York: AMACOM, 1979), pp. 401–429.

employees is high should also be viewed from the standpoint of a scenario where such competencies are rather low. This helps determine whether a given factor in a theory (such as office worker competency) is a necessary or sufficient factor in a given application of the theory. Each component of the theory is altered—viewed through its opposite state—using Tables 2.2 and 2.3 in Chapter 2.

### Reality Tests and Other Criteria

The various reality tests discussed in Chapter 7 also represent summary evaluative criteria. Such questions as: does it work? whose theory is it? are frequently used criteria for evaluating theories. We might also suggest the considerations expressed in Table 1.2 in Chapter 1 as useful criteria. For example, does the theory enable us to understand ongoing, evolving processes? Is the theory relevant to both academic and practitioner communities? On this last question we are cautioned against mathematistry, which is the "development of theory for theory's sake, which since it seldom touches down with practice, has a tendency to redefine the problem rather than solve it."[21] This, of course, has nothing to do with mathematics per se. In fact, the ability to easily express a theory in mathematical terms is another important criterion.[22]

## The Reader's Turn

Reference was made earlier in this chapter to a discussion of distribution channels as political economies (footnote 18 in this chapter). This particular view of distribution channels is reprinted in Appendix 1 as the basis of an exercise: to apply the various criteria discussed in this chapter to the framework offered by Louis W. Stern and Torger Reve. This exercise has three purposes. One is to provide the reader with an opportunity to apply these criteria to an existing system of ideas. The second, and perhaps more important purpose, is to provide the reader with an opportunity to use these criteria in a formative evaluation mode. That is, the reader should use the criteria to develop further the ideas contained in the framework. Professors Stern and Reve are careful to suggest that they offer a framework, *not* a theory. They believe that there is an important difference between a framework and a theory and that the one should not be confused with the other. It might be useful for the reader to attempt to define those differences. Here, we are asking you to apply evaluative criteria that appropriately should be laid against a theory. In this instance, the reader is therefore encouraged to use various evaluative criteria to develop a theory out of

---

[21] Box, *op. cit.*, p. 797.
[22] Thomas J. Fararo, "The Task of the Formal Theorist," Paper presented at the Annual Convention of the American Sociological Association, New York, 1980.

the framework. These new ideas might serve as the basis for further contributions to the marketing channels area and may be the source of useful future research. The third purpose is to demonstrate how different people may judge a theory differently with respect to a given criterion. This third purpose requires readers to compare their evaluations.

## *Summary*

This chapter has introduced several traditional and nontraditional criteria for evaluating theories. In nearly all cases considerable subjectivity is involved in applying these criteria. Additionally, with respect to a given theory, different evaluators may assign rather different importance weightings to particular criteria. When theory builders are sensitive to these criteria and the frames of reference and truth tests of their audience (see Chapter 7), they are likely to develop more readily accepted theories. Presumably these theories will also be better as measured by these criteria. Applying these notions is not always easy. The explicit use of any large subset of these criteria is extremely rare. In fact, the reader is cautioned in their use. It may be best to select only a small number of what you judge to be the most important criteria and to work to satisfy only these at the outset. As these criteria come under control, another two or three might be attended to. Trying to do all things well at the outset may stifle creativity while unduly stimulating despair.

# NINE

# POSTSCRIPT:
# A COMMENCEMENT

*The contents of this book represent starting points for further reflection and action. In this concluding chapter we present a brief review of some of the main topics considered in earlier chapters and also indicate some important topics or issues that were necessarily underdeveloped.*

Now this is not the end. It is not even the beginning of the end. But it is, perhaps, the end of the beginning.

**Winston Churchill**[1]

Because of its dynamic nature, the field of marketing has substantial need for creative thinking. The world of marketing is in frequent change due to competitive, governmental, and other institutional actions and social forces. Marketers must also contend with new situations that are the direct result of their own actions. Many changes require new understandings and new interpretations concerning the nature of markets and responses to markets. Even in the absence of change, many marketers require better understandings of their current situations or fields of interest. Developing better understandings and interpretations of new or existing situations involves a process of inquiry we have referred to as "theory building." As indicated in the Preface, theory building—the development and use of interrelated ideas for purposes of explaining, predicting, and/or controlling events—is an inherent human activity. Because of the dynamic nature of marketing phenomena and the costs of not being creative, the development of skills in theory building should be given special attention. Like so many inherent human characteristics, they can be improved upon. This book has tried to highlight a selection of issues and skills involved in building theories. In this postscript we would like to review briefly some of the basic messages conveyed. This book could not touch upon or, in some cases, develop adequately a number of other important messages. These too will be reviewed briefly. It is hoped that the reader will treat all messages referred to in this postscript and in preceding chapters as a sort of commencement address. They are starting points for further reflection and action.

## A Brief Review

One purpose of this book is to "unfreeze" current ways of viewing marketing problems and situations and encourage people active in marketing to play with alternative thinking styles and to develop their own set of "thinker toys." In developing one's own set of thinker toys one should keep in mind a number of considerations.

[1]This point is well illustrated by comparing such books as Thomas Cook and David T. Campbell, *Quasi-Experimentation: Design and Analysis Issues for Field Settings* (Chicago: Rank McNally, 1979); Kenneth Leiter, *A Primer on Ethnomethodology* (New York: Oxford, 1980); Frederick Hartwig and Brian E. Dearing, *Exploratory Data Analysis* (Beverly Hills, CA: Sage, 1979); Edward G. Carmines and Richard A. Zeller, *Reliability and Validity Assessment* (Beverly Hills, CA: Sage, 1979); David Held, *Introduction to Critical Theory: Horkheimer to Habermas* Berkeley, CA: University of California Press, 1980).

1. There is no one approach for developing explanations of marketing phenomena that is "best" for all individuals and situations. If anything, the stress should be on developing a generative capacity that allows divergent perspectives to arise when one is developing explanations.

2. Theory building is not unbiased and value-free. This fact does not reduce its usefulness, but recognizing it does encourage one to surface his or her own preferred mode of thinking about a particular problem by breaking down perceptual and intellectual blocks. It permits richer and better-understood insights which are the starting points for developing more valid and reliable theories. The benefits of methodological rigor in testing theory are enhanced or restricted in direct proportion to the artistry contained in ideas. And artistry is very much a matter of values and healthy bias.

3. A major problem in theory development is not the generation of ideas, but the generation of interesting ideas. These are ideas that challenge taken-for-granted assumptions. Various perceptual and intellectual blocks contribute to this problem. Interesting ideas need not be complex. They may, in fact, be quite simple. What are important are the consequences of ideas if they are accepted as valid and reliable. Would many people have to change much of their thinking and many of their actions if the idea were accepted? Developing interesting ideas does not alter the importance of conventional tests of validity and reliability but merely provides a broader spectrum of ideas to which these tests might be applied.

4. Although not all events need be construed using causal imagery, it is useful for marketing managers to construct marketing explanations in terms of how changes in one marketing variable can affect another. The importance of causality lies in developing one's own "map" or "blueprint" of how the marketing system works so that decisions can be made more efficiently and effectively.

5. When constructing maps of marketing systems, marketers should develop their own "thinker toys," that is, concepts, propositions, and models. One's own thinker toys may often be a blend of those used by others and those that are unique to one's own particular circumstance.

6. Using concepts and propositions to develop marketing maps requires a constant interplay between deductive and inductive thinking—between generating concepts and propositions and assessing their logical and actual consequences. This process is more one of a series of iterative learning experiences where the marketing manager moves back and forth between ideas and observed facts until a conclusion can be reached.

7. Explicating theories-in-use, a kind of personal cartography of marketing phenomena, may yield new insights into those phenomena for the theory holder and the theory builder. It is also a way of constructing maps so that their intellectual content may be more easily shared with others.

8. A "good" theory-in-use or theory produced in any other way is one which can pass a number of reality tests. There is not necessarily one best theory to explain a particular marketing phenomenon. Rather, different theories may be useful depending on what tests are used to validate them. What is considered "real" or "true" depends on one's own particular frame of reference. A key point, however, is that marketing managers and scholars must realize that a number of different reality or truth tests might be used to assess the solution to a particular marketing problem or question.

9. Evaluating a theory relies on a constant interplay between traditional and nontraditional criteria. The focus of evaluation is to develop a more accurate "goodness of fit" between one person's particular theory and those that might be held by others with regard to a particular marketing phenomenon.

## Some Underdeveloped Issues

As we have said, many important issues in theory building could not be addressed at least to the degree their importance may warrant. This is beyond the possibility of a multivolume encyclopedia of the philosophy of science. A few of these topics are identified here.

1. The unique role in theory building of each of the various ways of designing and conducting research has not been treated. Different research designs and data analytic methods often produce different kinds of insights. They also tend to emphasize different types of validity and reliability criteria.[1] Apart from design and data analytic issues, the important role of measurement in the operationalization of concepts has not been treated. We refer not to technical matters concerning test construction and interpretation, although these too are significant, but rather to the philosophy of measurement and observation.[2]

2. A positivist approach to science dominates the philosophical landscape in marketing research and theory. This includes the ideas that theories are expressible by first-order mathematical logic, that correspondence rules can link theory to phenomena, that a theory has a high degree of confirmation if it passes a number of empirical tests, that theories are expanded by encompassing more events, and that seemingly disparate but

---

[2]Frederick Suppe, "The Search for Philosophic Understanding of Scientific Theories," in F. Suppe (Ed.), *The Structure of Scientific Theories* (Urbana, IL: University of Illinois Press, 1977), pp. 3–232, esp. pp. 45–49 and 62–118; Peter Achinstein, *Concepts of Science* (Baltimore: Johns Hopkins University Press, 1968).

apparently well-supported theories can be reduced to a more comprehensive theory. These ideas and others go virtually unchallenged in marketing. They have, however, come under severe attack by philosophers of science. It is correct to say that some of the most prevalent and dearly held ideas in marketing about the philosophy of science are largely disparaged outside of marketing.[3] Perhaps the best available statement in defense of this last sentence is to be found in the essays and commentaries by leading scholars contained in *The Structure of Scientific Theories*. (The reader who may now be a bit offended cannot in good conscience suffer or express dignified indisposition without reading seriously that volume or other current treatises on the philosophy of science.)

3. The major premise of this book, that thinking about thinking is constructive, has not been challenged within the context of the book. There is, however, a challenge suggested by Theodore Levitt.[4] This is the idea that reflection upon certain creative processes may actually constrict those processes. If artists or poets, for example, begin to analyze why they are creative in the ways that they are, they may in some cases begin to be less creative. A kind of inhibitory self-consciousness develops. Certainly anecdotal evidence exists to the effect that this problem occurs. The prevalence of the problem is not clear and we do not feel that on balance it poses any threat to the marketing profession. However, the idea cannot be lightly dismissed. It can also manifest itself in other ways. Increased competency in critical analysis (whether in one of the positivistic traditions or in one of the contemporary schools of thought) can produce a reluctance to put forth new sets of ideas since the ease with which any idea can be criticized is more fully appreciated. Understanding the ultimate frailty of theories may daunt creativity at least for some of those who feel science is primarily a means for obtaining reliable knowledge rather than a means for extending perception.[5] No prescriptions have been offered (or will be) for creating a synergy between critical and creative abilities. This is clearly another commencement point. The prescriptions may well lie in sociological and psychological analyses of knowledge production.

4. Two related themes which have been touched upon only in passing are of such substantial importance in marketing that they require special mention here. One has to do with what is called the "social construction of reality."[6]

---

[3]Frederick Suppe (Ed.), *The Structure of Scientific Theories*, 2nd ed. (Urbana: University of Illinois Press, 1977).

[4]Theodore Levitt, personal communication.

[5]Cf. David Bohm, "Science as Perception: Communication," in F. Suppe (Ed.), *Structure of Scientific Theories*, pp. 374–391.

[6]Burkart Holzner, *Reality Construction in Society* (Cambridge, MA: Schenkman, 1968); P. Berger and T. Luckman, *The Social Construction of Reality* (Garden City, NY: Doubleday, 1967); B. Latoca and S. Woolgar, *Laboratory Life: The Social Construction of Scientific Facts* (Beverly Hills, CA: Sage, 1979).

This idea holds that reality emanates not from nature but from the structure of society, that is, social positions and relationships impact our concepts, frames of reference, and reality tests, and thus our processing of information. Because of diverse positions and relationships, there are multiple realities which guide activity in any particular setting. The idea of multiple social constructions of reality is especially relevant if one accepts the exchange theory approach to the study of marketing. The second theme which deserves further inquiry is the notion that for many phenomena the act of observation as well as understanding (see Bohm, *op. cit.*) constitutes an intervention.[7] This is sometimes referred to as Heisenberg's principle of uncertainty (with reference to subatomic physics): The influence of the observer makes it impossible to know precisely both the position and the momentum of a particle. *Either* can be known precisely (but nothing of the other) and *both* can be known only approximately. This principle is not confined to quantum mechanics but operates in the context of social exchange as well.[8] What is at issue here is something quite beyond Hawthorne effects phenomena.

A wide variety of ideas have been touched upon in varying degrees in this book. It is hoped some of these ideas will invite further inquiry and perhaps augment the ways in which readers think about and systematize their ideas about marketing issues. While this book is not in any way a comprehensive review of contemporary thinking in the philosophy of science and related fields, we hope it will encourage further reading in these fields. We hope also this book and the subsequent inquiry it might stimulate will lead to broader points of view. A quote which might have fittingly introduced Chapter 1, "Points of View," is also appropriate for closing this Commencement.

Oh foolish people and without understanding: which have eyes and see not; which have ears and hear not.

**Jeremiah 5:21**

---

[7] Werner Heisenberg, *Across The Frontiers* (New York: Harper, 1974); Niels Bohr, *Atomic Theory and Human Knowledge* (New York: Wiley, 1958); David Bottem, "Science as Perception: Communication," in F. Suppe (Ed.), *Structure of Scientific Theories*, pp. 375–408; and David Bohm, *The Special Theory of Relativity* (New York: Benjamin Press, 1965), Appendix.

[8] Walter A. Weisskopf, "The Method Is the Ideology: From a Newtonian to a Heisenbergian Paradigm in Economics," *Journal of Economic Issues*, 13, no. 4, 869–884; Eric Voegelin, "What Is Political Reality?" in G. Niemeyer (Ed.), *Anamnesis* (South Bend, IN: University of Notre Dame Press, 1978); Burkart Holzner and John Marx, *Knowledge Application: The Knowledge System in Society* (Boston: Allyn & Bacon, 1979).

# Appendix 1

## Distribution Channels as Political Economies:
## A Framework for Comparative Analysis

Published studies related to distribution channels present, collectively, a rather disjointed collage. This is due, in part, to the absence of a framework which can accommodate the various paradigms and orientations employed in performing research on distribution channel phenomena. What is needed is a comprehensive mapping of the field which depicts the various paths one could follow, the likely places where one might end up, and the boundaries of the various places within the entire conceptual space. If this mapping were successfully accomplished, then those individuals already within the field would have a better understanding of where their work stood relative to others' and would, hopefully, be encouraged to seek out complementary paradigms to those which they have adopted. The mapping would also indicate to many of those who perceive themselves as standing outside the field that much of what they are doing could easily have relevance to the substance of the field. They might even be motivated to advance the field themselves. And, most importantly, the mapping would be helpful to prospective scholars who, to a large extent, do not have a very solid understanding of the research opportunities available within the field. While no single article is ever likely to accomplish such a comprehensive mapping, there is

Source. Louis W. Stern and Torger Reve, *Journal of Marketing*, 44 (Summer 1980), 52–64. Reprinted with permission. Published by the American Marketing Association.
Louis W. Stern is A. Montgomery Ward Professor of Marketing and Chairman, Department of Marketing, J. L. Kellogg Graduate School of Management, Northwestern Univerisity, Evanston, IL. Torger Reve is Assistant Professor of Business Administration, Norwegian School of Economics and Business Administration, Bergen, Norway. The authors gratefully acknowledge the contributions of J. L. Heskett, Richard Bagozzi, Nikhilesh Dholakia, Ravi Singh, Orville Walker, and three anonymous reviewers to the development of this article. A special thanks to Lynn W. Phillips, who was instrumental in helping to structure the conceptual framework presented here.

clearly a strong need to make a beginning. If a meaningful start at ordering the field can be undertaken, then this will likely encourage others to pursue the completion and refinement of the ordering process.

Despite the centrality of distribution channels in marketing, there exist three major deficiencies in the current status of distribution channel theory and research. *First*, analyses of distribution channels have largely focused on the technologies (e.g., sales force incentive systems, pricing procedures, and the like) employed by individual organizations in their efforts to structure and control channel activities (cf., Gattorna 1978; McCammon and Little 1965; McCammon, Bates, and Guiltinan 1971). These analyses have adopted a *micro* orientation in keeping with traditional problem-solving approaches in marketing management. Little attention has been given to questions of the maintenance, adaptation, and evolutions of marketing channels as competitive entities.

*Second*, channel theory is fragmented into two seemingly disparate disciplinary orientations; an *economic* approach and a *behavioral* approach. The former attempts to apply microeconomic theory and industrial organization analysis to the study of distribution systems and has been essentially "efficiency" oriented, focusing on costs, functional differentiation, and channel design (cf., Baligh and Richartz 1967; Bucklin 1966; Bucklin and Carman 1974; Cox, Goodman, and Fichandler 1965). The latter borrows heavily from social psychology and organization theory and has been essentially "socially" oriented, focusing on power and conflict phenomena (cf., Alderson 1957; Stern 1969). Rarely have there been attempts to integrate these two perspectives. Indeed, they should be viewed as complementary, because the former deals mainly with economic "outputs" while the latter is concerned with behavioral "processes."

*Third*, empirical studies of distribution networks have been extremely limited in their scope and methodological sophistication. The vast majority of empirical works in the channels area has been purely descriptive in nature, with little or no testing of formal hypotheses derived from theory (cf., McCammon and Little 1965). Although more recent studies evidence a trend toward more systematic testing of theoretical relationships, these investigations have typically been confined to an analysis of a single distribution channel within a particular industry (exceptions include Etgar 1976a, 1978; Hunt and Nevin 1974; Porter 1974; Weik 1972.)[1] Future channel research must focus on making systematic *comparisons* of different distribution networks within and between various environmental conditions, irrespective of whether the different networks are found in the same industry or across industries.

A promising framework for addressing these issues is provided by the *political economy* approach to the study of social systems (Benson 1975; Wamsley and

---

[1] Methodologically, many of the studies fall short due to the incorrect use of informant methodologies as well as insufficient and often single-item operationalizations of constructs, thus not allowing for reliability checks and construct validation. For an excellent critique, see Phillips (1980). Thus, more emphasis needs to be given to careful research designs and improved measurement.

Zald 1973, 1976; Zald 1970a, 1970b). Basically, the *political economy approach views a social system as comprising interacting sets of major economic and sociopolitical forces which affect collective behavior and performance*. The purpose of this article, therefore, is to present a political economy framework which can be applied to gain deeper understanding of the *internal* functioning of a distribution channel. Such a framework also permits comprehension of the processes where distribution channels are influenced by and adapt to environmental conditions. It is, however, recognized that this framework is only one of many that might be suggested. It has been selected because of its strong potential for comprehensively mapping this area of marketing inquiry.

The political economy framework outlined here should be viewed as the first step in the direction of identifying and dimensionalizing the major variables influencing and ordering channel structure and behavior. A premise of the framework as initially formulated is that complex socioeconomic interrelations involve multilateral interactions as opposed to "simple" cause-effect mechanisms, such as those between power use and conflict or between channel design and costs. Given the present state of channel theory development, the initial task to be performed in accomplishing methodological and interpretive rigor is to lay out the relevant channel dimensions in terms of "fields," e.g., external-internal; economic-sociopolitical; structural-process. Otherwise, theoretical research in the area will continue to suffer from ad hoc operationalizations, where researchers select independent measures and globally hypothesize some dependent outcome without indicating or even being aware of which other interacting variables are being held or assumed constant. Hence, the political economy framework should be seen as an attempt to *chart out* or classify the total field of channel interaction. The political economy perspective as an organizing framework impels the generation of significant research questions and, therefore, has the potential for producing new theoretical insights.

As an aid to exploring the promise of the framework, a number of *illustrative* propositions have been generated throughout this article. They should be helpful in stimulating future research because they provide some insights into the kinds of meaningful relationships among core concepts which are motivated by employing the framework. However, it should be noted that there has been no attempt to specify research designs to "test" the propositions. This is because the propositions can be operationalized in a variety of ways. Given the existing state of knowledge in the channels area, it might be misleading for us to suggest specific operationalizations and would, almost certainly, deflect attention from the main purpose of the article due to the controversy they might evoke. As an aid to the reader, we have provided an appendix which conceptually defines a few of the key constructs used. This "glossary" only serves to suggest the conceptual boundaries of the constructs; it is not intended to provide operation allegations.

In the following section, the full political economy framework is broadly outlined. Then, the remainder of the paper explores, in considerable detail, the *intra*-channel variables included in the framework.

## The Political Economy Framework

The political economy framework is capsulized in Figure 1. As indicated, there are two major systems: (I) the *internal political economy*, i.e., the internal structuring and functioning of the distribution channel, and (II) the *external political economy*, i.e., the channel's task environment. Both systems are divided into two component parts: an *economy* and a *polity*. The major relationships which need to be explored are indicated by arrows with capital letter notations (see Figure 1).

***The Internal Political Economy.*** Distribution channels are interorganizational "collectivities" of institutions and actors simultaneously pursuing self-interest and collective goals (Reve and Stern 1979; Van de Ven, Emmett, and Koenig 1974). As such, the actors interact in a socioeconomic setting of their own, called an internal political economy. To comprehend fully the relevant internal dimensions and interactions, the framework suggests that a channel be analyzed in relation to its (1) *internal economy*, i.e., the internal economic structure and processes, and its (2) *internal polity*, i.e., the internal sociopolitical structure and processes.

The internal economic structure is described by the type of transactional form linking channel members, i.e., the vertical economic arrangement within the marketing channel, while the internal economic processes refer to the nature of the decision mechanisms employed to determine the terms of trade among the members. On the other hand, the internal sociopolitical structure is defined by the pattern of power-dependence relations which exist among channel members, while the internal sociopolitical processes are described in terms of the dominant sentiments (i.e., cooperation and/or conflict) within the channel.

Identifying that marketing channels consist of an internal economy and an internal polity is not a major departure from prior approaches to channel research. The contribution of the political economy framework is the explicit

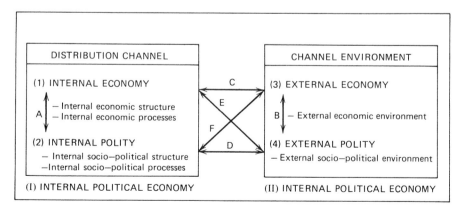

**Figure 1.** A political economy framework for distribution channel analysis.

insistence that economic and sociopolitical forces not be analyzed in isolation. By considering the interactions between the economy and the polity, it is possible to understand and explain the internal structuring and functioning of distribution systems and to derive a number of illustrative propositions for channel research.

*The "External" Political Economy.* Organizations always operate within an environment. The environment of a distribution channel is a complex of economic, physical, cultural, demographic, psychological, political, and technological forces. In the political economy framework, such forces are, as shown in Figure 1, incorporated in (3) *the external economy*, i.e., the prevailing and prospective economic environment and (4) *the external polity*, i.e., the external sociopolitical system in which the channel operates. The external economy of a distribution channel can be described by the nature of its vertical (input and output) and horizontal markets. The external polity can be described by the distribution and use of power resources among external actors (e.g., competitors, regulatory agencies, and trade associations) (cf., Palamountain 1955; Pfeffer and Salancik 1978; Thompson 1967; Yuchtman and Seashore 1967). An analysis of the external sociopolitical environment entails specification of the type of actors exercising power in the environment (Evan 1965), the power relations and means of control used between the external actors and the focal channel (Thompson 1967), the power relations between external actors (Terreberry 1968), and the extent to which the activities of channel members are actually controlled by environmental forces (Benson 1975).

The external economic and sociopolitical forces interact and define environmental conditions for the channel. The external political economy thus influences the internal political economy through adaptation and interaction processes (Aldrich 1979). Furthermore, channels not only adapt to their environments, but also influence and shape them (Pfeffer and Salancik 1978). The arrows in Figure 1 which indicate interactions between the component systems therefore point in both directions.

Attention is now turned to an elaboration of the internal political economy of distribution channels. The focus on intra-channel variables is a natural starting point, given that virtually all existing channel research has dealt with internal channel phenomena. Knowledge of environmental variables and their impact is fragmentary at best (Etgar 1977). Future examinations of the political economy framework must, however, focus on environmental variables and on the interactions between the internal and external economies.

## The Internal Political Economy of Distribution Channels: An Elaboration of the Framework

In this section the major internal economic and sociopolitical forces at work in distribution channels are described. These forces interact in shaping channel arrangements and in affecting marketing channel behavior and performance.

*Internal Economy of Distribution Channels.* Distribution channels are primarily set up to perform a set of essential *economic* functions in society, bridging the gap between production and consumption. Thus, it is no surprise that a substantial proportion of channel research, especially the earlier studies, has focused on an analysis of the *internal economy* of distribution channels (see Gattorna 1978; McCammon and Little 1965 for reviews).

As already indicated, the internal economy of a distribution channel may be divided into two components. The *internal economic structure* refers to the vertical economic arrangements or the transactional form in the channel. These arrangements range from a series of independently owned and managed specialized units which transact exchanges across markets to complete vertical integration where exchanges between wholly owned units are conducted within a hierarchy (Williamson 1975). Whereas market transactions rely primarily on the use of the price mechanism, hierarchical transactions rely on administrative mechanisms. Between these two extreme economic arrangements lies a wide variety of structures in which the market mechanism is modified through some kind of formal or informal contractual arrangements between the parties involved (Blois 1972; Liebeler 1976).

Operating within each internal economic structure of a channel are certain *internal economic processes* or decision mechanisms. Thus, agreement on the terms of trade and the division of marketing functions among channel members may be reached in impersonal, routine, or habitual ways; through bargaining; or via centralized planning processes. The type of processes used to allocate resources in any given channel is likely to conform to or, at least, be constrained by the transactional form of the channel. Typically, competitive, price-mediated mechanisms are dominant in those market transactions where information is relatively complete and products are undifferentiated, as in soybean trading, while centralized planning is dominant in most hierarchical transactions. But competitive, price-mediated mechanisms have also been simulated in hierarchical structures through mathematical programming models using computed shadow prices as terms of transfer (Jennergren 1979). For other transactions which fall in between the two structural extremes, the allocation of many marketing activities is largely determined through bargaining among the parties.

Of critical importance for channel analysis is the need to compare the efficiency and effectiveness of various transactional forms or structures across each of the three decision-making mechanisms. It is also important to consider cases where a specific economic process is employed across economic structures. For example, an illustrative proposition dealing with centralized planning processes might be:

**P1.**   The more contralized planning processes predominate, irrespective of the transactional form, the more efficient and effective the marketing channel for a product or service is likely to be.

In this sense, efficiency could be defined in terms of output to input ratios (e.g., sales per square foot) and effectiveness could be some external market referent (e.g., market share). A number of theoretical rationales underlie P1: (1) the likely constraints on suboptimization within the channel derived from joint decision making, (2) the exploitation of potential scale economies, (3) the possible cost advantages gained via increased programming of distributive functions, and (4) the reduction of transaction costs due to reduced uncertainties and lessened opportunism (cf., Etgar 1976a, Grønhaug and Reve ).

There are, however, a number of rationales working against P1's central premise: (1) the satisficing modes which operate when centralized planning processes predominate, (2) the danger of bureaucratization and loss of cost consciousness, and (3) the curbing of initiative at "lower" levels. Therefore, P1 demands investigation in concert with a second, counter proposition.

**P2.** The more centralized planning processes predominate, irrespective of the transactional form, the less likely is the marketing channel to be able to react quickly to external threats.

This proposition has its roots in the criticism which has often been directed at vertically integrated systems (cf., Arndt and Reve 1979; Sturdivant 1966). However, it may also apply to market transactions, because the more that the exchange process among channel members is organized, the more severe become trade-offs between efficiency and adaptiveness. On the other hand, while fast and specific adaptation to localized threats will likely be slow when centralized planning processes are prevalent, the adoption of such processes may permit better environmental scanning, more opportunities to influence external actors, and more ability to absorb shocks over the long run than those channels which are typified by bargaining or by routine or habitual decision making.

Analysis is also required within transactional forms across the various decision-making mechanisms. Especially significant are the issues which Williamson (1975) raises in his markets and hierarchies framework. He shows how market transactions may become very costly due to human factors, such as bounded rationality and opportunism, coupled with environmental factors, such as uncertainty and economically concentrated input or output markets (i.e., small numbers bargaining). When information is unequally possessed, opportunistic behavior is likely to prevail, and exchange may be commercially hazardous. An illustrative proposition drawn from this line of reasoning is:

**P3.** Market transactions in oligopsonistic situations are likely to lead to information imbalances, opportunistic behavior, and high transaction costs. Impersonal, routine, or habitual decision-making mechanisms in such situations will not suffice to overcome opportunistic behavior within the channel.

For example, when the members of atomistic industries, such as those found in the manufacture of maintenance, operating, and repair items, rely on open market forces to determine the terms of trade between themselves and the members of oligopolies, such as in the aerospace or automotive industries, the latter may withhold relevant information regarding demand projections and manipulate the exchange process by distorting any information passed along in order to achieve inequitable advantages from their fragmented suppliers. Extensive theoretical rationales underlying P3 are provided by Williamson (1975), Arrow (1974), and Lindblom (1977). Empirical research, using this internal economy perspective, is required to test the large number of Williamsonian hypotheses dealing with why channel structures based on market transactions may tend to fail.

***Internal Polity of Distribution Channels.*** As has been noted by several channel analysts (e.g., Alderson, Palamountain), distribution channels are not only economic systems but also social systems.[2] This observation has led to research on the behavioral aspects of distribution channels and the intra-channel sociopolitical factors (Stern 1969; Stern and El-Ansary 1977). In a political economy framework, these forces are referred to as the *internal polity* of distribution channels. The economy and the polity of channels are basically allocation systems, allocating scarce economic resources and power or authority, respectively. Both the economy and polity of channels can also be viewed as coordination systems (Hernes 1978) or ways of managing the economics and politics of interorganizational systems.

The polity of a marketing channel might be seen as oriented to the allocation and use of authority and power within the system. Similar to the internal economy, there are also structural and process variables which describe the working of the internal polity. Adopting Emerson's (1962, 1972) notion of power relationships as the inverse of the existing dependency relationships between the system's actors, the *internal sociopolitical structure* is given by the initial pattern of power-dependence relations within the channel. The limiting cases of dependence are minimal power and completely centralized power. Power is a relational concept inherent in exchange between social actors (Emerson 1962, 1972). There will always be *some* power existing within channels due to mutual dependencies which exist among channel members, even though that power may be very low (El-Ansary and Stern 1972). However, power can also be fully concentrated in a single organization which then appears as the undisputed channel administrator (e.g., Lusch 1976). Such a power constellation can be referred to as a unilateral power system (Bonoma 1976). Because of the numerous marketing flows which tie the channel members together, the more common case is a mixed power situation where different firms exercise control over different flows, functions, or marketing activities (e.g., Etgar 1976b). The

---

[2]Simply observing that many marketing channels are loosely aligned (e.g., McVey 1960) does not invalidate their systemic nature. For argumentation supporting the perspective that channels are social action systems, see Reve and Stern (1979).

latter can be referred to as a mixed power system (Bonoma 1976).[3] Careful analysis is required to assess correctly the power-dependency patterns in a marketing channel (cf., El-Ansary and Stern 1972; Etgar 1976b; Frazier and Brown 1978; Hunt and Nevin 1974; Wilkinson 1973), because sociopolitical structures alter over time. Changing bases of power, coalition formations, and evolving linkages with external actors are among the factors causing such dynamism and creating measurement problems.

The various patterns of power-dependence relationships in a distribution channel are thought to be associated with various *sociopolitical processes*. The sociopolitical processes primarily refer to the dominant sentiments and behaviors which characterize the interactions between channel members. Although channel sentiments and behaviors are multidimensional constructs, two major dimensions in channel analysis are cooperation and conflict. Cooperation can be represented as joint striving towards an object (Stern 1971)—the process of coalescing with others for a good, goal, or value of mutual benefit. Cooperation involves a combination of object- and collaborator-centered activity which is based on a compatibility of goals, aims, or values. It is an activity in which the potential collaborator is viewed as providing the means by which a divisible goal or object desired by the parties may be obtained and shared. Conflict, on the other hand, is opponent-centered behavior (Stern 1971) because in a conflict situation, the object is controlled by the opponent while incompatibility of goals, aims, or values exists. The major concern in such situations is to overcome the opponent or counterpart as a means of securing the object. Conflict is characterized by mutual interference or blocking behavior.[4]

While they are highly interrelated, cooperation and conflict are separate, distinguishable processes. Exchange between social actors generally contains a certain dialect varying between conflictual and cooperative behavior (Guetzkow 1966). A common example is found in customer–supplier relationships ordered by long-term contracts. They reflect basically cooperative sentiments, but conflicts regularly take place regarding the interpretation of contractual details and problem-solving approaches.

---

[3] Bonoma (1976) also proposes a third power constellation—the bilateral power system—in which the interactants are in a unit relation jointly determining unit policy for individual and group action. Such systems, which are held together by social altruism, have not yet been examined in distribution channel settings.

[4] In the social sciences in general and the conflict literature in particular, there has been a considerable amount of controversy surrounding the distinction between conflict and competition. We believe that competition is distinguishable from conflict. Competition can be viewed as a form of opposition which is object-centered; conflict is opponent-centered behavior. Competition is indirect and impersonal; conflict is very direct and highly personal. In competition, a third party controls the goal or object; in conflict, the goal or object is controlled by the opponent. A swim meet is competition; a football game is conflict. For a discussion of the distinction between the two terms in a distribution channel context, see Stern (1971). For an excellent comprehensive review of the controversy, see Fink (1968).

At one extreme, dysfunctional conflict processes—those aimed at injuring or destroying another party—will severely impede any existing or potential cooperative behaviors among the parties. However, the absence of confrontation will not necessarily produce maximal joint-striving, because the complacency and passivity which may be present in the relationship may cause the parties to overlook salient opportunities for coalescing (cf., Coser 1956; Thomas 1976). Indeed, because of the mutual dependencies which exist in channels, it is likely that conflict, in some form, will always be present (Schmidt and Kochan 1972; Stern and El-Ansary 1977; Stern and Gorman 1969). In addition, channels cannot exist without a minimum level of cooperation among the parties. Thus, conflictual and cooperative processes will exist simultaneously in all channels.

Having specified major structure and process variables in the internal polity, it now is possible to examine their interactions for illustrative propositions. For instance, there exists a relatively large number of situations in distribution where power is somewhat balanced, e.g., when department store chains deal with well-known cosmetic manufacturers, when large plumbing and heating whole-salers deal with major manufacturers of air conditioning equipment, and when supermarket chains deal with large grocery manufacturers. Drawing from political science theory, it can be proposed that:

**P4.** In marketing channels typified by balanced power relationships, inter-actions will be predominantly cooperative as long as the balance of strength is preserved (e.g., Kaplan 1957). However, the potential for dysfunctional conflict is higher than it would be if power were imbalanced (Gurr 1970).

The first part of P4 is primarily drawn from balance of power theories of international politics which predict peaceful coexistence as long as balance of strength remains. This position is congruent with the insights offered by bilateral oligopoly and duopoly theories in economics (Scherer 1970) which forecast the development of informal or formal interfirm agreements regarding pricing and competitive actions. The second part of P4 draws on relative deprivation theories of collective conflict (Gurr 1970) which predict that conflict potential and the magnitude of manifest dysfunctional conflict will be highest in balanced power situations.

Even though P4 is intuitively appealing, counter propositions can be offered which indicate that empirical verification is required. For example, Korpi (1974), a political scientist, argues that conflict potential is higher in slightly imbalanced than in balanced power constellations while Williamson (1975), an economist, posits that a centralized power pattern—the extreme form of imbalanced power—will tend to exhibit predominantly cooperative modes of exchange when compared to a more balanced pattern. Furthermore, in an imbalanced situation, ideology is often used as a unifying and cooperation-inducing force by the more powerful party. The seeming cooperation in a balanced power constellation may be of a deterrent nature. Thus, there is a need to distinguish between detente-type cooperation and ideologically induced cooperation.

As with the variables specified for the internal economy, there is clearly a need to compare structural sociopolitical conditions across processes and vice versa in order to generate propositions which can permit predictions for channel management. At the same time, it is important to understand that conflict and cooperation processes are activities conducive to some economic end; they are not ends in themselves. Furthermore, the way in which power is used within a channel will clearly affect the sociopolitical processes. For example, it may be proposed that:

**P5.** In marketing channels characterized by imbalanced power, the use of coercive power will produce a dysfunctional level of conflict.

Additionally,

**P6.** Marketing channels characterized by imbalanced power and dominated by coercive influence strategies will be inherently unstable, resulting in decreased competitive viability.

To some extent, the works of Raven and Kruglanski (1970): Stern, Schulz, and Grabner (1973); and Lusch (1976) examining the relation between bases of power and resulting conflict point in the direction of these propositions.

Alternately, in line with findings generated by Wittreich (1962), Kriesberg (1952), and Weik (1972), it is possible to propose that:

**P7.** Marketing channels characterized by minimal power will exhibit low levels of cooperation.

This is supported by McCammon (1970), who has argued that conventional marketing channels, comprised of isolated and autonomous decision-making units, are unable to program distribution activities successfully. If power is low, so is dependence. Thus, two or more relatively independent entities may not be motivated to cooperate.

The above propositions indicate a few of the expected relations within the internal polity of distribution channels. As mentioned, they are merely illustrative of the meaningful insights for channel theory and management available in this kind of analysis.

***Interaction between Internal Economy and Internal Polity of Distribution Channels.*** The essence of the political economy framework for the analysis of marketing systems is that economic and sociopolitical forces are not analyzed in isolation. Therefore, it is imperative to examine the interactions between the economy and the polity. To illustrate the potency of the combination, it is again possible to generate a series of propositions. Each of these propositions draws upon the variables enumerated previously.

The constellation of a given economic structure with a certain sociopolitical structure within a marketing channel will influence the economic and sociopolitical processes which take place. Considered first is the intersection between various power structures and economic structures typified by market transactions.

**P8.** In marketing channels in which market transactions are the predominant mode of exchange and in which power is centralized, centralized planning processes will emerge.

A relative power advantage within a channel is often used to program channel activities, and in such situations, decision making with respect to at least certain functions (e.g., promotion, physical distribution) tends to be centralized. Indicative of these types of channel arrangements are those found in the food industry where manufacturers, such as Nabisco and Kraft, develop shelf or dairy case management plans for supermarket chains; in the automotive aftermarket where warehouse distributors, such as Genuine Parts Company, evoke inventory management programs for jobbers (e.g., NAPA); in lawn care products where manufacturers; such as O. M. Scott, engage in detailed merchandise programming with the various retailers of their products; and in general merchandise retailing where retailers, such as Sears, Wards, and Penneys, preprogram the activities of their private label suppliers.

In addition to economic efficiency considerations, several behavioral considerations underlie P8. Thus, following Williamson (1975), some form of organizing process (in this case, centralized planning or programming) is required in order to overcome the tendencies toward opportunistic behavior present in market transactions and to cope with the bounded rationality of each channel member. The means to achieve centralized planning may be centralized power, although this is not always likely to be the case. For example, even in cases where there are balanced power structures in channels, centralized planning processes have emerged. This was the case when the Universal Product Code was developed jointly by retailers and manufacturers operating through their food industry trade associations.

P8 can be elaborated by considering the sociopolitical processes which are likely to prevail in market transactions with centralized planning.

**P9.** Under the conditions specified in P8, marketing channels will exhibit a relatively high level of conflict, but they will also exhibit highly cooperative processes. Such channels will tend to be more competitively effective than others where market transactions are also the predominant mode of exchange.

Following Korpi's (1974) reasoning, P9 predicts that conflict potential will be high due to the imbalanced power situation. The expectation with respect to cooperation is based on the ability of the channel administrator to mitigate opportunistic tendencies among the units in the channel and to establish superordinate goals. The overall effect of the combination of interacting variables in P9 will be to produce effective channel systems in which programmed merchandising is likely to be the rule rather than the exception. Such channels are likely to be more successful in improving their market shares relative to other channels typified by market transactions.

Anecdotal evidence supporting P8 and P9 can be found in the construction and farm equipment industries. In these industries, market transactions are the predominant means of exchange between the various manufacturers and their dealers. However, Caterpillar and Deere have gained sizable leads over their rivals by developing highly efficient and effective systems of distribution through the use of their considerable power in their channels. They have achieved an unusual amount of success by programming their networks and by managing conflict within them.

Another proposition in line with the discussion above is that:

**P10.** In marketing channels in which hierarchical transactions are the predominant mode of exchange and in which power is centralized, conflict processes are more likely to be effectively managed, superordinate goals are more likely to be established, and efficiency is more likely to be achieved relative to any other marketing channel.

The underlying rationale for this proposition is supplied by Williamson (1975):

Unlike autonomous contractors, internal divisions that trade with one another in a vertical integration relationship do not ordinarily have pre-emptive claims on their respective profit streams. Even though the divisions in question may have profit center standing, this is apt to be exercised in a restrained way. For one thing, the terms under which internal trading occurs are likely to be circumscribed. Cost-plus pricing rules, and variants thereof, preclude supplier divisions from seeking the monopolistic prices to which their sole supply position might otherwise entitle them. In addition, the managements of the trading divisions are more susceptible to appeals for cooperation. Since the aggressive pursuit of individual interests redounds to the disadvantage of the system and as present and prospective compensation (including promotions) can be easily varied by the general office to reflect noncooperation, simple requests to adopt a cooperative mode are more apt to be heeded. Altogether, a more nearly joint profit maximizing attitude and result is to be expected. (p. 29)

However, it should be noted that, even within a vertically integrated channel, opportunism and bounded rationality may still be found. In addition, the large size of many vertically integrated organizations often creates problems of bureaucratization and inflexibility. Thus, P10 isolates centralized, as opposed to decentralized, power. For example, the power which Sears' field operations held with regard to inventory levels within its stores was one of the major reasons for the disastrous inventory situation the company faced in 1974. In order to reduce the opportunistic behavior which existed among Sears' various divisions (e.g., the retail stores refused to hold their rightful share of the inventories which were building to abnormal levels in Sears' distribution centers), the entire company was reorganized and power was centralized more firmly in its Chicago headquarters. Now it remains to be seen whether Sears' management is equal to the task of successfully controlling the organization. Clearly, the advantages of such an internal political economy can dissipate as increasing degrees of vertical integration lead to more complex organization, more impersonal relationships, less perception of the relationships between actions and results, less moral involvement, generally more self-serving behavior, and greater toleration for substandard performance.

It should be noted that the political economy framework also encourages the examination of more narrowly focused propositions than those already stated. Given the difficulties associated with researching channel issues (due primarily to the lack of accessibility to and the sensitivity of the data involved), it is likely that research using the political economy framework should start with relatively manageable tasks. Illustrative of such propositions are:

**P11.** The more that relationships between channel members are characterized by cooperative behavior, the greater the level of profits attainable to the channel as a whole.

**P12.** The greater the proportion of relative power possessed by any channel member, the greater the proportion of the channel's profits that member will receive.

Central issues in political economies are (1) how surpluses are generated and (2) how they are distributed among the members. These "processes" provide critical links between the "political" and "economic" aspects of the system. P11 suggests a positive relationship between the level of cooperation within the channel and the joint profits obtained by it. The rationale is that cooperative behavior facilitates coordination and programming of activities within the channel which, in turn, provides potential cost advantages and improved competitive strength. In some cases, cooperation is likely to be informal, requiring a minimum of interaction. In these cases, environmental factors such as professional or trade norms, the role of trade associations, and the impact of government regulations may play significant roles in encouraging joint striving behavior. In other cases, cooperation may take the form of ad hoc consultations, the formation of committees, the establishment of federative coordination bodies, or the construction of bilateral contracts, joint ventures, or other types of formal long-term agreements (Pfeffer and Salancik 1978).

P12 addresses the critical issue of the allocation of joint profits within the marketing channel. The division of returns clearly is a matter of relative power and bargaining skill. Thus, the benefits obtained in the economic arena are divided in the political arena, a situation which is analogous to the income reallocation problem in welfare economics. Porter (1974) has found some empirical support for P12 using mainly secondary data.

Focusing on the interaction between the economy and polity of marketing channels may also produce insights into the evolution and adaptation of channel institutions. Innovative distributive institutions, such as limited line–limited service grocery stores (e.g., Aldi) and catalogue showrooms (e.g., McDade) may emerge due to differential cost advantages achieved by improved logistical systems or sharper positioning relative to specific consumer segments. The initiative for such innovations often comes from "outsiders" who are at odds with traditional channel norms and practices (Kriesberg 1955; McCammon and Bates 1965). Thus, the innovations result, at least in part, because of functional conflicts within existing channels. As the new institutions mature, they tend to hire personnel from competitors, thereby gradually changing their professional orientation. At the same time, they become preoccupied with quality, add services, and begin to cater to broader market segments, thus moving towards the same practices as their competitors. The functional conflicts with other channel members tend to disappear, and opportunities for new outsiders to innovate emerge. Such scenarios as the "wheel of retailing" simply illustrate how sociopolitical circumstances often influence economic activities within a marketing channel. In turn, the economic form influences the sociopolitical sentiments surrounding the emerging transactions which lead, in turn, to further changes in economic activities.

### Conclusion

Analysis of distribution channels as political economies provides a framework in which to incorporate and integrate the variety of approaches and findings found in the existing channel literature. More importantly, the emergent framework provides a basis for future research by isolating the critical dimensons determining transactional effectiveness and efficiency in distribution. It also provides a conceptual mapping which may be useful to anyone with an interest in channel relationships.

The framework, including the illustrative propositions developed from it, presents a preliminary, general look at distribution channel structuring and functioning. In particular, the propositions advanced above serve to underscore the caveat that the economy and the polity of such systems are inseparably linked and cannot be studied in isolation (Frey 1978; Lindblom 1977; Thorelli 1965; Tivey 1978). Choosing an internal economic structure for a channel seems to have clear implications for the internal sociopolitical structure involved. The constellations formed by the intersection of the various economic and sociopolitical structures also have implications for the type of sociopolitical processes to be expected within channels. An internal economic structure may have certain benefits in terms of the economic performance and the competitive effectiveness of the channel. On the other hand, the sociopolitical processes associated with a given internal economy may vary both in the transaction costs and in the rationality of decision making for the channel as a whole. All of these factors directly influence channel performance. Another general implication which may be drawn from this type of analysis is that the various political economies of channels require different interorganizational management strategies for maintaining and expanding channel operations and for dealing with channel conflicts.

Clearly, factors in the external political economy will have a profound influence on a channel's internal political economy. Any propositions generated by adopting the political economy framework, including those outlined here, need to be modified by circumstances in the external economy and polity. A description of the impact of external forces and internal-external interactions then emerges as a topic for future work. However, this directive must be kept in proper perspective. In the only published empirical research focusing directly on the latter topic, Etgar (1977) has indicated that certain aspects of the internal political economy of channels can be expected to explain more of the variance in channel behavior than environmental factors. Following his findings, the strongest emphasis in future research should probably remain focused on achieving a deeper understanding of the internal political economy. The framework provided in this article should, hopefully, be of some assistance in this respect.

## Appendix

### *Definitions of Key Concepts in the Political Economy Framework (See Fig. A-1).* Political economy = collectivity comprised of an economic system

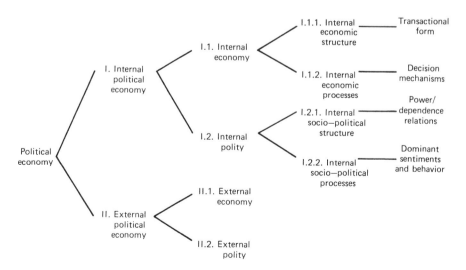

**Figure A.1.** Key concepts in the political economy framework.

(economy) and a sociopolitical system (polity) which jointly influence collective behavior and performance.

*I. Internal political economy* = the internal structuring and functioning of an organized collectivity (e.g., marketing channel) analyzed in terms of an internal economy and an internal polity and their interactions.

*II. External political economy* = the task environment of an organized collectivity (e.g., marketing channel) analyzed in terms of an external economy and an external polity and their interactions.

*I.1. Internal economy* = the internal economic allocation system analyzed in terms of the internal economic structure and processes.

*I.2. Internal polity* = the internal sociopolitical allocation system analyzed in terms of the internal sociopolitical structure and processes.

*II.1. External economy* = the economic task environment of an organized collectivity (e.g., marketing channel) described by the nature of its vertical (input and output) and horizontal markets.

*II.2. External polity* = the sociopolitical task environment of an organized collectivity (e.g., marketing channel) described by the distribution and use of power resources among external actors and their prevailing sentiments.

*I.1.1. Internal economic structure* = the economic arrangements or transactional form within an organized collectivity (e.g., marketing channel) set up to complete internal exchanges.

*I.1.2. Internal economic processes* = the decision-making processes within an organized collectivity (e.g., marketing channel) which determine the terms of trade and the division of labor, functions, and activities among the internal actors.

*I.2.1. Internal sociopolitical structure* = the pattern of power/dependence relations within an organized collectivity (e.g., marketing channel).

*I.2.2. Internal sociopolitical processes* = the dominant sentiments and behaviors which characterize the interactions between actors within an organized collectivity (e.g., marketing channel).

*I.1.1. Transaction form* = internal economic arrangements ranging from markets to hierarchies (e.g., vertical integration).

*I.1.2. Decision-making processes* = internal collective choice processes ranging from inpersonal determination of terms of trade through the price mechanism, through bargaining processes, and centralized planning processes.

*I.2.1. Power/dependence relations* = internal power/dependence pattern ranging from minimum power (low dependence), through mixed power constellations of balanced and imbalanced power (mutual-dependence), to centralized power (unilateral dependence).

*I.2.2. Dominant sentiments and behaviors* = internal sentiments and behaviors of cooperation and functional or dysfunctional conflict characterizing internal exchange, ranging from minimum cooperation, high dysfunctional conflict to maximum cooperations, functional conflict.

# References

Alderson, W. (1957). *Marketing Behavior and Executive Action.* Homewood, IL: Irwin.

Aldrich, H. A. (1979), *Organizations and Environments.* Englewood Cliffs, NJ: Prentice-Hall, Inc.

Arndt, J. and T. Reve (1979), "Innovativeness in Vertical Marketing Systems," in *Proceedings of Fourth Macro Marketing Conference,* P. White & G. Fisk, eds., Boulder CO: University of Colorado Press.

Arrow, K. J. (1974), *Limits of Organizations.* New York: John Wiley and Sons.

Baligh, H. H. and L. E. Richartz (1967), *Vertical Market Structures.* Boston: Allyn and Bacon.

Benson, J. K. (1975), "The Interorganizational Network as a Political Economy," *Administrative Science Quarterly,* 20 (June), 229–249.

Blois, K. (1972), "Vertical Quasi-Integration," *Journal of Industrial Economics,* 20 (July), 253–260.

Bonoma, T. V. (1976), "Conflict, Cooperation and Trust in Three Power Systems," *Behavioral Science,* 21 (November), 499–514.

Bucklin, L. P. (1966), *A Theory of Distribution Channel Structure.* Berkeley, CA: Institute of Business and Economic Research, University of California.

———— and J. M. Carman (1974), "Vertical Market Structure Theory and the Health Care Delivery System," in *Marketing Analysis of Societal Problems,* J. N. Sheth and P. L. Wright, eds., Urbana-Champaign, IL: Bureau of Economic and Business Research, 7–41.

Coser, L. A. (1956), *The Functions of Social Conflict.* Glencoe, IL: Free Press.

Cox, R., C. Goodman and T. Fichandler (1965), *Distribution in a High Level Economy.* Englewood Cliffs, NJ: Prentice-Hall, Inc.

El-Ansary, A. and L. W. Stern (1972), "Power Measurement in the Distribution Channel," *Journal of Marketing Research,* 9 (February), 47–52.

Emerson, R. M. (1962), "Power-Dependence Relations," *American Sociological Review,* 27 (February), 31–41.

———— (1972). "Exchange Theory, Part II: Exchange Relations and Network

Structures," in *Sociological Theories in Progress*, J. Berger, M. Zelditch Jr., and A. Anderson, eds., Boston: Houghton Mifflin.

Etgar, M. (1976a), "The Effect of Administrative Control on Efficiency of Vertical Marketing Systems," *Journal of Marketing Research*, 13 (February), 12–24.

——— (1976b), "Channel Domination and Countervailing Power in Distribution Channels," *Journal of Marketing Research*, 13 (August), 254–262.

——— (1977), "Channel Environment and Channel Leadership," *Journal of Marketing Research*, 14 (February), 69–76.

——— (1978), "Differences in the Use of Manufacturer Power in Conventional and Contractual Channels." *Journal of Retailing*, 54 (Winter), 49–62.

Evan, W. M. (1965), "Toward a Theory of Inter-Organizational Relations," *Management Science*, 11 (August), B-217–230.

Fink, C. F. (1968), "Some Conceptual Difficulties in the Theory of Social Conflict." *Journal of Conflict Resolution*, 12 (December), 412–460.

Frazier, G. L. and J. R. Brown (1978), "Use of Power in the Interfirm Influence Process," in *Proceedings*, Eighth Annual Albert Haring Symposium, Indiana University, 6–30.

Frey, B. S. (1978), *Modern Political Economy*. Oxford, England: Martin Robertson.

Gattorna, J. (1978), "Channels of Distribution," *European Journal of Marketing*, 12, 7, 471–512.

Grønhaug, K. and T. Reve (1979), "Economic Performance in Vertical Marketing Systems," *Proceedings of Fourth Macro Marketing Conference*, P. White and G. Fisk, eds., Boulder: University of Colorado Press.

Guetzkow, H. (1966), "Relations Among Organization," in *Studies in Organizations*, R. V. Bowers, ed., Athens, GA: University of Georgia Press, 13–44.

Gurr, T. R. (1970), *Why Men Rebel*. Princeton, NJ: Princeton University Press.

Hernes, G., editor (1978), *Forhandlingsøkonomi og Blandingsadministrasjon*, Bergen, Norway: Universitetsforlaget.

Hunt, S. D. and J. R. Nevin (1974), "Power in a Channel of Distribution: Sources and Consequences," *Journal of Marketing Research*, 11 (May), 186–193.

Jennergren, L. P. (1979), "Decentralization in Organizations," to appear in *Handbook of Organizational Design*, P. G. Nystrom and W. H. Starbuck, eds., Amsterdam; Elsevier.

Kaplan, M. A. (1957), "Balance of Power, Bipolar and Other Models of International Systems," *American Political Science Review*, 51 (September), 684–695.

Korpi, W. (1974), "Conflict and the Balance of Power," *Acta Sociologica*, 17, 2, 99–114.

Kriesberg, L. (1952), "The Retail Furrier: Concepts of Security and Success," *American Journal of Sociology*, 58 (March), 478–485.

—— (1955). "Occupational Control Among Steel Distributors," *American Journal of Sociology*, 61 (November), 203–212.

Liebeler, W. J. (1976), "Integration and Competition," in *Vertical Integration in the U.S. Oil Industry*, E. Mitchell, ed., Washington DC: American Enterprise Institute for Public Policy Research, 5–34.

Lindblom, C. E. (1977), *Politics and Markets*. New York: Basic Books.

Lusch, R. F. (1976), "Sources of Power: Their Impact on Intrachannel Conflict," *Journal of Marketing Research*, 13 (November), 382–390.

McCammon, B. C. Jr. (1970), "Perspectives for Distribution Programming," in *Vertical Market Systems*, L. P. Bucklin, ed., Glenview, IL: Scott, Foresman, 32–51.

—— and A. D. Bates (1965), "The Emergence and Growth of Contractually Integrated Channels in the American Economy," in *Economic Growth, Competition, and World Markets*, P. D. Bennett, ed., Chicago: American Marketing Association, 496–515.

—— and R. W. Little (1965), "Marketing Channels: Analytical Systems and Approaches," in *Science in Marketing*, G. Schwartz, ed., New York: John Wiley and Sons, 321–384.

—— A. D. Bates, and J. D. Guiltinan (1971), "Alternative Models for Programming Vertical Marketing Networks," in *New Essays in Marketing Theory*, G. Fisk, ed., Boston: Allyn and Bacon. 333–358.

McVey, P. (1960), "Are Channels of Distribution What the Textbooks Say?" *Journal of Marketing*, 24 (January), 61–65.

Palamountain, J. C. Jr. (1955), *The Politics of Distribution*. Cambridge, MA: Harvard University Press.

Pfeffer, J. and G. R. Salancik (1978), *The External Control of Organizations*. New York: Harper & Row.

Phillips, L. (1980), "The Study of Collective Behavior in Marketing: Methodological Issues In the Use of Key Informants," unpublished doctoral dissertation, Evanston, IL: Northwestern University.

Porter, M. (1974), "Consumer Behavior, Retailer Power, and Market Performance in Consumer Goods Industries," *Review of Economics and Statistics*, 56 (November), 419–436.

Raven, B. H. and A. W. Kruglanski (1970), "Conflict and Power," in *The Structure of Conflict*, P. Swingle, ed., New York: Academic Press, 69–109.

Reve, T. and L. W. Stern (1979), "Interorganizational Relations in Marketing Channels," *Academy of Management Review*, 4 (July), 405–416.

Scherer, F. M. (1970), *Industrial Market Structure and Economic Performance*. Skokie, IL: Rand McNally.

Schmidt, S. M. and T. A. Kochan (1972), "Conflict: Toward Conceptual Clarity," *Administrative Science Quarterly*, 17 (September), 359–370.

Stern, L. W., editor (1969), *Distribution Channels: Behavioral Dimensions*. Boston: Houghton Mifflin.

―――― (1971), "Antitrust Implications of a Sociological Interpretation of Competition, Conflict, and Cooperation in the Marketplace," *The Antitrust Bulletin*, 16 (Fall), 509–530.

―――― and A. I. El-Ansary (1977), *Marketing Channels*. Englewood Cliffs, NJ: Prentice-Hall, Inc.

―――― and R. H. Gorman (1969), "Conflict in Distribution Channels: An Exploration," in *Distribution Channels: Behavioral Dimensions*, L. W. Stern, ed., Boston: Houghton Mifflin, 156–175.

――――, R. A. Schulz, and J. R. Grabner (1973), "The Power Base-Conflict Relationship: Preliminary Findings," *Social Science Quarterly*, 54 (September), 412–419.

Sturdivant, F. D. (1966), "Determinants of Vertical Integration in Channel Systems," in *Science, Technology and Marketing*, R. M. Hass, ed., Chicago: American Marketing Association, 472–479.

Terreberry, S. (1968), "The Evolution of Organizational Environments," *Administrative Science Quarterly*, 1 (March), 590–613.

Thomas, K. (1976), "Conflict and Conflict Management," in *Handbook of Industrial and Organizational Psychology*, M. D. Dunnette, ed., Chicago: Rand McNally, 889–935.

Thompson, J. D. (1967), *Organizations in Action*. New York: McGraw Hill.

Thorelli, H. B. (1965), "The Political Economy of the Firm Basis for a New Theory of Competition?" *Schweizerisch Zeitschrift fur Volkwirtschaft und Statistik*, 101, 3, 248–262.

Tivey, L. (1978), *The Politics of the Firm*. Oxford: Martin Robertson.

Van de Ven, A., D. Emmett, and R. Koenig, Jr. (1974) "Framework for Interorganizational Analysis," *Organization and Administrative Sciences*, 5 (Spring), 113–129.

Wamsley, G. and M. Zald (1973), "The Political Economy of Public Organizations," *Public Administration Review*, 33 (January-February), 62–73.

―――― and ―――― (1976), *The Political Economy of Public Organizations*. Bloomington, IN: Indiana University Press.

Weik, J. (1972), "Discrepant Perceptions in Vertical Marketing Systems," in *1971 Combined Proceedings*, P. Allvine, ed., Chicago: American Marketing Association, 181–188.

Wilkinson, I. (1973), "Power in Distribution Channels," *Cranfield Research Papers in Marketing and Logistics*. Cranfield, England: Cranfield School of Management.

Williamson, O. E. (1975), *Markets and Hierarchies: Analysis and Antitrust Implications*. New York: Free Press.

Wittreich, W. (1962), "Misunderstanding the Retailer," *Harvard Business Review*, 40 (May–June), 147–155.

Yuchtman, E. and S. Seashore (1967), "A System Resource Approach to

Organizational Effectiveness," *American Sociological Review*, 33 (December), 891–903.

Zald, M. (1970a), "Political Economy: A Framework for Comparative Analysis," in *Power in Organizations*, M. Zald, ed., Nashville: Vanderbilt University Press, 22, 261.

——— (1970b), *Organizational Change: The Political Economy of the YMCA*. Chicago: University of Chicago Press.

# INDEX

MARQUETTE UNIVERSITY LIBRARIES
MEM. 658.8001Z14
Theory construction in marketing : some

3 5039 00077543 4

SUBJECT TO

DATE DUE LIBRARY CALL

AU